Schriften zum
Internationalen Privatrecht
und zur Rechtsvergleichung

Band 51

Herausgegeben im
European Legal Studies Institute /
Institut für Europäische Rechtswissenschaft /
Institut pour le droit en Europe
der Universität Osnabrück

von
Professor Dr. Dr. h. c. mult. Christian von Bar, FBA, MAE,
Professor Dr. Christoph Busch,
Professor Dr. Hans Schulte-Nölke, MAE, und
Professor Dr. Dr. h. c. Fryderyk Zoll

Shaun Charlton

The Distinction of Land and Goods in English, French, German and EU Law

The Use of a 'Universal' Classification through
the Example of Standing Timber and other Things
agreed to be severed from Land

V&R unipress

Universitätsverlag Osnabrück

MIX
Papier aus verantwor-
tungsvollen Quellen
FSC® C083411

Bibliografische Information der Deutschen Nationalbibliothek
Die Deutsche Nationalbibliothek verzeichnet diese Publikation in der Deutschen
Nationalbibliografie; detaillierte bibliografische Daten sind im Internet über
https://dnb.de abrufbar.

**Veröffentlichungen des Universitätsverlags Osnabrück
erscheinen bei V&R unipress.**

The views expressed in this study are those solely of the author and do not represent those of
the Court of Justice of the European Union.

Druck und Bindung: CPI books GmbH, Birkstraße 10, D-25917 Leck
Printed in the EU.

Vandenhoeck & Ruprecht Verlage | www.vandenhoeck-ruprecht-verlage.com

ISSN 2198-7041
ISBN 978-3-8471-1392-8

Contents

Acknowledgements 9

Introduction 11

Chapter 1. Land and Goods, Movables and Immovables 19
A. Land and goods: an apparently universal distinction of European
    private law 19
B. General theories of classification: physical attachment and intention 21
    1. German law 21
    2. French law 23
    3. English law 24
C. General characterisations of various things growing out of the
    ground 26
    1. English law 26
    2. French law 27
    3. German law 27

Chapter 2. Tax law: 'now you see they see them, now you don't!' 29
A. Purchase of land with appurtenances 30
    1. The national land acquisition taxes 30
    2. Charged on the value of 'land' 30
    3. A British exception: growing crops 31
B. Purchase of appurtenances without the land 33
    1. A sale of goods, not an acquisition of land – French law 34
    2. A contractual licence to appropriate future goods, not an
       acquisition of presently-existing goods or land – German law . . 35
    3. Once an acquisition of land, now a sale of goods – English law . . 36
       a. Appurtenances sold separately from the land as taxable
          acquisitions of land 37

      b. Appurtenances sold separately from the land not taxable
         acquisitions of land 38
  C. Purchase of appurtenances and then of the land 40
    1. French law 40
    2. German law 42
    3. English law 44
  D. Conclusions 46

Chapter 3. Requirements of form for sales contracts in land 49
  A. Distinctions and Delimitations 50
  B. Characterisations 51
    1. French law 52
      a. Validity inter partes – a signed description of the property
         gifted 52
      b. Third parties – publication? 53
    2. English law 55
      a. Emergence of the problem 56
      b. A spectrum of classifications 57
      c. Whether the SGA operated a change in the law 59
      d. Effect of the duality 62
      e. Academic accounts of English law 64
      f. Synthesis of the various statements of the law 68
      g. Brief comparative overview of Anglo-American jurisdictions . 69
    3. German law 71
  C. Conclusions 74
    1. Relevancy and application of the distinction 74
    2. Profit à prendre and usufruct/life-interest analyses 75

Chapter 4. A conceptual framework for the application of the distinction
outside of property law 77
  A. Policy considerations and *ratio legis* 77
    1. Expediency/Solemnity 78
    2. Ordinary/Extraordinary 79
    3. Immediacy/Long-term 80
    4. German law: third party protection and commercial expediency . 81
  B. Systemics and purpose 82
    1. A conceptual framework 82
    2. English law 84
  C. Conclusion 87

Chapter 5. Nursery plants, German Christmas trees and transplantation . 89
A. France. 90
   1. Doctrinal discussion 90
   2. Case-law 96
B. Germany 102
   1. Legislative framework 102
   2. Case-law illustrations 103
   3. Systemics: transplantation and Christmas trees 106
C. England 111
   1. Superficies solo cedit 111
   2. View of Amos & Ferard 112
   3. Reconciliation with Elwes v. Maw 113
   4. Bilateral relationships: removal during the currency of the
      landlord-tenant relationship 115
   5. Third party situations 118
   6. Conclusion 120

Chapter 6. The distinction of land and goods in EU law 123
A. The relevant provisions of the VAT Directive 124
B. Factual permutations and outcomes 125
C. Reasoning. 126
D. Policy considerations 131
E. Interim summary 132
F. Purpose 133
   1. Difference in purpose between national law and EU VAT law . . 133
   2. The purpose behind the distinction of land and goods in EU
      VAT law 134
G. Recalibration 135

Conclusion 141
A. Executive summary: taking stock 141
B. Main conclusions: a need for recalibration 144
C. Propositions: a new framework 145
D. Perspectives: international and interdiscipinary 146
   1. Geographical scope 146
   2. Regulatory scope 147
E. A final word 148

Bibliography. 149
   Table of Cases 149

  Common Law decisions   150
  German decisions   152
  French decisions   153
  Decisions of the CJEU   156
Literature   157
Legislation and International Conventions   161

Acknowledgements

I would like to thank Professor Schulte-Nölke for his time, patience, *bienveillance* and the opportunities he gave me as one of his doctoral students. My thanks also go to Professor von Bar for allowing me to attend his weekly seminar on *gemeineuropäisches Sachenrecht* and the chance to rewrite an earlier version of this thesis in the light of his criticism. The *Institut suisse de droit comparé* provided me with an ideal research stay at a crucial drafting stage and the Young Property Lawyers' Forum unique settings to reflect and discuss. To Laura and my family I am forever grateful for all your love and support over the years.

Introduction

The distinction of land and goods is universally accepted in the legal systems of Europe and elsewhere in the world. English, French and German law are typical examples of that universality. The scope of this distinction is not limited only to the law of property but is used to varying degrees throughout other fields of private law as well as beyond.

The universality of the distinction is betrayed, to a certain extent, by the rules determining whether, according to the general theories of national law, something is goods or land. All three legal systems, for instance, certainly coalesce around a combination of firmness of connection, on the one hand, and permanency of intention, on the other. However, despite such similarity, fundamental differences do appear, such as whether greater emphasis is laid on objective or subjective intention. These cracks in the seemingly universal distinction of land and goods then become plain to see upon further analysis of the national legal discussion and judicial decisions on whether certain (tangible) things are regarded as parts of land or goods.

The diversity in classification is prima facie readily apparent in respect of standing timber and other things contractually agreed to be severed from land, such as this year's crop and nursery plants. For instance, in English, French and German law, a conveyance of land will include trees growing from the plot of land conveyed. Yet, in France, once agreed to be severed, the same trees become goods, sometimes as of the time of the conclusion of the contract, at other times when marked for felling and, in any event, certainly once cut down.[1] In Germany, despite the clear cut-off point of physical separation from land,[2] Christmas trees growing on a plantation have been held by the courts – without criticism in any

---

1 Articles 520 and 521 Code civil; Fréjaville, *Des Meubles par Anticipation* (1927) (Thesis); Mestrot, 'Le rôle de la volonté dans la distinction des biens meubles et immeubles' [1995] 3 RRJ 809.

2 § 94 BGB (cf. in respect of transfer of ownership, § 953–957 BGB), Salier, G., *Verkauf von Bäumen auf dem Stamm* (Berlin: von Struppe & Winckler, 1903) and Pufe, W., *Der Kaufvertrag von Holz auf dem Stamm* (Breslau, 1928) (Thesis).

legal literature – to be goods.[3] English law, for its part, has no definitive answer: the rules are openly considered to be riddled with inconsistency.[4]

Standing timber is perhaps a difficult borderline case; the rules on crops have, to varying degrees, always been exceptional vestiges of medieval law; the same goes for nursery plants. Any similarity is not, however, necessarily any greater regarding other things affixed to land. Easily removable factory machinery fixed to the factory-floor (of saw-mills or printing presses),[5] period tapestries, wain-scoting[6] and chimney fire-backs in stately homes,[7] wooden dwellings or pre-fabricated constructions,[8] statues placed in niches,[9] central heating elements[10], are variously regarded as sharing the legal fate of the land to which they are attached, or not. If not regarded as parts of land (or of the buildings upon land) they are considered to be goods. There is thus a clear incongruity between a distinction which is universally drawn, yet supported by different underlying theories and, ultimately, one which characterises differently the same things in factually similar circumstances.

In recent years, comparative law research has moved from its traditional fields of study, contract law and then more widely the law of obligations as a whole,[11] to

---

3 OLG Hamm (28.02.1992): NJW-RR 1438.

4 E.g., in the legal literature, Megarry & Wade, *The Law of Real Property* (1984, 5ᵗʰ ed.), p. 574–575. Guest, *Anson's Law of Contract* (Oxford, Clarendon Press, 1969, 23ʳᵈ ed.), p. 73. The decisions of the courts admit the same: *Rodwell* v. *Phillips* (1842): 9 M&W 501, 505 *per* Lord Abinger: 'taking the cases altogether … no general rule is laid down in any one of them that is not contradicted by some other'; *Marshall* v. *Green* (06.11.1875): (1875) 1 CPD 35, 38 per Lord Coeridge CJ: 'high authorities have said that it is impossible to reconcile all the decisions on the subject'.

5 *Hobson* v. *Gorringe* CA (19.12.1896): [1897] 1 Ch. 182, *Schnellpressenfabrik* v. *W. Ehel* RG (02.11.1907, V 53/07): 67 RGZ 30, 34, *M* v. *Aktiengesellschaft R & Co* RG (05.03.1902, V 413/01) 50 *RGZ* 241; see, generally, Charlton, S., 'How far factory machinery follows the land in England, France and Germany' in Apers et al., *Property Law Perspectives III* (2015), 217–237.

6 *Spyer* v. *Phillipson* CA (01.27.1931): 2 Ch 183; *Gesamthaus Braunschweig-Lüneburg* v. *Land Braunschweig* RG (14.11.1938): 158 RGZ 362.

7 *Harvey* v. *Harvey* 2 Strange 1141; 93 ER 1088; *Augier de Moussac* v. *Ramare* CA Poitiers (23.04.1968): [1969] 2 JCP 15857; [1969] RTD civ 585, case-note Brédin.

8 Bundesfinanzhof (BFH) (27.10.1978, VI R 8/76): 126 BFHE 217; [1979] NJW 392; *Nouvel* v. *Yves Jacobelli* (15.02.1985): [1985] 2 Gaz Pal 442, case-note Dureuil; *Elitestone Ltd.* v. *Morris and Another* [1997] 1 W.L.R. 687.

9 *D'Eyncourt* v. *Gregory* (07.12.1866): L.R. 3 Eq. 382; art. 525(4) Code civil, CA Paris (27.03.1963): 1964 D 27; Civ³ (03.07.1968): [1969] D 161; von Bar, *Gemeineuropäisches Sachenrecht* (2015), [251], fn. 1155.

10 *Melluish (Inspector of Taxes)* v. *BMI (No. 3) Ltd* [1996] A.C. 454; *Bouillette* v. *Armandon* Cass. Soc. (01.12.1944) [1946] D 56; Civ. 3ᵉ (23.01.2002): [2002] D 2365, case-note Depadt-Sebag; 2504, case-note Reboui-Maupin; [2002] 1 JCP 176, case-note Périnet-Marquet; *K* v. *B GmbH* BGH (13.03.1979, V ZR 71/67): 53 BGHZ 324.

11 Zimmerman, 'The present state of European private law' (2009) 57 *American Journal of Comparative Law*, 479.

property law.[12] In the seminal work, *Gemeineuropäisches Sachenrecht*, von Bar has explored and developped numberous fundamental principles of European property law, including that of 'property' – or 'thing' and the (novel) distinction between 'normative things with a physical substratum', i. e. land, and 'real things' or goods *in a property law sense*.[13] This study aims to return from some of that relatively newly-trodden terrain in property law in respect of a distinction which, whilst ultimately derived from property law, is nevertheless broader in scope.

Undeniably, in a legal system which admits of private ownership, the property of one person must be separated from that of another. I must be able to ascertain where my property ends and that of my neighbour's begins. And if there is to be private ownership of land and goods, then the two must be spacially delimited: does standing timber form part of a plot of land, a young sapling recently transplanted from a tree nursery, an olive tree in a pot? This is the primary purpose for which the distinction of land and goods may be drawn and, when drawn, it is an elemental yet fundamental question of property law.[14]

The distinction of land and goods has, however, also been applied to other ends. A number of rules of law are based on the premiss that land is more valuable than goods, or, on the other face of the same coin, that commercial expediency requires greater transactional freedom in goods. That rule of thumb has, for instance, led to greater legal protection for transactions in land. These other purposes are secondary to the primary purpose of the distinction in that the latter cannot exist without the former but the latter need not necessarily exist at all. It would be perfectly coherent for land and goods to be distinguished yet subject to the exact same transactional rules regarding acquisition, inheritance, tax, claims for damage to such property, and so on. However, a requirement of writing for contracts of sales of land would be partially meaningless without something other than land being capable of individual ownership.

---

12 van Erp, *European and National Property Law: Osmosis or Growing Antagonism?* (2007); van Erp and Akkermans, *Cases, Materials and Text on Property Law* (2012); Ramaekers, 'Classification of Objects by the European Court of Justice: Movable Immovables and Tangible Intangibles' (2014) 39 ELRev 447; Rieländer, *Sachenrechtliche Erwerbsrechte: Eine rechtsvergleichende Untersuchung monopolisierter Eigentumserwerbsrechte in England und Deutschland* (2014); Sliwka, *Herausgabeansprüche ALS Teil Des Zivilrechtlichen Eigentumsrechts?* (2012).

13 von Bar, *Gemeineuropäisches Sachenrecht*, especially in volume I 'Grundlagen, Gegenstände sachenrechtlichen Rechtsschutzes, Arten und Erscheinungsformen subjektiver Sachenrechte' (2015), but see also volume II, 'Besitz, Erwerb und Schutz subjektiver Sachenrechte' (2019).

14 von Bar, 'Why do we need Grundstücke (land units), and what are they?' (2014) 22 *Juridica International* 1, 6: '[without land units] no-one would know which part of Earth is the subject matter of the relevant property right'.

Taking a property law distinction of land and goods as a starting point,[15] the present study explores the extension of the distinction, in three legal systems, to other fields of law. Unsurprisingly, the extension of the distinction to other fields of law, for purposes other than delimiting the boundaries of independent third party rights, is far from uniform in the three legal systems.[16] Moreover, its relevance is largely dictated by the wider system of patrimonial rights within the particular national law. A combination of different function with differing legal systemics gives rise, first, to different characterisations in the same factual circumstances of things such as standing timber as (integral parts of) land or as (separately-existing) goods. Secondly, different function and systemics result in certain factual circumstances being more or less relevant to outcome.

The thrust of the argument in this study is that a key element of the distinction of land and goods in national law accounts is either missing or overlooked. In focusing predominantly on physical criteria and intention in determining whether something is a part of land or goods, less attention is paid to the reason why resort has been had to the characterisation of the object of litigation as land or goods. It shall be argued that, once the legal purpose of the distinction is integrated into the criteria for determining whether something is land or goods legal discussion is enriched and answers to certain questions become more apparent.

To take the mundane example of standing timber, such trees must be attached to the soil for their living existence. They are attached firmly enough to land such as to pass their entire lifespan in one place. Whilst 'firmly' attached, they are nevertheless relatively easily chopped down, at least without resorting to complex technical solutions and at little cost. However, the trees of a primeval forest may regarded as never intended to be felled, whereas the timber of a commercially-exploited rotationally-managed tree plantation will inevitably be felled, and that that timber may even be spoken of in an economic sense as only temporarily

---

15 For which it would, from a comparative perspective and for the benefit of clarity in analysis, be necessary to separate the terms relating to what can form the subject matter of (third party) property rights (Grundstück/reale Sachen) from the 'classificatory' function of the distinction (Mobilien/Immobilien), von Bar, *Gemeineuropäisches Sachenrecht* (2015), [219], p. 308: 'Dem Immobiliarbegriff geht es in seiner aktuellen Ausgestaltung durch die meisten Rechtsordnungen, die ihn verwenden, um bestimmte Folgefragen der Grundstücksbildung, z. B. um die Modalitäten des Erwerbs und der Übertragung von registerpflichtigen Rechten oder darum auszudrücken, dass jemand, der ein Nutzungs- oder Verwertungsrecht an einem fremden Grundstück hat, daraus auch auf die Habe seines Schuldners zugreifen darf, die der Bewirtschaftung des Landes dient'.

16 von Bar, *Gemeineuropäisches Sachenrecht* (2015), [219], p. 308: 'Solche Regeln freilich müssen nicht nur von subjektivem Recht zu subjektivem Recht und in einem europäischen Kontext außerdem von Rechtsordnung zu Rechtsordnung separat entfaltet werden'.

attached to the land, until mature enough to be cut down.[17] Such considerations of physical attachment or human intention are, however, meaningful in a legal sense only when seen through the prism of a certain legal context, such as third party rights, contractual freedom, the acquisition and loss of ownership and so on.

Legal purpose may itself take several forms, each of which is important. The most fundamental of its forms is the legal purpose underlying a particular legal institution, such as the distinction of land and goods. Given that the distinction of land and goods is used beyond its primary legal purpose of delimiting what may form the subject matter of third party rights, the other legal purposes for which it is drawn may require different solutions. Different policy considerations therefore underlie each use of the distinction.

Another form of legal purpose is the wider system of private law, the 'systemics' of the legal system in question. For instance, national law on the sale of goods may provide that the allocation of risk of destruction be presumed to lie with the passing of ownership from the seller to the buyer. Ownership being, in principle, a third party right, to ask who owns standing timber is to ask whose right of ownership encompasses the timber. Nevertheless, consensual systems of the transfer of ownership allow ownership to pass as soon as the price and thing sold are agreed. For the purposes of determining whether the buyer must still pay the agreed price when the standing timber sold has been destroyed in an accidental fire, it is easily conceivable that asking who holds a third party right over the timber or whether the timber has been individualised and the price calculable may result in different answers.

At the very least, an awareness of the different purposes served by the distinction of land and goods shines a light on a potential tension at national level between two competing forces. On the one hand, the coherency and consistency of the distinction pulls in favour regarding property in factually similar circumstances as either land or goods whenever the distinction is used. On the other hand, a difference in function may equally justify a characterisation of property as land or goods in factually similar circumstances departing from the characterisation prevailing in respect of a different function, thereby reflecting the different interests at issue and different policy considerations.

A comprehensive comparative consideration of the distinction of land and goods in European law would require a complete catalogue of all rules distinguishing land and goods across all fields of law where it applies, an overview of all rules relating to accession to, and severance from, land, a number of related areas, such as the law of accessories, and full in-depth analysis of the case-law on

---

17 This is important, given that, globally, approximately 40% of land has been put to agricultural use, http://www.fao.org/food-agriculture-statistics/en/.

things as distinct as residential bathtubs, industrial machinery and grapes hanging by the vine, in all legal systems in Europe. At the expense of the accuracy which would result from such an analysis, this study is limited, first of all, to three legal systems only, to only several fields of law (or purposes for which the distinction has been drawn), to the severance of parts of land, and, in the main, factually to standing timber. It completely ignores a number of subjacent questions, not least of which is whether the distinction may be regarded as applicable to intangible property. The attempt has been made to find a compromise between a sufficient level of abstraction so as to contribute to transnational legal debate on the distinction of land and goods whilst including sufficiently pin-pointed detail to support the propositions made. Other extensions of the distinction of land and goods outside of property law in the strictest sense of the law governing third party rights, in at least one of the legal systems under consideration, include, *inter alia*, limitations on capacity to contract and transfer title,[18] the allocation of the risk under a sale of goods contract,[19] the effect of a deadline for performance,[20] and sale prior to attachment by buyer's creditors.[21]

The first chapter in this study introduces the distinction of land and goods in English, French and German law in terms of the comparability and universality

18 Particularly, in French law. In respect of frescos severed from a church: *Ville de Genève et Fondation Abegg* v. *Consorts Margail* Cass. Assemblée plénière (15.04.1988, n° 85-10262, 85-11198): [1988] Bull. AP 5 (n° 4); [1988] D. 325 (Opinion Cabannes), case-note Maury; (1989) 78 Rev. crit. dr. int. pr. 100, case-note Droz; [1988] 1 JCP 21066, case-note Barbieri. *Ville de Genève et Fondation Abegg* v. *Consorts Margail* CA Montpellier (18.04.1984): [1985] D 208, case-note Maury. In respect of standing timber, *Legigan* v. *Legigan* Tribunal de la Seine (12.06.1844), aff. in Cass req (01.05.1848): [1848] 1 S 501; 1 D 220. See also, Josserand, *Les mobiles dans les actes juridiques du droit privé* (1928), [307] and Mestrot, 'Le rôle de la volonté dans la distinction des biens meubles et immeubles' in (1995) *Revue de la recherche juridique*, vol. 3, 809, 817–818.

19 It is relevant in English, Commonwealth and Scots law: *Kursell* v. *Timber Operators and Contractors ltd* [1927] 1 KB 298; *Morison* v. *Lockhart* [1912] SC 1017 (Scots law); *Smith* v. *Daly and Booth Lumber Ltd* Ontario Supreme Court (29.06.1949): [1949] 4 D.L.R. 45 (Canada). It is also relevant in French law: *Millien* v. *Gay* Req (18.03.1902): [1902] 1 DP 190; *Sté de la blanchisserie de Thaon* v. *Le Gonidec* Cass. Req. (13.06.1925): [1925] 1 S 251; *HVB Ostertag GmbH* v. *Office national des forêts* CA Nancy (13.05.2008): [2008] Juris-Data n°372089. German law may – although the view to the contrary has also been expressed – acheive a similar result by way of the doctrine of segmental possession (*Teilbesitz*), cf. Salier, *Verkauf von Bäumen auf dem Stamm* (1903), p. 28; Wirtgen, *Der Kaufvertrag über Bäume auf dem Stamm* (1931), pp. 18 and 22; OLG Naumburg, 5. Zivilsenat (14.11.1929, 5 U 211/29): [1930] JW 845, case-note Wolff.

20 Article 1657 Code civil; *Mallet et Uro* v. *Le Visage* Cass. civ. (03.04.1922): [1923] 1 S 14. Also, CA Rennes (31.05.1917): [1917] 1 *Receuil de Nantes* 278; [1912–1920] *Gazette du Palais* (tables), Vente, [339bis]. In respect of English law: *Jones & Sons* v. *Tankerville* [1909] 2 Ch 440; 78 LJ Ch 674; however, see also Scots law decision in: *Munro* v. *Liquidator of Balnagown Estates Co* (16.11.1948): [1949] SC 49.

21 In French law: *Guillot* v. *Abel-Coindoz & Durand* Cass. Com. (21.12.1971, n° 70-12033), [1971] Bull civ 290.

behind the national law terminology, the national theories underlying the rules for determining whether something is (a part of) land or goods and various legal characterisations of standing timber and other things agreed to be severed from the land. The second chapter explores the application of the distinction of land and goods in tax law, specifically in relation to the national land acquisition taxes as far as standing timber is concerned. That chapter explores the interrelation between, on the one hand, maintaining the uniformity of a distinction borrowed from one field of law when applied in another and, on the other, admitting exceptions for the specific purposes for which the distinction is drawn in that other field of law. A third chapter considers whether the requirements of form for the conclusion of contracts in land apply to contracts for the severance of parts of land. A conceptual framework is developed in Chapter 4 for the comparative analysis of the distinction of land and goods, which is then applied in the final two chapters. Chapter 5 focuses on the curious example of the legal position of plants in a tree nursery, particularly in relation to differing factual character-isation resulting from different underlying legal structures. The final substantive chapter provides a practical example of the working of the new framework in its application to the case-law of the Court of Justice of the European Union (CJEU) on the distinction of land and goods, which has primarily been drawn for the purposes of European Union legislation on value-added tax (VAT).[22]

---

22 Council Directive 2006/112/EC of 28 November 2006 on the common system of value added tax (OJ 2006 L 347, p. 1).

Chapter 1.
Land and Goods, Movables and Immovables

A.   Land and goods: an apparently universal distinction of European private law[23]

French and German law distinguish, on the one hand, between movable and immovable property. In French law, the distinction is expressed in legislative form in the Code civil as the introductory article to the rules on different types of property. Thus, Article 516 states that 'all property is movable or immovable' (*'Tous les biens sont meubles ou immeubles'*).

Whilst both movable and immovable property is distinguished in both French and German law, their taxonomies are inverted. Thus, in French law, property is first movable or immovable and then movables are either corporeal or incorporeal, in the latter case comprising, for instance, debts for sums certain and shares. In German law, on the other hand, objects such as rights are initially excluded from the notion of property, which is limited to corporeals, and then (exclusively corporeal) property is divided into movables and immovables.

In German law, having restricted the scope of third party rights solely to corporeal objects, the Bürgerliches Gesetzbuch distinguishes more specifically, and terminologically, between *Grundstücke* (plots of land) and *bewegliche Sachen*. §§ 94 and 95 BGB set out a number of rules for ascertaining what a particular plot of land is comprised of in a property law sense. Movable property is both defined implicitly and negatively. The distinction is implicitly drawn through the scheme of the civil code: certain rules or concepts apply both to land and goods (e.g. possession and the nature and protection of ownership) whereas in other areas there is one set of rules for land and another for goods (e.g. acquisition of ownership).[24] No article of the BGB defines corporeal *'bewegliche*

---

23 von Bar, *Gemeineuropäisches Sachenrecht* (2015), [149]–[154], and his critical conclusion, '*Viel kruder kann man kaum vorgehen*'.

24 Cohn, *Manual of German law*, vol. 1, General Introduction Civil Law (London: Oceana Publications, 1968, 2nd ed.), p. 171, [345].

Sachen', goods are defined negatively in the sense that everything which is not a part of land is movable property.

English law is somewhat confused terminologically. It uses almost interchangeably land and realty[25] (or real property), on the one hand, and goods or (tangible/corporeal) personalty (or personal property), on the other. The land/goods couplet is perhaps best seen as a convenient shorthand for the broader original common law distinction of real and personal property. Here, from a *summa divisio* of realty/personalty, as in French law, the notion of personalty is comprised, on the one hand, of choses in possession (i. e. goods) and, on the other hand, of choses in action (e. g. shares, etc.).[26] A certain amount of ink has been spilt on the question of whether or not the movable and immovable property of the Civil Law systems corresponds to that of personalty and realty in Common Law systems. This study sidesteps that fundamental question of legal theory,[27] thereby avoiding a protracted discussion of the incremental evolution of the English concepts,[28] and the many cursory comparisons in English-language legal literature, predominantly in private international law, concluding only that they are either functionally equivalent or different.[29]

Two points are relatively clear from this brief sketch of the distinction of land and goods in English, French and German law. First, all three distinguish land from goods. Each legal system considers it expedient to set plots of land apart from other property, and more specifically corporeal movable property, that is to say 'goods'. In this sense, the distinction can be regarded as 'universal'. Nevertheless, it is also clear that even at this high level of abstraction the universality of the distinction is punctuated by a number of differences, principally relating to the national law notion of 'property' and even what is comprised in each category. These differences thus give a foretaste of the myriad of differences in the

---

25 With a few exceptions, for instance, although all land is realty, certain property, such as heirlooms, were for the purposes of the law of inheritance regarded as realty.

26 Bell, *Modern law of personal property in England and Ireland* (London, Butterworths, 1989).

27 For a comprehensive overview, see von Bar, *Gemeineuropäisches Sachenrecht* (2015), [155]–[163].

28 As well as the developments of the continental distinction from the ius commune scholarship to that of the Pandectists. See, for instance, in relation to French customary law, the couplets of *meuble/immeuble* (movable/immovable) and *hereditagia/catalla* (hereditament in English law and 'heritable' in Scots law/chattels in English law), Castaldo, 'Beaumanoir, les cateaux et les meubles par anticipation' (2000) 68 *Tijdschrift voor Rechtsgeschiedenis* 1.

29 As regards their equivalence, even in private international law, see: European Commission, *The law of property in the European Community* in Studies: Competition – Approximation of Legislation Series 27, (Brussels: 1976), p. 149; Story, *Commentaries on the Conflict of Laws, foreign and domestic, in regard to marriages, divorces, wills, successions, and judgments* (Boston, Hilliard, Gray & Co., 1834), [374]; Dicey & Morris, *The Conflict of Laws* (London: Sweet & Maxwell, 2000, 13th ed.), vol. 2, [22–002]; Cheshire & North, *Private international law* (London: Butterworths, 1999, 13th ed.), pp. 923–924.

extended use of the distinction for purposes extraneous to property law which will be explored in Chapters 2 to 5.

B.   General theories of classification: physical attachment and intention

Leaving aside the broader nature of the distinction of land and goods or immovables and movables and homing in on the rules for determining when something (corporeal) is "part and parcel" of a plot of land or independently-existing goods, the rules and principles in English, French and German law are broadly similar. As will be seen, all accounts of the rules focus on the twin criteria of physical attachment and intention, be it subjective intention or objectively-ascertained intention. This natural world view – appearing as a simple scientific enquiry as to what is constituted by a particular plot of land as a whole – does not incorporate any of the variety of legal purposes for which the distinction of land and goods is drawn.

As set out in von Bar's *Gemeineuropäisches Sachenrecht*, in determining what forms a part of land, all European systems combine criteria of 'firm attachment', whether determined by means of the degree of expenditure of energy in, or cost of, severance, and (objective) permanency of intention, be it economic or aesthetic. The legal systems differ, however, in terms of what combination is applied, or relative weight attributed to, each criterion.[30]

1.   German law

The German law rules on combination of things and particularly, accession of goods to land are essentially contained in §§ 93 to 95 of the BGB. At the most general level, German law provides, in § 93 of the BGB, that a single item of 'property' is comprised of every part which cannot be separated from something without destroying or essentially changing that part or that thing itself.[31] Whilst the firmness of an attachment can be determined by the expenditure of energy or cost of separating one thing from another, the criterion of the nature of something is a direct point of reference for objective intention. Objective intention determines whether the essence or nature (*Wesen*) of something would be de-

---

30 Von Bar, *Gemeineuropäisches Sachenrecht* (2015), [183–208].
31 'Bestandteile einer Sache, die voneinander nicht getrennt werden können, ohne dass der eine oder der andere zerstört oder in seinem Wesen verändert wird (wesentliche Bestandteile), können nicht Gegenstand besonderer Rechte sein.'

stroyed by the removal of a part thereof. Thus, according to statements of settled case-law, an aggregate only becomes a single whole when, from a general, natural point of view (*natürliche Anschauung*), the individuality of the aggregate is lost in place of indistinguishable parts of a greater whole.[32] The relationship between physical attachment and objective intention is that of a continuum, whereby weakness in the former criterion may be compensated by the strength of the latter and visa-versa. Thus, circumstances may lead to things only loosely attached being regarded as having lost their corporeal individuality for such a time as they are, for instance, particularly adjusted to accommodate one another.[33]

Specifically in relation to land, § 94 BGB provides that everything firmly attached to land becomes an integral part thereof, including buildings, (natural) products of the land for as long as they are still attached to the land, and that seeds and plants become integral parts of the land once sown and planted. Such *wesentliche Bestandteile* ('integral or essential parts') of the land cannot form the subject-matter third party rights other than as third party rights in the land to which they are attached. This is a legislative statement of the general principle of *superficies solo cedit*. The criterion of 'firm attachment' is reiterated, supplemented by things growing from the soil of land and things affixed for the completion of a building.

§ 95 BGB sets out an exception to the rule of *superficies solo cedit* where certain things are attached to the ground only temporarily. Such temporary fixtures are only "apparent component parts" (*Scheinbestandteil*). They are therefore goods and, as a result, rights can exist in those objects in their severed, movable form separately from rights in the land despite the fact that they are generally firmly attached to the land (or another part thereof). Lastly, it is important to note the institution of 'accessories' (*Zubehör*) which, without being parts of land and thus, in essence, goods with a propensity to be the subject matter of distinct third party rights, are presumed to follow the legal fate of the principle object to which they stand in a close functional relationship.

---

32 *Elektrizitätslieferungsgesellschaft in B* Reichsgericht (2.6.1915, V 19/15): 87 RGZ 43, 45: 'Jedoch ist ... ein aus bisher selbständigen Sachen zusammengesetztes Ganze nur dann als eine einzige Sache zu erachten, wenn das Ganze sich nach allgemeiner natürlicher Anschauung als eine Körpereinheit darstellt und die zu dem Ganzen verbundenen Gegenstände ihre frühere Eigenschaft als selbständige Sachen durch die Verbindung dergestalt verloren haben, dass sie fortan nur als unselbständige Stücke jener Körperinheit erscheinen'.

33 Idem.: 'in der Regel wenigstens, ein besonderer Umstand vorliegen müssen, der zu der Anschauung führt, dass die zusammengesetzten Gegenstände trotz der nur losen Verbindung ihre körperliche Selbständigkeit verloren haben und, solange die Verbindung dauert, nur noch unselbständige Stücke des Ganzen sind; so namentlich, wenn die Gegenstände einander besonders angepasst oder zur Herstellung des Ganzen verfertigt sind'.

2. French law

As far as concerns the rules in French law under which goods are regarded as parts of land, there are two broad classifications. Property is, on the one hand, immovable by 'nature' (*immeuble par nature*) or, on the other, immovable by purpose (*immeuble par destination*). 'Natural' in this sense effectively means attachment. Thus, *par excellence*, immovables *par nature* are comprised of a plot of land (*'fonds de terre'*) and buildings.[34] To avoid doubt from diverging views from the *Ancien Droit*, Article 519 specifies that water mills and wind mills fixed on pillars to buildings are also innately or 'naturally' immovable. From a slightly different perspective, specifically with regard to the extent of ownership over property, Article 552 of the Code civil, paraphrased, states that ownership of the soil extends to things (attached) above and below its surface (*'La propriété du sol emporte la propriété du dessus et du dessous'*). As regards vegetation, Articles 520 and 521 of the Code civil consider the enumeration of 'natural' parts of land from a temporal perspective, laying down that ripened crops and fruits and trees remain immovable until harvested, and become movable property as and when physically separated from their attachment to the earth.

The second broad classification – property which is part of land by way of purpose – is further subdivided into two forms of conceptual attachment, utility and permanency. In the former case, the first form of purpose regards goods the use of which has been earmarked for the better exploitation of the use to which the land has been put as immovable (*'Les objets que le propriétaire d'un fonds y a placés pour le service et l'exploitation de ce fonds'*). Although there is no restriction on the form of commercial exploitation of land or business operated in a particular building, the goods must, however, be necessary for the better exploitation of the use of that land or building in order to be transformed into immovable property.

The other form of conceptual attachment is permanency. Goods which can be objectively regarded as intended to remain in a close aesthetic relationship with the land are considered to form part of that land. This category of parts of land is termed land by way of permanency (*'immeuble à perpétuelle demeure'*). A specially-created niche in a building to house a statue or picture frame establishes a clearly-discernible objective intention that the picture placed in that niche is intended to remain there permanently.

In these forms of 'intellectual' attachment, the rule of accession does not apply automatically as with 'natural' incorporation. Instead, the person earmarking the goods for the use of the land must own both land and goods to effect

---

34 Article 518 of the Code civil: *'Les fonds de terre et les bâtiments sont immeubles par leur nature'*.

the immobilisation.[35] Once immobilised, however, the dominant view in legal scholarship is that they cannot be the subject of third party rights unless the functional relationship with the land has come to an end, either through a change of exploitation of the land or the physical removal of such immobilised goods elsewhere.

Lastly, reference must be made to the principle of anticipatory 'mobilisation' of a part of land into goods prior to its physical separation from the land (*mobilisation par anticipation*). This theory has no legislative basis and even appears to run counter to the abovementioned rule laid down in Articles 520 and 521 of the Code civil. It is, however, long-established settled case-law, fully accepted in the literature,[36] that the conclusion of a contract for the severance of parts of land (whether by way of nature or purpose), if individualised, effects the immediate transformation of such parts of land into goods, at least *inter partes* and in many cases vis-à-vis certain third parties. Third parties are furthermore bound by constructive or actual notice of such contractual severance. Contractually severed parts of land continue, however, to be immovable to a third party transferee of the land without notice of the contract in respect of the parts of land transformed into goods. The tension resulting from what is regarded in French law as the influence of party autonomy on the distinction of land and goods is reflected in two rules of case-law, potentially reconcilable but only to a point. On the one hand, the movable or immovable character of property 'is determined primarily by the perspective of the parties to the contract',[37] yet, on the other, it is 'laid down in law and cannot be influenced by the agreement of contracting parties'[38].

3.   English law

As far as English law is concerned, the rules or principles themselves are straightforward, simple and unanimously accepted. Their application in individual cases is, however, extremely unclear and casuistic. Latin epithets abound, the effect of which is that everything attached to land is part and parcel of it (*cuius est solum eius est usque ad coelom et ad inferos, superficies solo cedit, quicquid plantatur solo solo cedit*). The requisite degree of attachment is de-

---

35 Cass. 1e civ., (5.3.1991): JCP 1991, IV, 169.

36 Fréjaville, *Des Meubles par Anticipation* (1927) (Thesis).

37 'le caractère mobilier ou immobilier des biens se détermine avant tout par le point de vue auquel les ont considérés les parties contractantes'.

38 'La nature, immobilière ou mobilière, d'un bien est définie par la loi et la convention des parties ne peut avoir d'incidence à cet égard'; cf. 1879: 'la destination résulte de faits determines par la loi et ne saurait dépendre de stipulations entre le propriétaire de ces objets et son créancier'.

termined by a combination of strength of physical attachment and purpose of attachment.[39] Thus, 'if an object cannot be removed without serious damage to, or destruction of, some part of the realty, the case for its having become a fixture is a strong one'[40] These twin criteria have been subsumed within an overarching single test, that of permanency of intention or purpose in the sense that strength of attachment does, to a certain extent, often demonstrate that something is intended to be a part of land permanently.[41] Weak physical attachment is not precluded if the objectively ascertainable intention behind that weak attachment is the better enjoyment of the object as a chattel or a permanent improvement to the land.

No goods can become part of land by way of purely intellectual attachment alone. There must always be a modicum of physical attachment. There is therefore no *immobilisation par destination*, as in French law, or theory of accessories (*Zubehör*), as in German law, by way of which goods with a strong intellectual attachment will follow the land for certain legal purposes. There is also no place for subjective intention alone. 'The subjective intention of the parties cannot affect the question whether the chattel has, in law, become part of the freehold.'[42] Thus, it is stated that 'contractual autonomy is overridden by objective legal reality.'[43] It is 'the purpose which the object is serving which has to be regarded, not the purpose of the person who put it there.'[44]

However, the application of these rules of thumb in specific cases is not so clear. It has therefore been stated that, '[i]n reality, however, the differentiation of fixtures and chattels may now depend so heavily upon the circumstances of each individual case that relatively few guidelines remain in the modern law which are capable of unambiguous application to particular facts'.[45] Stated simply, '[t]he case-law is neither uniform nor consistent.'[46]

Crucially, none of these criteria for determining when something is a part of land or goods take account of the variety of legal purposes for which the distinction of land and goods is drawn and whether – or to what extent – different legal purposes affect the criteria for characterising something as land or goods.

---

39 cf. *Eastwood* case and *Holland* v. *Hodgson*.
40 *Berkley* v. *Poulett* [1976] CA (29.10.1976) EWCA Civ 1.
41 Gray, K., & Gray, S., *Elements of Land Law*, p. 28, [1.53]: 'all such factors merely subserve or illuminate the primary analysis, which relates to the objectively demonstrable intention or purpose which underlies the construction'.
42 *Elitestone Ltd.* v. *Morris and Another* HL (01.05.1997): [1997] 1 W.L.R. 687.
43 Gray, K., & Gray, S., *Elements of Land Law*, p. 29, [1.54].
44 *Elitestone* v. *Morris*.
45 Gray, *Elements of Land Law*, p. 39, [1.71].
46 Gray, *Elements of Land Law*, p. 43, [1.80].

C.   General characterisations of various things growing out of the ground

1.   English law

In English law, as far as crops are concerned, emblements are generally considered to be goods.[47] For instance, it has been stated that 'corn and other products of the earth which are produced annually by labour and industry ..., having been sown with the intention of being afterwards separated from the realty, are held to partake of a personal nature.'[48] Nevertheless, there are some situations in which they belong to the land under the rule *quicquid plantatur solo, solo cedit.*[49] Standing timber has also been characterised, along with crops, as 'chattels vegetable,[50] that is to say as goods. They have thus been regarded as a 'chattel in the vendee',[51] but the view has also been taken that they may be the subject of a freehold interest, that is to say that they are land distinct from the land of the soil.[52] In other cases, they are integral parts of land.[53] Nursery plants have been assimilated as emblements,[54] *a priori* goods, yet they have also been regarded as trade fixtures, in which case they clearly accede to the land subject to a right of removal.[55]

---

47 Comyn's Digest, Biens, (G) Emblements; 'Emblements upon the land at the death of the tenant, are chattels, and go to the executor or administrator'; Co. Litt. 55b.

48 *Amos & Ferard on the Law of Fixtures* (London: Sweet & Sons, 1883, 3rd ed.), p. 266.

49 As counsel argued in *Knevett* v. *Pool*, (1594) Cro. Eliz 463, 463–464; 78 ER 701 [(464)], that 'he who should have the land shall have the corn; for quicquid plantatur solo, solo credit; and therefore if a man sow land, and lets it for life, and the lessee for life dies before the corn be severed, his executor shall not have them, but he in reversion; but if he himself sowed the land and died, it were otherwise'.

50 Burge, *Commentaries colonial and foreign laws* (London: Saunders and Benning 1838), vol. 2, p. 8; Grady, *Law of fixtures* (London: O. Richards, 1845), p. 83, [170]; Lehr, *Eléments De Droit Anglais* (1906), vol. 2, [609].

51 *Liford's Case* (1615): 11 Co. Rep. 46b, 50b; 77 ER 1206, 1214.

52 Gray & Gray, *Elements of Land Law* (Oxford: OUP, 4th ed., 2005), [1.104]: 'realty is capable of horizontal division and it is, in this sense, feasible to own and to convey a freehold or leasehold estate in a tree which is separate from estate ownership of the subjacent soil, provided that the tree has not yet been severed from the realty.'

53 *McDonnell Estate* v. *Scott World Wide Inc* Nova Scotia Court of Appeal (16.07.1997): 149 DLR (4th) 645, persuasive Common Law authority.

54 *Amos & Ferard on the Law of Fixtures* (London: Sweet & Sons, 1883, 3rd ed.), p. 266.

55 Grady, *Law of fixtures* (London: O. Richards, 1845), p. 84, [173].

2.   French law

Generally, in French law, all these entities have been variously considered to be integral parts of land[56] and/or[57] goods. The degree of acceptance of such propositions nevertheless varies depending on whether standing trees, both timber[58] and coppice,[59] this year's crop[60] and nursery plants are at issue.[61]

3.   German law

In German law, these entities are almost without exception considered to be integral parts of land.[62] In this sense, they are legally inexistent, otherwise than as parts of a greater whole. Whilst classified as integral parts of land under the *Bürgerliches Gesetzbuch*, the rules applicable to the attachment of goods apply to crops and fruits prior to physical separation in the time immediately preceding the time at which they would ordinarily be harvested.[63] Certain doubts may be expressed in respect of the classification of nursery plants in so far as the courts have held them to be goods in connection with different prerogatives in land shared between persons,[64] tortious claims for damage to property where the

---

56 Laurent, *Principes de droit civil* (Bruxelles: Bruylant-Christophe; Paris: A. Durand et Pedone-Lauriel, 1869–1878), vol. 5, [432], p. 536: 'Il est certain aussi qu'à l'égard des tiers, les choses vendues restent immeubles, aussi longtemps que l'incorporation subsiste.'

57 Fréjaville, *Des Meubles par Anticipation* (1927) (Thesis), p. 266.

58 *Péchin-Gourdin et Aubert* v. *Meurisse* CA Paris (12.04.1851): [1853] 2 Journal du Palais 184.

59 *Lambert* v. *Saint* Cass. Req. (21.06.1820): [1820] S 257.

60 Demolombe, *Cours de Code Civil*, vol. 9, [183], p. 90 *contra* Fréjaville, *Des meubles par anticipation*, pp. 213–214.

61 Pothier, *De la communauté* (Paris: Debure, 1770), [46]: 'Suivant la règle, que nous venons d'exposer, les arbres des pépinières, qui tiennent encore à la terre qui les a produits des pépins qui y ont été semés, sont censés faire partie de cette terre, et ne faire qu'un seul et même tout avec elle. Mais, lorsqu'ils ont été arrachés et séparés, ils deviennent une chose meuble, distinguée de cette terre. Ils conservent même cette qualité de chose meubles, lorsqu'ils sont haubinés, c'est-à-dire, transplantés dans une autre, où ils sont mis en dépôt, pour s'y fortifier quelque temps, jusqu'à ce qu'on les en arrache pour les vendre; car n'étant que comme en dépôt dans cette terre, ils n'en font pas partie'.

62 *Vermögensverwaltungsstelle für Offiziere und Beamte* v. *Z* Reichsgericht, II. Zivilsenat (24.03.1905): 60 RGZ 317.

63 § 810(1) ZPO: 'Früchte, die von dem Boden noch nicht getrennt sind, können gepfändet werden, solange nicht ihre Beschlagnahme im Wege der Zwangsvollstreckung in das unbewegliche Vermögen erfolgt ist. Die Pfändung darf nicht früher als einen Monat vor der gewöhnlichen Zeit der Reife erfolgen.'

64 *T und Gen.* v. *R und Gen.* Reichsgericht (27.04.1907): 66 RGZ 88.

nurseryman is a lessee[65] or the plants have been uprooted and re-planted with a view to their immediate sale.[66]

In is indeed curious that in an area characterised by a high degree of similarity between legal systems[67] that these relatively mundane entities of the social world be treated so differently.

65 *Akt.-Gesellschaft Wollwäscherei und Kämmerei v. R* Reichsgericht, V. Zivilsenat (04.10.1922, V 611/21): 105 RGZ 213.
66 Hoffmann et al., *Das bürgerliche Gesetzbuch: mit besonderer Berücksichtigung der Recht- sprechung des Reichsgerichts* (Nürnberg: Sebald, 1910); Busch et al., *Idem* (1923), § 95 [2]: 'auch die Pflanzenbestände einer Baumschule, die nur solange im Boden bleiben sollen, bis sie verkaufsfähig geworden sind, und die als lebende Pflanzen verkauft werden sollen'.
67 von Bar, 'Real Things' Loss of Capacity to be owned when subsumed within a Parcel of Land' 126 (2013) *Tidsskrift for Rettsvitenskap* 429–448, 447–448: '[i]n the law on attaching real things to parcels of land, however, it only requires a quite low altitude to discover the very many similarities'.

Chapter 2.
Tax law: 'now you see they see them, now you don't!'

Tax law – a field far removed from the scope of private law, and property law in particular – provides an obvious and straightforward example of the use of distinctions for purposes other than those for which they were initially drawn. The reason for this is simple. In taxing particular economic transactions, tax law hones in on the particular distribution of rights and obligations which make up a legal construct. It is therefore often convenient in framing tax law provisions to rely, in the first instance, on a private law distinction in the relevant field. For instance, inheritance tax is charged on what devolves onto an heir according to the law of succession and corporation tax is charged from the starting point of the legal definition of a corporation, or of ownership within a group of companies. In turn, tax law distinguishes clearly movable and immovable property. To name but two taxes, on the one hand, contracts for the sale of goods and for services are frequently charged with value-added tax (VAT), whereas, on the other, land acquisition taxes are charged on sales of land.

As clear as the use of notions of private law in tax law is, it is equally apparent that such notions are put to a very specific purpose. For instance, property law questions of whether standing timber may be the subject of an independent real right and, if so, whether such property is movable or immovable pose different policy considerations from the issue of whether a transaction for the felling of that timber should be subject to a tax for the acquisition of land. Furthermore, whilst economic reality frequently coincides with legal reality, the latter of which provides the formal substratum of the former, the two perspectives may diverge. If that does happen, a tension will arise in tax law as to whether a given tax is to be charged according to the strict legal position or whether allowance should be made for economic reality. If such allowance is made, this is recognition of the specific purpose to which a private law distinction is being put. If not made, a one-size-fits-all distinction arises and there will – at least formally – be a mismatch between the policy considerations which justify the original distinction and the policy considerations underlying its use in tax law.

The following venture into the realms of tax law will be as brief as it is illustrative. The English, French and German land acquisition taxes are charged on acquisitions of (rights in) land to the exclusion of (rights in) goods. When land is purchased with its appurtenances such as produce growing from that land, tax is charged, with minimal exceptions, on the full economic value of the land; when appurtenances are purchased without the land – although strictly speaking still legally attached to the land – no tax is charged, according to the law as it currently stands in English, French and German law; when first purchased without the land and – at a later point in time – the land is subsequently purchased but, for instance, the timber previously sold has not yet been felled, the economic value of the produce is sometimes added to the tax base of the land acquisition tax. Despite no physical change to appurtenances such as standing timber, and as for as the tax authorities are concerned, 'Now they see it, now they don't!'

A.   Purchase of land with appurtenances

1.   The national land acquisition taxes

All three legal systems provide for a tax charged on the acquisition of land. Originally known simply as Stamp Duty, the present-day English tax was, in 2003, renamed the Stamp Duty Land Tax.[68] Although its nomenclature has hardly changed, the present-day tax is now charged on the land transactions themselves rather than the documents effecting them. The French law equivalent is variously known as *droits d'enregistrement* (registration tax) or *taxe de publicité foncière* (land registration tax)) and, in a broader sense, *droits de mutation* (transfer tax). Previously a direct translation of the English stamp tax, *Stempelsteuer*, the modern-day German equivalent is known as *Grunderwerbsteuer* (land acquisition tax).

2.   Charged on the value of 'land'

Each of these national taxes has in common that they are charged on transactions in land, to the exclusion of transactions in goods or intangible property. In England, according to s. 48 of the Finance Act 2003, the land acquisition tax thus

---

68 s. 14, Stamp Act 1891. This bears tribute to the historical origins of these taxes whereby documents requiring a stamp were not admissible as evidence in court or for recording transactions in land unless the relevant tax had been paid and, thus, properly stamped.

applies to 'an estate, interest, right or power in or over land'[69] as well as 'the benefit of an obligation, restriction or condition affecting the value of any such estate, interest, right or power.'[70] In France, the *Code général des impôts* (General Tax Code) expressly provides that 'private and court transfers of the ownership of, or usufruct in, immovable property for consideration' are subject to the land acquisition tax.[71] The German land acquisition tax is charged on sales contracts, or any other juridical acts which give rise to a right to the transfer of ownership, and, in the alternative, the transfer of ownership itself, in land situated in Germany.[72] For the purposes of that tax and subject to certain limited exceptions,[73] German law expressly applies the civil code definition of land,[74] albeit tempered by a hierarchically superior rule that tax law may, for its own purposes, diverge from the strict position in other fields of law.[75] Thus, as a general rule, to paraphrase the relevant provisions of the BGB, land acquisition tax is due on the value of the plot of land as well as all permanent integral parts of the land, including buildings, natural produce, fixtures for the completion of a building provided that they are not brought onto the land by a lessee.[76]

3.   A British exception: growing crops

Whilst not relating to standing timber, mention must also be made to an exception applied by the UK tax authorities regarding growing annual crops, known as *fructus industriales* or emblements. In Scottish and English property law, crops have traditionally been considered for certain purposes, but not all, as goods. The present-day practice of the UK tax authorities is no exclude the value

---

69 s. 48 (1)(a), Finance Act 2003.

70 s. 48 (1)(b), Finance Act 2003.

71 Art. 683, Code général des impôts (CGD). For a recent case-law divergence from the private law classification of fixtures, which are immovable (by destination), to exclude machinery from the reference in the scope of the French shares acquisition tax (*droits d'enregistrement sur la cession d'actions et de parts sociales*) to 'land or rights in land' ('*immeubles ou de droits immobiliers*', see *Directeur départemental des finances publiques du Pas-de-Calais* v. *Bernard Escande et cie*, Cass. Comm. (2.12.2020; 18-25.559).

72 § 1, (1) & (3), Grunderwerbsteuergesetz (17.12.1982) BGBl I, 1777 as modified on 26.02.1997 (BGBl. I, 418 & 1804) and with minimal changes through Art. 14, *Gesetz zur Anpassung des nationalen Steuerrechts an den Beitritt Kroatiens zur EU und zur Änderung weiterer steuerlicher Vorschriften* (25.07.2014; BGBl. I, 1266).

73 E.g., relating to rights for the extraction of minerals.

74 § 2, (1) Grunderwerbsteuergesetz: 'Unter Grundstücken im Sinne dieses Gesetzes sind Grundstücke im Sinne des bürgerlichen Rechts zu verstehen.'

75 § 39 (Zurechnung), *Abgabeordnung* (1976), according to version in [2002] 1 BGBl. 3866 and [2003] 1 BGBl. 61.

76 §§ 93–95 BGB.

of *fructus industriales* or emblements from the land acquisition tax on the ground that, along with 'felled timber and plants or trees growing in pots', they are goods.[77] It is worth noting that such a view would not run according to the French doctrinal construct of mobilisation by anticipation, described in the previous chapter and below. French law requires a contract to 'mobilise' crops which, in the absence of such a contract, are otherwise part of the land. In French law, it has also been held, albeit in an old decision, that the value of nursery plants is also subject to land tax when the land is sold,[78] but this decision has been claimed not to apply where plants are re-planted into the soil of a nursery in order to be sold at a later time.[79]

Although the tax treatment of annual crops is supposedly based upon the decision in *Saunders* v. *Pilcher*, in fact, the judges in that case expressed opinions to the contrary. For instance, Jenkins LJ said that 'even if the cherries were *fructus industriales*, ... it by no means follows that the distinction [as between a life tenant's executor and heir or remainderman, or between landlord and tenant] has the same materiality as between vendor and purchaser.'[80] In fact, it was even said that where 'the contract is silent as to such matters, and there is simply an out-and-out sale of a farm in hand from an absolute owner to a purchaser, then, I apprehend, the crops in the ground, whether they be *fructus industriales* or *fructus naturales*, pass with the land in the ordinary way.'[81]

Whilst not relating to the UK land acquisition tax, Scottish precedent has for tax purposes regarded crops sold with land as goods (movables). In *Gunn* v. *Inland Revenue*, land farmed by the landowner was sown prior to its sale and it was a condition of the sale that the purchaser take the resulting crop at valuation immediately before harvest.[82] The seller claimed that the purchase price of the crops ought to be taxed in the tax year following the sale of the land, not the year in which the land was sold. The seller was said to remain the owner of the crops as movable property and the crops only ascertained after valuation. The UK tax authorities, however, contended that the crops were sold as part and parcel of the land and, since the obligation to pay the price arose upon the conclusion of the sale of the land, the income from the crops was taxable in the year of the land's sale. Lord President Clyde resolved the case on the basis of the year in which title

---

77 [2014] *Stamp Taxes Bulletin* (Issue 2), p. 3; https://www.gov.uk/hmrc-internal-manuals/stamp-duty-land-tax-manual/sdltm04010.
78 Championnière & Rigaud, *Droits d'enregistrement*, vol. 4, [3166]; Ministre des finances (10.06.1810): JE 3881.
79 Championnière & Rigaud, *Droits d'enregistrement*, vol. 4, [3166].
80 [1949] All ER 1097, 1104F-1105.
81 [1949] All ER 1097, 1105A per Jenkins LJ.
82 CSIH (11.03.1955): (1955) SLT 266.

passed in the crops.[83] If title passed upon the conveyance of the land with the land itself then income was taxable in that year, whereas if title passed upon the valuation of the crop the resulting income was taxable in the year of the valuation. Although Lord Sorn refused to resolve the case on the basis of whether the crop was *pars soli* or not,[84] if title passed independently of the land, the crop must necessarily have been considered movable property. Here the law ignores the characterisation of the crops as part of the land, by which the sale would have been that of a capital asset, and taxes the profit from the crop's value independently from the land.

To conclude this section, whether termed land (England), immovable property (France), or plot of land (Germany), each national tax law refers to the corresponding general private law notion of land. As far as transactions concerning the purchase of land with its appurtenances are concerned, the systems of tax law do not make any allowance for the deduction of the value of appurtenances which might otherwise have been considered as part of the working capital of enterprise, but instead favour a clear-cut rule imported from private law. To apply this to the leitmotiv for the comparison of the three legal systems, land acquisition tax falls due on the full value of land, including any standing timber. Even if, for example, the value of such timber were to exceed that of the land itself, the tax would also be due on the value of those growing trees in that they are part and parcel of the land. Clear-cut adherence to the definition of land in private law has, with regard to English (and Scottish) law, meant that hesitations regarding the classification of growing crops in private law are carried over lock, stock and barrel into tax law.

B.   Purchase of appurtenances without the land

As far as French and German law are concerned, appurtenances of land, such as standing timber, which are contractually agreed to be sold under a sales contract are not subject to land acquisition tax. There is no sale of land, therefore no transaction chargeable to a land acquisition tax. The legal reasoning underpinning that outcome is, however, different in each case. French law specifically characterises the sale as one of goods (and therefore not one of land) whilst German law regards such transactions as mere contractual licences to appropriate parts of property. English tax law has oscillated between charging transactions for the severance of parts of land to a land acquisition tax and exempting them from the scope of that tax. In the latter case – the law as it currently stands –

---

83 (1955) SLT 266, 269.
84 (1955) SLT 266, 269–270.

the reasoning for not charging such contracts to that tax is that they are contracts for the sale of goods.

1.   A sale of goods, not an acquisition of land – French law

A sale of parts of land for severance has consistently and continuously been deemed a sale of goods contract for the purposes of French tax law.[85] This has been held, in particular in the case of sales of standing timber, almost from the moment of the inception of the Code civil.[86] Prior to codification, diverging views had been expressed. On the one hand, there was the view that the sale of timber, presently growing from the land, should be subject to land acquisition tax because the subject matter of the contract is an integral part of land and, a disposition of a part of the value of the land, thereby disposes of the land itself.[87] On the other hand, the view to the contrary was based upon the consideration that, ultimately, the buyer of standing trees will only acquire property in goods, once the trees are chopped down and the performance to which the buyer is obliged under the contract is fulfilled.[88] The latter view prevailed and continues to be the law today.

In French law, the subject-matter of the contract, such as standing timber, would otherwise be immovable, that is to say relate to a part of land. However, when sold, even if not yet physically separated from the land, such trees are 'mobilised by anticipation'. The doctrinal explanation runs that the intention of the parties expressed in their contract is to regard the trees presently in their future severed state, as goods. Tax law takes cognizance of that contractual intention and, on that basis, the buyer is exempted from any liability to land

---

85 Rigaud & Championnière, *Traité des droits d'enregistrement* (Paris, Cosson, 1839), vol. 4, [3170]-[3173], pp. 296–300.

86 *La Régie de l'enregistrement* v. *Rocquigny* Cass. req. (08.09.1813): [1816] 1 S 15.

87 Pothier, *Traité des fiefs* (1776), ch. 5, section 2, § 1; Bugnet (ed.) *Œuvres de Pothier*, vol. 9 (Plon, Paris, 1861, 2nd ed.), [478], p. 621: 'La raison de douter est que ces bois, tant qu'ils sont sur pied, font partie du fonds féodal auquel ils tiennent; que le fief, par la vente qui en est faite, doit être diminué; d'où il paraît résulter que cette vente de partie de fief doit produire les profits de quint[e].'

88 Pothier, *idem:* 'Les raisons de décider au contraire sont que ces bois ne font partie du fonds ou du fief qu'en tant qu'ils y tiennent; que, dès qu'ils sont coupés, ils deviennent de simples meuble: l'acheteur, ne les achetant pas avec le fief auquel ils tiennent, mais à la charge de les en séparer, ne peut, en vertu de cette vente en acquérir la propriété qu'à mesure qu'ils sont coupés; cette vente qui lui est faite n'est qu'une vente de simples meubles, laquelle ne peut opérer aucune mutation dans le fief, puisque l'acheteur n'acquiert que des meubles, et non aucune partie du fief, le fief demeure au vendeur de cette coupe dans toute son intégrité; il est seulement déprécié de valeur…'

acquisition tax in that the subject matter of the contract is presently existing goods.[89]

2. A contractual licence to appropriate future goods, not an acquisition of presently-existing goods or land – German law

German law coincides in outcome with French law, but differs in reasoning. This is well illustrated by an early 20th century case. In *K* v. *preußischer Fiskus*, a number of houses were bought for demolition. The Prussian tax authorities pursued the payment of the applicable land acquisition tax on the basis that the houses were bought whole (and were therefore to be taxed as *unbewegliche Sachen* (immovable things)).[90] The buyer claimed that the sale was one of *bewegliche Sachen*, that is to say goods (in contemplation of the future state of the building materials once the houses were demolished), and was therefore not liable to land acquisition tax.[91] At first and second instance,[92] the courts rejected the buyer's claim that the sale was 'not one of immovable property since the purpose for which the houses were connected to the ground became temporary when they were earmarked for demolition,'[93] holding, on the contrary, that 'the subject matter of the sales contract was the houses, not the materials to be obtained from their demolition.'[94] In effect, the contract was relied on as demonstration of the temporary nature of the attachment of the houses to the land. However, the Reichsgericht overturned the decision of second instance but in doing so it upheld the outcome that the transaction was not liable to the tax. In the grounds for its decision, it rejected the buyer's reasoning, instead characterising the sale as one of future materials from the demolition ('*Verkauf zu-*

---

89 Mestrot, 'Le rôle de la volonté dans la distinction des biens meubles et immeubles' [1995] 3 RRJ 809, 818: '[Lorsque les diverses conditions de mobilisation par anticipation sont satisfaites, les volontés des parties] sont alors souveraines pour convertir un immeuble en meuble et pour soumettre leur convention au régime juridique des opérations mobilières... D'un point de vue fiscal, le droit d'enregistrement est celui applicable aux ventes mobilières...' cf. Cass. Com. (23.01.1978, n° 76-13.175) where sale of standing trees in a public sale was held taxable as the sale of corporeal movable property.
90 Reichsgericht (08.12.1905): 62 RGZ 135, 136: 'die Häuser als Ganzes gekauft [wurden]'.
91 Ibidem: '[Es] ist geltend gemacht, es handele sich bei dem Kaufgeschäft um eine Menge von beweglichen Sachen, nämlich Abbruchsmaterialien'.
92 Following a line of argumentation reflecting practically word-for-word the prevailing doctrinal position in French law.
93 Ibidem: 'es [handelt] sich ... nicht um den Verkauf von unbeweglichen Sachen [...], da der Zweck, für welchen die Verbindung der Häuser mit dem Grund und Boden bestehe, ein dauernder zu sein aufhöre, wenn die Baulichkeiten zum Abbruch bestimmt seien'.
94 Ibidem: 'die Häuser, nicht aber die aus denselben zu gewinnenden Materialien, ... [bildeten] den Gegenstand des Kaufgeschäfts'.

künftiger Abbruchsmaterialien').[95] The subject matter of such sales contracts was that of a future thing, and not therefore formed by its unsevered state as (a part of) land.

That there be direct references in *K* v. *preußischer Fiskus* in 1905 to legal argumentation evoking the idea of 'mobilisation' can certainly be attributed to the persistence of ideas valid prior to the entry into force of the German civil law codification in 1900. Contractual exploitation or extraction rights are, in modern times, unanimously characterised as contractual licences for the appropriation of parts of a legal thing (*Gestattungs-/ Aneignungs-verträge*).[96]

The outcome of that 1905 decision of the Reichsgericht has not budged. The same view was also taken in a gravel extraction case where the Bundesfinanzgericht held that, although the right to extract the minerals was an enduring burden ('*eine dauernde Last*'), it only bound the grantor contractually.[97] In the absence of third party effect, the price of such sales contracts is not subject to land acquisition tax.[98] German law does not therefore base the exclusion of contracts for the sale of parts of land sold for severance from liability to land acquisition tax on their characterisation as movable property. It does, however, refuse to characterise such contracts as for immovable property, thereby excluding them from the scope of the land acquisition tax.

3.   Once an acquisition of land, now a sale of goods – English law

The position in English law has historically pivoted from regarding sales of parts of land for severance, such as standing timber, as sales of land, and therefore subject to land acquisition tax. It now characterises such contracts as one for the sale of goods, falling outside the scope of land acquisition tax. The former characterisation may be considered to be the position at common law – judge-made law in the absence of legislative intervention. A more accurate account would be to describe this earlier period as the judicial interpretation of the stamp

---

95 Ibidem: 'Es ist auch rechtlich ausgeschlossen, etwas anderes als diese für den Gegenstand des Kaufgeschäfts anzusehen'.

96 § 956 BGB.

97 BFH (22.06.1966, II 130/62): [1966] 3 BStBl 552.

98 [1966] 3 BStBl 552, 554: 'Verpflichtungen, die den Grundstückseigentümer persönlich belasten, fallen dagegen nicht unter § 11 (2)(2)[2] GrEStG, weil ihnen der Charakter der dauernden Last mit dinglicher Wirkung fehlt.' See also, BFH (25.03.1958, II 193/56): [1958] 3 BStBl 239; BFH (01.06.1950, II 181/57): [1960] 3 BStBl 294 and BFH (22.06.1966, II 74/63): [1966] 3 BStBl 552 where a real servitude/easement had been granted to the adjacent (dominant) tenement. However, cf. the aforementioned decision of the House of Lords in *Hood Barrs v. Inland Revenue Commissioners* which held a personal right to extract timber as 'enduring right' in land (13.03.1957): [1957] 1 WLR 529.

duty legislation prior to the codification brought about by the Sale of Goods Act 1893. The so-called position at common law is important to the rest of the common law world outside of England and Wales because it has been contended to provide persuasive authority, if not an actual statement of the law as it should be applied, in certain legal systems such as Australia. As such it has influence the characterisation of things sold for severance in private law and beyond.[99]

a.   Appurtenances sold separately from the land as taxable acquisitions of land

Under the Stamp Duties Act 1783, an exception from the English predecessor to the modern land acquisition tax, stamp duty, was made for 'any m[em]orandum, letter or agreement, made for or relating to the sale of any goods, wares or merchandises.'[100] Similarly in the Stamp Act 1891, contracts for goods, wares and merchandise were taxed differently from conveyances on sale of 'any equitable estate or interest in any property whatsoever.'[101] However, stamp duty applied to all contracts for the sale of land as well as initially all executory contracts and only excluded (present) sale of goods contracts. For that reason, it is not possible to regard some of the older cases in which it was held that sales of parts of land for severance, such as *fructus naturales*, require a stamp,[102] as authority for the proposition that acquisition tax was due on account their characterisation as land.

　　Thus, in 1801 in *Waddington* v. *Bristow*, it was held that the sale of the whole produce of the vendor's land in the nature of hop-grounds would not fall under the exception of 'goods, wares and merchandises'. The *ratio decidendi* may, however, be found either in the proposition that such a sale of hops was a sale of land, or that, at the time when the hops were sold, they had not been physically separated from the land into goods.[103] It should also be noted that the Stamp Duty Acts served a dual purpose, on the one hand, the taxation of certain transactions, on the other, the formalities for the conclusion of such transactions since un-stamped documents could not be admitted as evidence in court.[104]

99　*Ashgrove Pty Ltd* v. *DFCT* [1994] 28 ATR 512 (Australia); *Smith* v. *Daly and Booth Lumber Ltd* Ontario Supreme Court (29.06.1949): [1949] 4 D.L.R. 45 (Canada).
100　s. 4, Stamp Duties Act 1783 (23 Geo. 3), c. 58.
101　s. 59 (1), Stamp Act 1891 (54 & 55 Vict.), c. 39. cf. Stamp Act 1815 (55 Geo. 3), c. 184.
102　cf. Blackburn, *Sale of Personal Property* (1887), p. 5.
103　cf. the account of Chambre J's dictum from that decision in *Evans* v. *Roberts* (1826) 5 B&C 829, 835; 108 ER 309, 311 *per* Bayley J. Even Rooke J., who looked to the intention of Parliament in the exception as not to impede commercial transactions, found that, as a speculative bargain, it did not fall within the exception, Common Pleas (09.06.1801): 2 Bos. & Pul. 452, 454–455; 126 ER 1379, 1381.
104　s. 14, Stamp Act 1891; cf. Chapter 3. Requirements of form for sales contracts in land.

It is not until the case of *Teall* v. *Auty* that the nature of a contract for the sale of *fructus naturales* was definitively characterised as one for an interest in land rather than as a contract in general not being for the sale of presently-existing goods. With regard to the then interconnected question of admissibility in evidence, Dallas LC held, of the sale of young growing trees, that '[t]he agreement was originally for the purchase of an interest in land, for when it was made, the poles were growing.'[105] Thus, a present disposition of something in the nature of real property must effect the sale of an interest in land. This rule was re-affirmed in *Rodwell* v. *Phillips* where fruit and vegetables in the nature of *fructus naturales* were the subject of a contract for sale made in writing but which had not been stamped.[106] On the basis that the contract was not admissible in evidence as it was not stamped, the seller justified his refusal to allow the buyer to harvest and remove the ripened hanging fruit. In giving the judgment of the court, Lord Abinger CB held that 'this was a sale of that species of interest in the produce of the lands which has not been excepted by the Stamp Act, and that it is not a sale of goods and merchandize; and the contract is of a sufficient value to require a stamp.'[107]

b.   Appurtenances sold separately from the land not taxable acquisitions of land

The 19th century position of English law[108] was not followed in the second half of the 20th century. The codificatory reform brought about by the Sale of Goods Act 1893, inter alia in decoupling the formalities for the conclusion of sale of goods contracts from the Stamp Duties Acts, had a slow-burning evolutionary effect on the scope of stamp duty. It thus come to be held in 1964 in *Hopwood* v. *CN Spencer Ltd* that the purchase by a timber merchant of standing timber was a purchase of goods, rather than that of an interest in land.[109] Buckman J. qualified the trees as goods in which title had passed because the trees were both ascertained and in a deliverable state. Ascertained because title passed in all the trees of the forest and in a deliverable state given that they were already ripe for cutting and there 'was no advantage to be gained in leaving them standing, except the [buyer's] convenience.'[110] In reliance upon a venerable and relatively oft-cited[111] analogy

---

105 (14.06.1820): (1822) 4 Moore 542, 546–547.
106 (31.06.1842): M&W 500.
107 (1846) M&W 500, 504–505.
108 Tilsley, *A Treatise on the Stamp Laws* (London, Steven & Sons, 1871, 3rd ed.), vol. 1, pp. 41–45.
109 HC (19.11.1964): 42 *Tax Cases* 169.
110 42 TC 169, 181.
111 *Smith* v. *Surman* (1829) 9 B&C 561, 573; 109 ER 209, 213 *per* Littledale J.; *Marshall* v. *Green* HC (06.11.1875): (1875) 1 CPD 35, 39 *per* Lord Colderidge CJ; 44 *per* Grove J.

dating back to Sir Edward Vaughan Williams,[112] the timber merchant 'was, in effect, merely using the wood as a warehouse for its property from the time of the contract until the trees were felled and removed'.[113] As a result, 'the ownership of the timber was severed from the ownership of the surface of the land and [the taxpaying company] acquired a proprietary interest in the timber. The Company became the owners of the trees with, no doubt, such rights as were necessary to enable them to go on to the land to fell the trees'[114] and title passed 'from the moment of the agreement.'[115]

Although decided in relation to the distinction between capital expenditure (i.e. interests in land) and stock-in-trade (i.e. goods to be used in production process), that decision puts such transactions squarely within the scope of the previous stamp duty exception for goods, wares and merchandise. Accordingly, that statement of the law certainly applies to the scope of the present-day land acquisition tax.

Whilst the rule in *Hopwood* v. *CN Spencer Ltd* represents the current state of English law, the view has, however, been asserted that the old learning in *Teall* v. *Auty* and *Rodwell* v. *Phillips* is the position of the common law in the absence of the statutory intervention of the Sale of Goods Act. Under this view, sales of parts of land for severance are considered for all purposes other than those of the Sale of Goods Act as sales of immovable property.[116] In the absence of express pro-vision to the contrary, tax legislation in common law countries would therefore apply the supposed[117] immovable property characterisation of standing trees agreed to be severed and the price would be liable to land acquisition taxation. It is submitted that this is a misinterpretation of the rule in *Marshall* v. *Green*, and as Buckman J. said in *Hopwood* v. *CN Spencer Ltd* specifically for the distinction of movable and immovable property drawn in tax law, the word immediate ought not 'to be taken too literally.' It was there understood as ripe for severance and capable of severance within a reasonable time.[118]

---

112 Williams's case-note on *Duppa* v. *Mayo* KB (1669) 1 Wms. Saund. 275, 276; 85 ER 366, 395.

113 (1964) 42 TC 169, 181.

114 42 TC 169, 181.

115 42 TC 169, 182.

116 Hart, 'The impact of property law and contractual principles in taxation law' (2004) 14 *Revenue LJ* 92 (Australia): '[In *Ashgrove Pty Ltd* v. *DFCT* [1994] 28 ATR 512] Hill J held that the definition of 'goods' in the Sale of Goods legislation was only applicable for the purposes of the legislation, and for all other purposes the common law definition of goods which existed before 1893 was the relevant test.'

117 Hart, *idem*: 'At common law there was a sale of goods, if the parties agreed that the thing sold should within a reasonably short time be felled and removed from the land. On the other hand, there was a profit à prendre if the purchaser should benefit not only from the existing timber but from further growth of the thing sold, because this benefit truly arose from an interest in the land.'

118 (1968) 42 TC 169, 181 and 180.

Furthermore, a contract for the severance of parts of land must not, however, be capable of analysis as the grant of an interest in land in the nature of a profit à prendre. In *Hood Barrs* v. *Inland Revenue Commissioners*, the House of Lords held – once again specifically in relation to the distinction between capital and income revenue – that a sale of standing timber operated to grant 'an enduring right to cut timber.'[119] It must, however, be borne in mind that, under the contract, the taxpayer acquired a right to select, cut and carry away a certain number of trees standing in the seller's forest without any time-limit fixed within which to complete the felling operations.[120] Having not made the selection, the trees were unascertained and incapable of being mobilised by anticipation. It was for this reason that the later decision in *Hopwood* v. *CN Spencer Ltd* distinguished the decision of the House of Lords.[121]

To conclude this section on the purchase of appurtenances of land without the land itself, the positive law of all three legal systems has converged. Land acquisition tax is not charged on the consideration paid under such contracts. This convergence is, however, merely temporal as far as English law is concerned, demonstrating that an alternative outcome is certainly plausible, and has even been advocated for in other common law countries. However, what is significant in the grounds for the judicial decisions on this question is that they are almost entirely based on private law (property law) reasoning, to the exclusion of policy considerations pertaining specifically to tax law. There is, for instance, no mention of any disadvantage to the tax authorities of allowing a contract to dispose of what may be a significant portion of the economic value of land,[122] on the one hand, or, on the other, of any commercial expediency or unfair disadvantage to which industries concentrated on the extraction of natural produce might be put by the imposition of a land acquisition tax.

C.   Purchase of appurtenances and then of the land

1.   French law

In French law, doubt was originally expressed over sales of parts of land under a sale of goods contract followed by sales of the land 'bare' to the same purchaser either subsequently or contemporaneously with the sale of goods contract.

---

119 [1957] 1 WLR 529, 531.
120 [1957] 1 WLR 529, 531: '[to] mark, fell and carry away all the said trees and complete all the operations authorized at such times as he, the purchaser, shall consider convenient.'
121 42 TC 169, 180.
122 In particular when compared with transactions covered by the previous section, that is to say the purchase of land with its appurtenances.

Though originally deemed to be systematically fraudulent, from the mid-19th century onwards the French tax authorities accepted the legality of such sales, unless wholly artificial.

For instance, in the decision of *Enregistrement* v. *Laget-Valdeson*, decided in 1827, six years of successive cuts of coppice woodland (*bois taillis*) were sold first by immediate payment in full, and taxed as the sale of movable property on the basis of the doctrine of mobilisation by anticipation. However, two days later the same purchaser bought the same land upon which the mobilised trees grew.[123] The French tax authorities claimed that the two sales contracts, in fact, merely operated one single sale, that of the land and with its appurtenances (*avec toutes ses dépendances*), and that the cumulative price of both contracts should have been subject to the land acquisition tax, thus applying a higher rate of tax for the portion of the purchase relating to the successive cuts of coppice.

On appeal before the *Tribunal de Montpellier* the French tax authorities' claim for land acquisition tax on the sale of coppice was rejected on the ground that there was no fraud on the part of the buyer. In particular, since the land was matrimonial property owned by the wife yet managed by her husband, the separate sales contracts were held to be justified in that the contractual capacity to dispose of the produce of the land lay with the husband and that to dispose of the land itself belonged to the wife. The sale of the land separately was also justified by the fact that, as a sale of (anticipated) movable property which could not be the subject of a land charge, the sale of the bare land the price of which was not due until much later provided the buyer of the coppice with security.[124] The Cour de cassation upheld the appeal on a point of law on the sole ground that sales of coppice and timber are taxable as movable property[125] and, unless legislation was enacted to that effect,[126] the fact that separate sales contracts had not been concluded with the intention of evading the land acquisition tax, would not change the fact that the trees were movable under the first sales contract.

---

123 Cass. civ. (04.04.1827): [1827] S 563.

124 [1827] S 563: '[le paiement du prix comptant] ne pouvait se faire, sans négliger les précautions exigées par la prudence, exigée par la loi, qu'à l'égard d'une vente d'objets mobiliers non susceptibles d'hypothèque, tandis que le prix de la vente du domaine ne fut stipulé payable que dans le délai de six moins, temps plus que suffisant pour que l'acquéreur pût prendre ses précautions pour la validité de la libération'.

125 Art. 69(5)(1), Loi du 22 frim. An 7: 'les ventes de coupes de bois taillis et de futaie, et autres objets mobiliers.'

126 For example, in the Ancien Droit, although acquisition tax was owed to the feudal lord as under the custumals or collections of customary law of Paris and Orléans, such a separation of contracts was qualified as Norman fraud (*fraude normande*) and outlawed under a declaration of 27th July 1731, cf. Case-note on Cass. req. (08.09.1813): [1816] 1 S 15; Pothier, *Traité des fiefs* (1776), ch. 5, section 2, § 1; Bugnet (ed.) *Œuvres de Pothier*, vol. 9 (Plon, Paris, 1861, 2nd ed.), [478], p. 621.

In later years a certain degree of tolerance thus came to be accepted. The price of 'mobilised' parts of land are excluded from land acquisition tax in the presence of two separate contractual arrangements, provided there be no fraud on the part of the buyer. Thus, in the purchase of wooded land, a price attributed to all of the trees, irrespective of their age of maturity, under a sales contract and another price for the land considered bare of the trees would be regarded as tantamount to fraud and land acquisition tax would be due on the combined price of both contracts. If the sale of goods contract only granted a cut of all trees of felling age, to be felled as soon as possible, or there were objective reasons for such an arrangement, then the price stipulated in the sale of goods contract would not be charged to land acquisition tax.[127]

2.   German law

In German law, the rule that tax law follows the characterisation of property as land or goods according to the rules of property law is the principle of general application. Thus, if a person purchases parts of land sold for severance and subsequently the 'bare' land itself, the value of the parts of land remaining un-separated upon the transfer of title in the land is taxable with the price paid for the land 'bare'. To the argument that the transferee of the land would only acquire it, for example, bare in its future state once previously sold gravel had been extracted, the Bundesfinanzgericht has answered that, since the 'right to extract gravel is a power falling within the scope of the right of ownership over the land, and thereby merely a part of the land's ownership,'[128] the 'transfer of title in the land made the performance of the obligation to suffer another's removal of the gravel impossible.'[129] Unquestionably, an individual cannot forbear his or her own actions.

Tax law does not, however, always follow the property law classification. An exception from the general principle is made where the appurtenances and bare land are sold to different persons. If, for instance, land is sold of which some parts have already been sold for severance and the purchaser of the land also contracts to allow the previous purchaser of the parts to continue the exploitation of the

---

127 Guyot, *Droit forestier* (Berger-Levrault, Nancy, 1921), [68].
128 BFH (22.06.1966, II 130/62): [1966] 3 BStBl 552, 553: 'Das Recht zur Kiesgewinnung ist also nur eine im Eigentumsrecht selbst enthaltene Befugnis und somit lediglich Teil des Grundstückseigentums mit der Folge, daß der Grundstücksübergang sich auch auf das Kiesvorkommen erstreck...'
129 Idem: 'die Veräußerer [hatten] mit dem durch den Grundstücksvertrag erstrebten Ei-gentumsübergang sich die Erfüllung der Gegenleistung (Duldung der Kiesausbeute) für die erhaltenen [Ausbeutungspreis] gleichzeitig unmöglich [gemacht]'.

land, then only the value of the land in its future state without the parts for severance is taxable under the land acquisition tax.[130] In strict property law terms, the purchaser acquires the land with all its integral parts, whether gravel, standing timber or houses for demolition. Any so-called reservation operates *in personam* only, binding the purchaser of the land for the benefit of the seller of the land's previous contracting party (i.e. the earlier purchaser of the parts of land). Nevertheless, to take account of the economic result of the transaction, tax law only attaches significance to the value of the land considered 'bare'. In doing so, an overall view of the legal relationships at issue is taken enabling a departure from the strict position in property for the specific purposes of the land acquisition tax.

German law does not, however, depart from the property law classification where, even if sold to two different persons, the relationship between those legal persons is such that they would not consider themselves bound to one another. In such a tripartite case, with a common seller, a buyer of parts of land and another buyer of the land 'bare', a price is set for the parts of land earmarked for severance, another price for the land, and the purchaser of the land is proprietarily entitled to the full economic value of the land but paid a lesser price for it. Where the first buyer will, in reality, not rely on its contractual rights, there is also no need for the tax authorities to do so. Accordingly, the second buyer pays land acquisition tax on the full economic value of the land.

The law is well illustrated by a 1966 case before the Bundesfinanzgericht the timber had been purchased first followed shortly after by the land bare.[131] In contradistinction to the French case of *Enregistrement* v. *Laget-Valdeson*,[132] where both sales contracts were concluded by the same purchaser, but on analogy with the facts in the English case of *Hopwood* v. *CN Spencer Ltd*,[133] where the directors bought the land with the company's money, a German partnership purchased standing timber first, whilst one of the partners purchased the 'bare' land the following day. The Bundesfinanzgericht held that, if the means of acquisition led to the partnership's economic control over the value (*wirtschaftliche Verwertungsbefugnis*) of both the land and its parts contractually and separately destined for severance, such as where a partner's property is treated between the partners as owned by the partnership, the land acquisition tax will apply to the whole value of the land.

---

130 BFH (22.06.1966, II 130/62) 86 BFHE 424; [1966] 3 BStBl 552. Also, the lease of land with power to remove its products – a personal right with third party effect in German law – is taken into account for the calculation of the land acquisition tax: (28.08.1963, II 150/61): [1964] Höchstrichterliche Finanzrechtsprechung (HFR) 245.
131 BFH (11.05.1966, II 171/63): [1966] BeckRS 21005621.
132 Cass. civ. (04.04.1827): [1827] S 563.
133 42 TC 169. As well as those alluded to in *Saunders* v. *Pilcher* [1949] All ER 1097.

These principles are settled case-law. In another case of the Bundesfinanzgericht decided in 1977, land was purchased which had already been leased with the right to extract peat to the partnership in which the purchaser was a partner.[134] The German tax authorities claimed that the purchaser ought to pay tax on the whole value of the land, including the part represented by the future rent due for the lease. In the negotiations for the sale of the land, the purchaser of the land had explained that the partnership would no longer consider itself bound by the term set for the end of the lease if it acquired ownership of the land itself. The Bundesfinanzgericht held that the principle whereby the taxable part of purchased land previously leased for mineral extraction is formed by the land in its future exploited state, i. e. without the value of the minerals, does not apply to the present case where it is not even certain whether the contractual future state of affairs would come to pass.[135]

3.   English law

There is no binding authority in English law on the consequences, in terms of land acquisition tax, of buying parts of land for severance and then, prior to severance, buying the land 'bare'. Certainly, in terms of private law, the re-unification of all the prerogatives under the same head would, in law, reunite the trees to the land.[136] However, there are recent *obiter dicta* which suggest that, for tax law purposes, the land acquisition tax would only stick to the price of the bare land subsequently acquired.

In the leading tax case of *Saunders* v. *Pilcher* discussing the characterisation of *fructus naturales*, a market gardener bought a cherry orchard with the year's crop of cherries and three weeks later picked the cherries.[137] Approximately half of the purchase price had been apportioned to that year's cherry crop. For the purposes of income tax, the purchaser sought to deduct the costs apportioned to the cherries from the price at which the fruit was subsequently sold. The Court of Appeal held that the cherries passed with the land as part and parcel thereof and, as a capital expenditure, were not deductible; the purchaser was charged to

---

134 BFH (22.06.1977, II R 22/71): [1977] 2 BStBl 703; 122 BFHE 565.
135 'Voraussetzung ist jedoch, daß die Gestaltung des Vertragsverhältnisses den Schluß auf den Erwerb des Grundstücksanteiles bzw. Grundstückes in seinem künftigen Zustand rechtfertigt. Dieser Schluß liegt nahe, wenn das Grundstück demnächst vom Verkäufer (durch Bebauung) in diesen Zustand versetzt werden soll. Er läßt sich jedoch in solchen Fällen wie dem vorliegenden nicht rechtfertigen, in denen beim Erwerb nicht einmal feststand, wann dieser künftige Zustand eintreten werde.'
136 *Herlakenden's case* 4 Co. Rep. 62a, 63b; 76 ER 1025, 1029.
137 [1949] All ER 1097.

income tax on the entire sales price of the cherries. Having held that *fructus naturales* was for tax purposes a part of land as a capital asset, the decision must *a fortiori* be authority for the view that the value of the land, inclusive of the cherries, is subject to land acquisition tax.

Views were also expressed in that case on two permutations to the facts of the case. The first was if the cherries had been purchased under a sales contract, followed by the land 'bare'. The second was in terms of the business activity pursued by the purchaser. As regards the former permutation, both Singleton LJ and Jenkins LJ considered that '[the purchaser] might easily have done what would have been in substance the same thing in a different way by buying the cherries separately from the land simply by a modification in the form of the transaction' and thereby '… he might not have had so great a liability to tax.'[138] The income tax liability for the price of the cherries would then have fallen upon the seller of the land.[139] The same view has also been stated regarding fixtures, such as machines attached to a factory, when the land is sold.[140]

The second permutation was a difference in the trade carried on by the purchaser. This obiter dictum is, however, more tentative in nature. Tucker LJ said, 'In the present case, I express no opinion – it is not necessary to do so – as to what the position might have been had the taxpayer been a dealer in fruit and nothing else. Different considerations possibly would have arisen in such circumstances, but that is not this case.'[141] This line of reasoning originates in the distinction drawn for income taxes between fixed and circulating capital in determining which expenses are deductible. Cherries hanging on a tree on land purchased by a dealer in fruit, as opposed to a market gardener, are necessarily purchased with a view to their severance and later sale. The dealer in fruit merely purchases stock-in-trade, as a crop of cherries already harvested, rather than the growing potential of the land itself. The reasoning is related to that underlying the exclusion of sale of goods contracts. Tax law looks to the intention of the parties to the transaction expressed in their contract in characterising a part of land as goods. Here that

---

138 [1949] All ER 1097, 1102D per Singleton LJ and 1106D-E per Jenkins LJ.

139 [1949] All ER 1097, 1106E per Jenkins LJ: 'One has to remember that this transaction concerned not merely the taxpayer, but also the vendor of the orchard. …The difference [between selling the cherries with or apart from the land] is obviously a material one from the vendor's point of view, because, dealing with the matter as he did, he was selling a capital asset, and the resulting capital receipt prima facie would attract no tax. If he had sold the cherries separately in the way of trade, he would at once have created an income receipt on which prima facie tax would have been exigible.'

140 Thomas, *Stamp Duty Land Tax* (CUP: Cambridge, 2006), [2.14], p. 16: 'If [a] chattel is attached to the land so as to be a fixture it is treated as forming part of the land… However, if a chattel which has been a fixture is sold separately rather than as a fixture together with land of which it forms part then no chargeable interest is acquired.'

141 *Saunders* v. *Pilcher* CA (24.11.1949): [1949] All ER 1097, 1107B-C.

outward expression of intention is inferred, not from the form of a contract, but from the trade conducted by the buyer.

Similar reasoning on the type of trade pursued by a purchaser could also apply to standing timber. However, that view has been eschewed in other common law decisions on the distinction between fixed and circulating capital. In such cases, the full price of land purchased for the purpose and trade of acquiring its appurtenances for severance is, as land and thereby fixed capital, not a deductible expense.[142]

Accordingly, there is strong authority in English law for the proposition that the price of a previously-concluded sale of goods contract for the severance of parts of a plot of land subsequently sold to the same buyer would not be subject to land acquisition tax.

D.   Conclusions

An historical and comparative analysis of the relevant judicial decisions in the use of the distinction of land and goods for the purposes of tax reveals a whole variety of divergence. That divergence lies behind the apparent convergence of three national taxes of the same nature charged universally on the acquisition of land.

First, when land is purchased with its appurtenances, such as produce growing from that land, tax is charged on the full economic value of the land. Here economic and legal reality coincide, at least as far as land acquisition tax is concerned. Accordingly, there is no tension between the policy considerations of property law and tax law; the latter follows the former. In English law, the hybrid characterisation of growing crops has given rise to a benefit-of-the-doubt practice in favour of the taxpaying purchaser of the land which, although presenting a *de minis* discrepancy between economic and legal reality, has nevertheless received judicial criticism as an inaccurate statement of the law.

Second, when appurtenances are purchased without the land – although strictly speaking still legally attached to the land – no tax is now charged according to the law as it currently stands in English, French and German law. However, in English law, contracts for the sale of standing timber were, over an extended period of time past, regarded as a sale of land, and taxed accordingly. This historical difference demonstrates the relationship between private law classifications and tax. Sales of standing timber were formerly taxed ultimately

---

142 *Alianza Co Ltd* v. *Bell (Surveyor of Taxes)* HC (01.07.1904): [1904] 2 KB 666 and *Kauri Timber Co Ltd* v. *Taxes Commissioner,* Privy Council (New Zealand) (10.07.1913): [1913] AC 771.

on the basis of the same rules governing the level of formality required for different contracts. Such sales fell into the category of high-value (i. e. relating to land) and speculative (i. e. prospective) sales contracts. When the rules on the formalities for sales of goods contracts evolved, so did the tax treatment of the same transactions. These great changes in tax treatment all occurred under the auspices of an unchanged universal distinction between land and goods.

Third, when first purchased without the land and – at a later point in time – the land is subsequently purchased but, for instance, the timber previously sold has not yet been felled, the economic value of the produce is sometimes but not always added to the tax base of the national land acquisition tax. Here lies the greatest tension between, on the one hand, private law and tax law and, on the other, legal and economic reality. It is, for instance, possible for a significant portion of the economic value of the land to escape taxation. On the other hand, to regard a contract concluded prior to the physical separation of parts of land, such as standing timber, as a taxable acquisition of land may appear as an over-zealous legalistic adherence to the characterisation of parts of land at a particular point in time, notwithstanding the purpose of such contracts to govern future events. This situation also results in the greatest divergence in outcome between the legal systems for comparison. French tax law adheres strongly to the private law construct whereby parts of land contractually agreed to be separated are separated in law prior to their physical separation, and only intervenes to tax such sales of goods in the case of wholly artificial – if not fraudulent – arrangements. Similarly, the better view of English law appears to be that the price of a pre-viously concluded sales of goods contract for the severance of parts of a plot of land subsequently sold to the same buyer would not be subject to land acquisition tax. German tax law, according to the particular factual permutation in question, generally follows the position of standing timber and analogous parts of land according to the private law distinction of land and goods, but diverges excep-tionally. Thus, when a person first purchases appurtenances without the land and then acquires the land and such appurtenances have not been physically sepa-rated from the land, the price stipulated for the appurtenances is reattributed to the price of the land and taxed accordingly. However, if the buyers of the ap-purtenances and of the land sold 'bare' are different persons, although from a strict property law point of view such appurtenances are still part and parcel of the land, and pass as such to the second purchaser, the second purchaser pays tax only on the value of the land 'bare'. In such a case, tax law looks more broadly to the overall picture of the legal relationship, and the fact that the second purchaser would be under an obligation to forbear performance of the first contract.

What is, however, perhaps more important than differences in outcome be-tween these national decisions, or even differences in legal argumentation, is the universal nature of the underlying reasoning for those decisions. That reasoning is, in the first instance, systematically couched in terms of property law, or private law in general, and not – or extremely rarely – in terms of any policy considerations proper to tax law. Tax law is a prime example of a parasitic use of a distinction in one field of tax law which has been carried over wholesale from another field of law. It is a "lazy" or "economical" lawmaker legislative technique. Rather than reinventing the wheel with a novel or perhaps necessarily detailed definition of material scope, the lawmaker relies on a definition picked off the shelf from another field of law. The corollary of the "lazy" lawmaker approach is a corresponding "lazy ratio", whereby the reason underlying a particular classification of factual circumstances is the ratio from the "host" field of law. This legislative technique is extremely effective for the majority of cases. It works provided that the real ratio of the parasitic field of law does not diverge too significantly from the outcome resulting from the rules of the host field of law. If so, a tension arises and a choice presents itself of taking a formalistic approach, sticking to the host distinction, or adapting the distinction to the ratio or policy consideration of the parasitic field of law.

Chapter 3.
Requirements of form for sales contracts in land

The purpose of this chapter is to examine the extension of the distinction of land and goods to formal requirements for the conclusion of a sales contract, specifically for standing timber and crops. Do additional requirements of form for the validity of contracts for land apply to contracts for the sale of standing trees or the present year's crop?

There are two limbs to this question. The first limb presupposes that there are differences in form in respect of contracts for land and goods, whilst the second limb concerns whether they apply to one particular type of contract, that is to say a contract the purpose of which is to uproot standing timber or harvest crops. As will be seen, the legal systems differ in their answers to both limbs and in the reasoning underpinning those answers. This difference allows the comparative approach to be helpfully brought to bear where there are diverging views at a national level.

The first section of this chapter concerns the first limb of the question posed, namely whether there is a legal requirement relating to the distinction of land and goods as far as the validity of a contract for the severance of things forming part of land. The next section sets out the characterisations of such contracts in English, French and German law in this area, including a detailed exposition of the complex state of English law. This is followed by an attempt at synthesising and conceptualising the policy considerations underlying the previous characterisations and, lastly, a section bringing the resulting whole into a suggested conceptual framework for analysing the law as it stands in a comparative perspective, in terms of the systemics and purpose for which the distinction of land and goods has been drawn.

A.   Distinctions and Delimitations

In England and Germany, there are additional requirements of form for the validity of a sales contract for land. In England, as far as goods are concerned, 'a contract of sale may be made in writing, or by word of mouth, or partly in writing and by word of mouth, or may be implied from the conduct of the parties.'[143] As regards land, on the other hand, 'A contract for the sale or other disposition of an interest in land can only be made in writing and only by incorporating all the terms which the parties have expressly agreed in one document or, where contracts are exchanged, in each.'[144] In Germany, a contract for the sale of land must be recorded by a notary in order to bind the contracting parties.[145] Sales of goods, on the other hand, are, in principle free in form, hence the need to stipulate in § 452 BGB that sales contracts for ships – which would otherwise be movable property – are governed by the relevant provisions on sales contracts for plots of land.

In France, as far as concerns the validity of a sales contract between the buyer and seller, there are in fact no additional requirements of form relating to whether or not the object sold is goods or land. Whether the contract purports to sell land or goods of the same value the same requirements of form are applicable. The additional requirements of form for sales of land – notarization and publication – do not affect the validity of the contract *inter partes* but the transfer of title vis-à-vis third parties.

The distinction of requirements of form in French law for the formation of a contract and for the validity of its effect on third parties is well illustrated by the decision in *Nouvel v. Yves Jacobelli* where a wooden cabin was sold to be taken away by the buyer who, after having removed it, refused to pay the price.[146] The buyer argued *inter alia* that the sale was void for not having been concluded according to the specific rules relating to sale of contracts for land. The Court of appeal of Aix-en-Provence, however, qualified the contract as one for movables by anticipation since the parties had intended title to pass in a construction which could be detached from the land in whole or in a number of parts. It also held that 'even had the sale been of immovable property there would have been no requirement of form since the parties had agreed upon a thing in existence and its

---

143 s. 4, Sale of Goods Act 1979.
144 s. 2(1), Law of Property (Miscellaneous Provisions) Act 1989.
145 § 311b, BGB.
146 CA Aix-en-Provence (15.02.1985): [1985] 2 Gaz Pal 442, case-note Dureuil. cf. *Compain* v. *Gillet* Cass. civ. (25.01.1886): [1886] 5 DP 39 (sale of a barn (*grange*)).

price.'[147] The necessity of requirements of form for the validity of the contract and the establishment of the respective rights and obligations of the parties are only determined by the value of the property sold, irrespective of its immovable or movable nature.

French law does, however, provide for requirements of form principally by way of publication in order for the contract to bind third parties (*opposabilité*).[148] For instance, although gifts of all forms of property must be authenticated by a notary,[149] gifts of land must be published,[150] whilst a gift of movable property need only provide a signed description of the property gifted annexed to the authenticated contract of donation.[151]

As far as requirements of form are concerned, the distinction of land and goods is applied in English and German law to sales contracts. There is at least one level of formality for land which is not applied to goods. In France, on the other hand, the distinction of land and goods is applied solely to gifts contracts, with a greater level of formality being required of gifts of land. In that light, a comparison of English, French and German law characterisations of standing timber for the purposes of contractual formalities does not always apply to the same legal transaction. It is therefore important to bear in mind that whilst the distinction may be the same, the factual circumstances and possibly similar doctrinal justifications, the underlying transaction thus varies between these three legal systems.

B.   Characterisations

As will be seen, the characterisation of a contract for the sale of standing timber in terms of formal requirements regarding its validity has proved problematic in English law, giving rise to a complicated area of law and fine distinctions over which there is no consensus. English law frames the question of whether to apply the requirement of writing applicable to contracts (for the sale) of land or the lack of formality applicable to contracts for the sale of goods in terms of whether the subject-matter of the contract is land or goods. For this reason, it is proposed to consider French law first, where the question of what formal requirements to

---

147 [1985] 2 Gaz Pal 442, 443: 'd'ailleurs, eût-elle dû être encore appréhendée comme concernant un immeuble, cette vente n'aurait encore été soumise à aucune forme, dès lors que les parties étaient d'accord sur la chose, dont l'existence ne peut être déniée, et sur le prix.'
148 Article 710-1, Code civil (Art. 9, Loi n° 2011-331 du 28 mars 2011 de modernisation des professions judiciaires ou juridiques et certaines professions réglementées).
149 Article 931, Code civil.
150 Article 939, Code civil.
151 Article 948, Code civil.

apply is framed in the same terms in an analogous legal transaction, gratuitous contracts (gifts) of standing timber. Once the various statements of the law in England have been exposed, and a brief mention has been made of the same problem repeated throughout the common law world, it is instructive to contrast the position in the previous legal systems with German law, where the same question of whether the formal requirements for contracts relating to land apply to contracts for the severance of parts of land, such as standing timber, is framed in different terms, avoiding altogether the characterisation of standing timber as land or goods at the time of the conclusion of the contract.

1.   French law

In French law, the effect of non-compliance with the requirement of a signed description of a gift of standing timber if considered goods and publication if considered land must be distinguished. The first requirement is necessary as far as concerns the validity of the contract between the contracting parties. Here there is a consensus in legal scholarship. The second requirement would only be necessary to bind third parties, but in that regard legal scholarship is divided.

a.   Validity inter partes – a signed description of the property gifted

The present-day condition of publication for gifts of immovable property does not affect the validity of the contract authenticated by a notary as between the parties,[152] contrary to the position in the Ancien droit.[153] According to Chaveau, a gift of standing trees to be felled by the donee is, as a gift of movables by anticipation, not subject to publication, but only the lesser formality of an annexed description.[154] In reference to other articles of the Code civil,[155] Picard, Planiol & Ripert also adhere to the theory of anticipatory mobilisation, by which contracts for parts of land are, as a general rule, regarded as goods. They write in relation to sales of movables by anticipation that as a general rule the provisions of the Code civil governing sales of goods must apply to the exclusion of those

---

152 Pillebout in: J.-Cl. Civil Code (2014), [26].
153 Pillebout in: J.-Cl. Civil Code (2014), [6].
154 Chaveau, 'Des meubles par anticipation' [1893] Rev crit 573, 575, [3]: 'Ainsi lorsqu'une disposition entre-vifs, à titre gratuit, porte sur des arbres à couper dans une forêt, une pareille donation a pour objet des meubles; on en doit conclure qu'elle n'est pas soumise aux formalités de l'art. 939 mais aux exigences de l'art. 948.'
155 Art. 1657 CC (effect of term for taking possession of goods sold): *Favier* v. *veuve Rochette de Lempdes* Cass. Req. (12.07.1922): [1923] 1 D 61; *Mallet et Uro* v. *Dame veuve Le Visage* Cass. Civ. (03.04.1922): [1924] 1 D. 12. Art. 1619 CC (margin of error of $^{1}/_{20}$ for stipulated quantity): *Lacombe* v. *Jay* Cass. civ. (17.12.1923): [1924] 1 DP 14.

relating to sales of land.[156] The same reasoning applies to gratuitous contracts. As a disposition of movable property, Colin-Delisle does not require the contract of gift to be published. Accordingly, pursuant to Article 938 of the Code civil, title passes from the donor to the donee without the need for delivery of the property gifted.

According to Fréjaville's theory of mobilisation by anticipation, the subject matter of such dispositions is in general movable *inter partes* whilst immovable as against third parties (*erga omnes*). As a result, a gift of unexploited standing timber trees (*arbres de haute futaie non mise en coupes réglées*) should meet the formal requirements of both movable and immovable transactions. A signed description of the property gifted must be annexed to the authenticated contract of donation so that the donee can enforce the contract as against a subsequently reticent donor and, in order to bind third parties, such as a mortgagee of the donor, the gift must be registered.[157] Non-compliance with the movable-formality leads to absolute invalidity, the gift binds neither the contracting parties nor third parties. If the movable formality is satisfied but not the immovable-formality this leads only to relative invalidity, namely validity between the contracting parties, but not vis-à-vis third parties.

b.   Third parties – publication?

Whilst early commentators of the Code civil's provisions on gifts (*donation*), such as Vazeille and Coin-Delisle, excluded gifts of the fruits of land from the condition of publication,[158] they considered that Article 939 Code civil applies to gifts of parts of land forming its substance. For instance, gifts of minerals to be extracted from land which has not yet been exploited would be dispositions of land and therefore subject to the formality of publication. As for gifts of building materials to be recovered from currently-existing buildings, Vazeille writes that 'it is advisable, and may even be necessary, to subject the gift of building materials

---

156 Picard in Planiol & Ripert, *Traité pratique de droit civil français*, [103]: 'les textes qui régissent les ventes mobilières doivent recevoir leur application, à l'exclusion de ceux relatifs aux ventes d'immeubles (Art. 1657, 1619 etc.).'

157 Fréjaville, *Des Meubles par Anticipation* (1927), p. 266.

158 Coin-Delisle, *Donations et Testamens* (1844), p. 226, Art. 936, [14]: 'La donation des récoltes prêtes à faire ou de bois mûrs pour la coupe, selon l'aménagement ou l'usage du propriétaire, ne paraît pas susceptible de transcription: c'est la disposition de fruits que la nécessité va placer au rang des choses mobilières.' Vazeille, *Les Successions, donations et testamens* (1837), vol. 2, p. 256, Art. 939, [2]: 'Ainsi la donation de fruits, la récolte faite ou prête à être faite, n'a pas besoin d'être transcrite. Ainsi, la donation, non plus que la vente de bois abattus, ou d'une coupe de bois mûr à faire, n'est pas sujette à la transcription.'

from a building to be demolished to publication.'[159] Similarly, for gifts of property which is immovable by destination and the delivery of which is to take place
at a much later date, Coin-Delisle thought publication necessary 'since at the time
of the gift the property was immovable and continues in its immovable state as
against third parties who ought never to be misled by a gift made in secret.'[160]

Vazeille also considered that contracts for the severance of successive crops of
land over a number of years and for minerals to be extracted from a quarry
already in operation would be movable regarding the crop and minerals to be
extracted of the current year, but immovable regarding that of the remaining
years. This conclusion is, however, drawn from an indirect classification of the
successive crops as immovable, since Vazeille considered such a disposition as
the grant of a life interest and thus as property capable of being mortgaged (*biens
susceptibles d'hypothèques*). Although also followed by Coin-Delisle,[161] Fréjaville
contested this characterisation, considering the donnee not as a usufructuary but
rather as a mere creditor of the donor and having only a personal right to harvest
the gifted future crops.

The corollary of Fréjaville's hybrid characterisation is that, as far as third
parties are concerned, a gift of parts of land for severance is immovable – a
contract in respect of land – , and therefore in principle subject to publication.
Fréjavaille nevertheless precludes gifts of the fruits of land, such as standing
crops or regularly-exploited forests, which would not be subject to the formal
requirement of registration as goods *erga omnes* once disposed of.[162]

As between the donee and the creditors of the donor who seize gifted corpse-
wood or crops still standing, Colin-Delisle gives priority to the creditors.[163] It is
not, however, clear whether Colin-Delisle is referring to all other creditors of the
donor or specifically mortgagees (*créanciers hypothécaires*), general creditors
(*créanciers chirographaires*), for example, in the case of the donor's insolvency,
or the donor's execution creditors. Even as against an execution creditor of
standing crops – since standing trees of any nature cannot be seized in execution

---

159   Vazeille, *Les Successions, donations et testamens* (1837), vol. 2, p. 256, Art. 939, [3]: 'Il est bon,
      il peut être nécessaire même, pour sa sûreté, de soumettre à la transcription la donation des
      matériaux d'un édifice dont le donateur ordonne ou autorise la démolition.'
160   Coin-Delisle, *Donations et Testamens* (1844), p. 226, Art. 936, [16]: 's'il se doit écouler un
      temps plus ou moins long avant [la] livraison [d'immeubles par destination donnés à titre
      gratuit], il faudrait [la] faire transcrire; car au moment de la donation, ils avaient la qualité
      d'immeubles, et ils la conservent à l'égard des tiers qui ne doivent jamais être trompés par
      une libéralité secrète.'
161   Coin-Delisle, *Donations et Testamens* (1844), p. 226, Art. 936, [14].
162   Fréjaville, p. 267.
163   Colin-Delisle, *Donations et Testamens* (1844), 226, art. 939, [14]: 'Il est cependant vrai que si
      les récoltes pendantes par racines ou les bois sur pied étaient saisis par les créanciers avant
      que d'être recueillis, le donataire perdrait tous ses droits: ce ne serait pas faute de tran-
      scription, mais parce que le donataire ne serait pas entré en possession.'

of a debt – this would run contrary to the position adopted for standing crops sold before seized by execution creditors.[164] Although a debtor's insolvency immobilises all of the fruits of land physically attached to it, the passing of title in the crops and trees mobilised by anticipation, would nevertheless generally bind the debtor's general creditors. Finally, as dispositions of fruits of land, gifts of standing crops or coppice would bind a mortgagee as acts of management which the mortgagor is entitled to make.

Presumably owing to the rarity of gratuitous contracts for severance of parts of land, there is no case-law specifically addressing this point of law. However, the Cour de cassation refuses to give priority to a buyer of movables by anticipation which would seriously reduce the value of land as against a mortgagee, especially where the latter has seized the land and the mortgagor is in arrears. In the case of sales of minerals, the court has justified that outcome on the ground that the sale is not published, although there appears to be no system of publication for such sales, and, in the case of standing trees, on the ground of the sale's immovable character as regards third parties, independently of case-law considerations of publication.

From the foregoing analysis, it can thus be concluded that the distinction in French law is irrelevant to the formal validity of a contract for the sale of property which is presently immovable and which is to be separated from the land under that contract. The distinction of movable and immovable property is therefore neither relevant to formalities for the conclusion of sales contracts in general, nor sales contracts specifically for the transformation of parts of land into movable property. A distinction has, however, been drawn for both purposes in relation to contracts of gift. As far as the donor and donnee are concerned, such a gift is unanimously regarded as one of goods, with the corresponding requirement being applied. In relation to third parties, however, differing views have been expressed and the discussion appears neither to have been resolved, nor continued to form the subject of present-day discussion.

2.   English law

In English law, the question of whether contracts for the sale of standing timber, still rooted in the soil at the time of the conclusion of the contract, must satisfy the conditions of form for a sale of land has been disputed since the early

---

164 In relation to sales contracts concluded prior to the attachment of this year's crop by the seller's creditors, cf. *Brisabois* v. *Ravel* Cass. civ. (02. 03. 1902): [1902] 1 Pand. 303; *Rumpler* v. *Diemert* CA Colmar (09. 11. 1802; 18 Brum, an 11): [1802] S 9; *Schott* v. *Wolff* Cass. civ. (02. 10. 1805, 10 vendémiaire an 14): [1805] S 166 and also Vanuxem, *Saisie de récoltes sur pied*, [34]. See also, Chapter 2. Tax law: 'now you see they see them, now you don't!'.

19th century and, at least as far as certain types of parts of land are concerned, continues to this day, despite the wording of the Sale of Goods Act 1893 which appears to regard all such contracts as sales of goods.

a.   Emergence of the problem

It was not until the enactment of the Statute of Frauds in 1677 that detailed rules were laid down distinguishing different levels of formality depending upon the object to which a particular transaction related.[165] From 1677 onwards, however, transactions relating to land required writing (s. 4) and only sales of goods below a certain price could be concluded by parole (s. 17). A complicated body of case-law developed around the requirements of form emerging from the Statute of Frauds, particularly in relation to sales contracts for parts of land sold for severance. In certain circumstances, the contract was held to purport to convey an interest in land, whilst in other cases the courts sanctioned parole contracts for parts of land sold independently of the land as valid.

Unfortunately, the rules themselves, and their interaction with one another, as developed in the cases have led to '…the most troublesome set of problems in connection with the definition of goods'[166] and, thereby, also the definition of land.[167] After searching for a guiding principle, Megarry & Wade resign themselves to the "truth" of inner contradictions within the case-law.[168] This is even recognised by the judicial pronouncements themselves.[169] The rules have even been said to be 'almost impossible to apply with absolute strictness.'[170] The difficulty has continued into the modern law and has, if anything, been further complicated. In updating Benjamin's Sale of Goods in 1974, Sealy was still able to

---

165 Earlier cases had well established, for instance, that a landowner's reservation of the right to cut down certain trees operated as a sale of goods and a disposition of the trees as chattels. See *Herlakenden's case*, KB (1589) 4 Co. Rep. 62a; 76 ER 1025; *Anon*, KB, (1604) Owen 49, 74 ER 891; *Stukeley v. Butler* (1615) Hobart 169; ER 316.

166 Ontario Law Reform Commission, *Report on sale of goods* (1979), vol. 1, p. 57.

167 Diamond et al., *Sutton and Shannon on Contracts* (London, Butterworths, 1970, 7th ed.), p. 242: 'Difficulty was always experienced in deciding whether a contract of sale under which something was to be severed from the land and taken away, as e.g., growing crops or a building which was to be demolished, was a disposition of an interest in land within s. 4 of the Statute of Frauds, now s. 40 of the Law of Property Act, 1925, or was a contract of sale of goods.'

168 Megarry & Wade, *The Law of Real Property* (1984, 5th ed.), p. 574–575. Guest, *Anson's Law of Contract* (Oxford, Clarendon Press, 1969, 23rd ed.), p. 73.

169 *Rodwell v. Phillips* (1842): 9 M&W 501, 505 *per* Lord Abinger: 'taking the cases altogether … no general rule is laid down in any one of them that is not contradicted by some other'; *Marshall v. Green* (06. 11. 1875): (1875) 1 CPD 35, 38 per Lord Coeridge CJ: 'high authorities have said that it is impossible to reconcile all the decisions on the subject'.

170 *Marshall v. Green* (06. 11. 1875) (1875) 1 CPD 35, 39.

write that '... there are curious inconsistencies in [the] interpretation [of the statutory definitions of land and goods]. This was particularly so under the Statute of Frauds, where the definitions left something of a hiatus, but the position is just as confused under the modern definitions which have replaced them ...'[171] The modern definitions still apply to this day.

The "difficulties" which have arisen in this area of law are fourfold. First, there is a spectrum of different classifications of contracts disposing of parts of land apart from the land. Second, diverging opinion has been expressed as to the interpretation of the codification of the case-law definition of goods in the Sale of Goods Act. Third, the effects of a duality in the applicable statutory regime are unclear. Finally, even the doctrinal accounts of the rules themselves differ.

b.   A spectrum of classifications

A spectrum of classifications of contracts disposing of parts of land separately from the land have been advocated ranging from treating contracts for the sale of parts of land apart from the land itself as either contracts for the sale of goods *or* land, of both land *and* goods and, finally, *only* contracts for the sale of goods. According to some authors, some contracts are contracts for an interest in land whilst others are for goods.[172] According to Goode, if there is no obligation upon the "buyer" to extract or where there is an obligation to extract, but the parties intended to grant an interest in the materials *in situ* 'the transaction amounts to the grant of a profit à prendre; and this is the case even if the consideration for the grant is directly related to the quantity of material extracted.'[173] It has, for instance, been argued that a contract whereby a young crop is disposed of, but the buyer is to tend to it, harvest it and which confers upon the seller an immediate right of re-entry upon a certain date, irrespective of the harvest's progress would pass an interest in the land.[174]

---

171 Guest et al (ed.), *Benjamin's Sale of Goods* (1974), [76].
172 Guest, *Anson's Law of Contract* (Oxford, Clarendon Press, 1969, 23rd ed.), p. 73: '*Fructus naturales*, on the other hand, may or may not come within the Statute ...' Sealy in Guest (ed.), *Benjamin's Sale of Goods* (1974), [81]: 'Here the principal question is whether a contract providing for the severance and removal of such commodities is a sale of goods or an agreement to grant an interest in the land in the nature of a profit à prendre.'
173 Goode, *Commercial Law* (London, Penguin, 1982), p. 155; a profit à prendre is a real right in land to appropriate natural parts of land (minerals, timber, fish, etc.) and remove them from the land, similar in nature to the rights of servitudes in civil law systems. If 'in gross', however, it is not ancilliary to ownership of adjacent land.
174 Anon, Growing Crops – the passing of property before severance' (1949) 93 The Law Journal 259: 'Suppose a contract made in July provided for the sale of a growing crop of onions for a lump sum, the buyer to be responsible for the thinning, weeding, etc., of the crop, which was to be harvested and carried away by him before a specified date, after which the seller was to have the right to re-enter upon the field whether or not the field was by that time cleared. That is,

Other authors maintain that a sale of parts of land for severance could, in certain circumstances, be both a sale of land and of goods. The strongest expression of this doctrine is provided by Sutton & Shannon where the view is taken that 'a contract might be a contract for the sale of goods within the Sale of Goods Act, 1893, while also being a contract for the sale of an interest in land within s. 40 of the Law of Property Act, 1925.'[175] Other authors refer to the duality of classification as a "possibility".[176]

Although the two authors question whether 'the same thing [can be] land for the purpose of one statute and goods for the purpose of another,' Megarry & Wade seem to admit that '[i]nconvenient as this result may be, there is no necessary impossibility about it.'[177] Whilst suggesting that the enactment of the Miscellaneous Provisions LPA in 1989, should be interpreted as having changed the ("irrational"[178]) law on this point, Harpum et al accept that the intermediary position of the law – from the enactment of the first SGA to its latest revamping in 1989 – was such that 'a contract could at one and the same time, be a contract for the sale of both land within the Law of Property Act 1925 and goods within the Sale of Goods Act 1979.' Similarly, the American Uniform Commercial Code also appears to have adopted the duality of transactions over parts of land for sev-

---

without doubt, a contract which passes a present interest in the crop while it is still growing and still has some time to grow, and since the buyer has to tend the growing crop as well, it would seem to be a contract which passes an interest in the land. The property in the onions undoubtedly passes before severance. The buyer would therefore be deemed to be a grower, for the purposes of the Onions (Maximum Prices) Order, 1942, SR & O., 1942, n° 1774.'

175 Diamond et al., *Sutton and Shannon on Contracts* (London, Butterworths, 1970, 7th ed.), p. 243. Guest et al (ed.), *Benjamin's Sale of Goods* (1974), [76]: '[the modern statutory definitions of land and goods] appear in some respects to overlap'; [83]: 'The definition of "goods" is wider [in the Sale of Goods Act] than that in the Statute of Frauds, and has in consequence removed many doubts as to the meaning of "goods" for the purposes of its own provisions, but it cannot affect the meaning of "land" or "an interest in land" for the purpose of the [Law of Property] Act of 1925. The result is that both statutes may apply to certain transactions.'

176 Atiyah et al., *The Sale of Goods* (2001, 10th ed.), p. 46–47: 'The fact that since 1893 these [i. e. *fructus naturales*] are 'goods' within the meaning of the Sale of Goods Act does not rule out the possibility that they may at the same time be land within the meaning of the Law of Property (Miscellaneous Provisions) Act or of the Requirements of Writing (Scotland) Act' and for whom, p. 47, fn 2., 'the question is not, 'goods or land?', but rather, 'goods only, or goods and land?' cf. Anon, 'Growing crops' (1943) 93 LJ 259: 'It must, however, be remembered that a contract which is primarily intended to dispose of a growing crop may have the effect of passing an interest in the land on which the crop is growing, and the property in the crop will then also pass, quite irrespective of any considerations arising under the Sale of Goods Act, 1893, although it may well happen that such a contract also falls within the definition of a contract of sale of goods in that Act by reason of some provision in the contract providing for the severance of the crop.'

177 Megarry & Wade, *The Law of Real Property* (1984, 5th ed.), p. 575.

178 Harpum et al., *Megarry & Wade: The Law of Real Property* (London, Sweet & Maxwell, 2012, 8th ed.), p. 634, [15-026].

erance. Nevertheless, this concerns, on the one hand, the relations between buyer and seller and, on the other hand, vis-à-vis third parties having rights in the land.

Finally, some authors assert that, since the enactment of the Sale of Goods Act in 1893, such contracts are *only* contracts for the sale of goods. This is the view adopted in later editions of Blackburn's *Treatise on the effect of the contract of sale on the legal rights of property and possession.*[179] Harpum et al suggest in *Megarry & Wade's Law of Real Property* that all parts of land sold separately, whether crops, fixtures, or building materials, should be considered goods rather than land for the purposes of the formal requirements relating to their validity.[180] This approach mirrors Fréjaville's theory of anticipatory mobilisation in French law.

The view as to the duality of classification provokes the question of its practical consequences. It must be noted that, although the underlying distinction remains the same, the specific requirements of form have been reformed. First, at least for England and Wales, the requirement of written form for contracts disposing of interests in land is no longer merely evidential. Since the enactment of the Law of Property (Miscellaneous Provisions) Act 1989 written form is a condition of validity and the equitable doctrine of part performance has therefore been abolished. Furthermore, the additional formalities of writing, earnest or part-performance relating to contracts for sale of goods above a certain value have been repealed with the effect that any such contract, regardless of its value, can be concluded by parole.[181] As a result, there are many more contracts which are capable of being invalidated solely on the ground that they relate to land.

c.   Whether the SGA operated a change in the law

The Sale of Goods Act defines "goods" as 'all personal chattels other than things in action and money…; and in particular "goods" includes emblements, industrial growing crops, and things attached to or forming part of the land which are agreed to be severed before sale or under the contract of sale.'[182] Whatever the position at common law may have been, many authors assert that 'the Sale of

---

179 Raeburn et al., *Blackburn on Contract of sale* (Stevens & Sons, London, 1910, 3rd ed.), p. 6: 'But the Sale of Goods Act appears to have altered the law to this extent, that so long as the contract provides for the severance from the soil of the thing sold, even though it is the buyer who is to effect the severance, or the property has passed before severance, it is a contract for the sale of goods.'

180 Harpum et al, *Megarry & Wade: The Law of Real Property* (London, Sweet & Maxwell, 2012, 8th ed.), p. 635, [15-026].

181 s. 1, Law Reform (Enforcement of Contracts) Act 1954. Mark, *Chalmer's Sale of Goods Act 1893* (London, Butterworths, 1967, 15th ed.), p. 32: 'As a consequence, the whole of the learning which had accrued round the section and its predecessor (s. 17 of the Statute of Frauds, 1677) has become obsolete.'

182 s. 62, Sale of Goods Act 1893; s. 61, Sale of Goods Act 1979 (wording unchanged).

Goods Act appears to have altered the law to this extent, that so long as the contract provides for the severance from the soil of the thing sold, although it is the buyer who is to effect the severance, or the property has passed before severance, it is a contract for the sale of goods.'[183] All parts of land[184] forming the subject-matter of a contract for sale whose purpose is their severance, whether immediately or at some time in the future,[185] are therefore goods.

Against the view that the Sale of Goods Act overturned the previously applicable position at common law, the argument is raised that the Sale of Goods Act definition must be restricted to the purposes of that Act.[186] Sutton and Shannon wrote, and the view was maintained in subsequent editions, that 'the fact that a wide definition of goods is given in the one Act cannot operate to restrict the meaning of an 'interest in land' in the other, or to overrule cases decided thereunder or under the statute which it replaces.'[187] As will be seen in the following paragraph, delineating the purposes of the Sale of Goods Act from those of the Law of Property Act is problematic.

The Sale of Goods Act 1893, the full title of which is 'An Act for codifying the Law relating to the Sale of Goods', was drafted by Chalmers with the aim of reproducing 'as exactly as possible the existing law.'[188] Nevertheless, there are areas where Chalmers innovated and it is said to be unclear whether the definition of goods was one of those areas. In the view of the Ontario Law Reform Commission, for example, '[i]t is not clear whether Chalmers intended to reproduce the narrow construction of the effect of *Marshall* v. *Green* ..., or whether, in contrast to his usual approach, he sought to establish an enlarged

---

183 Raeburn et al (ed.), *Blackburn's Contract of sale* (3rd ed.), p. 6. Also, see p. 16: 'It is to be observed that the Sale of Goods Act, 1893, s. 62, includes in the definition of "goods" 'things attached to or forming part of the land which are *agreed to be severed before sale or under the contract of sale*,' and thereby sanctions the conversion, by agreement of the parties, of a hereditament into chattels, which Chitty, J., in *Lavery* v. *Purcell*, declined to accept; and it is submitted that in this respect the Act has made a change in the law.'

184 Sealy, in Guest et al (ed.), *Benjamin's Sale of Goods* (1974), [89]: 'The definition of "goods" in the Sale of Goods Act seems to be sufficiently wide to include all contracts for the sale of fixtures where severance (not necessarily by the seller) is contemplated.'

185 Sealy in Guest et al (ed.), *Benjamin's Sale of Goods*, [91]: 'Looking to the words of the Act itself, it is submitted that whether severance is to be immediate or otherwise is no longer material.'

186 *Sutton and Shannon on Contracts* (1970), p. 243: 'this definition is a definition for the purpose of the Act only, not a general definition'.

187 Diamond et al., *Sutton and Shannon on Contracts* (London, Butterworths, 1970, 7th ed.), p. 244.

188 Raeburn et al, *Blackburn's Contract of sale* (1910, 3rd ed.) 'The Sale of Goods Act, 1893, was a codifying statute, which, except in a few points to be hereafter noted, made no alteration in the existing law, but merely gave it a final and definitive expression. That being so, decisions prior to the Act are still of value as indicating and illustrating the principles upon which the codification proceeded, and as explaining the application of the various sections of the Act.'

meaning of goods, beyond the meaning warranted by the case-law. Unfortunately, this part of the statutory definition of goods lends itself to both interpretations and is ambiguous in other respects.'[189]

The view has even been taken that, since the continuation of s. 4 of the Statute of Frauds is contained in the Law of Property Act 1925, the provisions of the later Act ought to take precedence as having impliedly repealed the definition of the Sale of Goods Act 1893. This particular argument cannot stand. It would mean that the consolidatory re-enactment of the Sale of Goods Act in 1979 would encapsulate Parliament's will to re-assert the primacy of that definitions of goods, and thereby reduce the scope of the definition of land in the 1925 Act. Such a roller-coaster argument would then also mean that the Law of Property (Miscellaneous Provisions) Act would have returned the previous status quo in 1989. It is patent that the legislation never directed its attention to the issue.

Guest argues that '[i]t would be convenient if [the] definition [of the Sale of Goods Act] was also adopted for the purposes of the Statute [i.e. s. 40, Law of Property Act, now s. 2 Law of Property (Miscellaneous Provisions) Act, 1989] and such crops [as *fructus naturales*] held to fall outside its provisions.'[190] In the 2012 edition of *Megarry & Wade's Law of Real Property*, Harpum et al suggest that in light of the fact that the formal requirements for contracts for the sale of land and interests in land have been tightened through the abolition of the doctrine of part performance as well as the resulting invalidity instead of mere unenforceability of such contracts, 'there is much to be said for rejecting these old distinctions…'[191] As a result, all parts of land sold separately, whether crops, fixtures, or building materials, would be goods rather than land for the purposes of s. 2 of the Law of Property (Miscellaneous Provisions) Act 1989. On the other hand, since in any case reference is frequently had to the prior position at common law when interpreting such a codifying Act of Parliament, and especially where the statute is unclear, many authors therefore assert that the previous law still stands.

In the leading case of *Marshall* v. *Green*,[192] decided eighteen years before the enactment of the Sale of Goods Act, a landowner had sold a specific number of trees for a certain price by parole to be felled and removed by the buyer and, although the buyer had already begun to fell and had even disposed of some of the resulting timber to another, the seller sought to repudiate the contract so that the terms of the contract might be changed, arguing that as the agreement was for an interest in land no contract had in fact been concluded for lack of form. The court held that a valid sale of goods contract had been concluded and, although

---

189 Ontario Law Reform Commission, *Report on sale of goods* (1979), vol. 1., p. 54.
190 Guest, Anson's Law of Contract (Oxford, Clarendon Press, 1969, 23rd ed.), p. 67.
191 Harpum et al, *Megarry & Wade: The Law of Real Property* (London, Sweet & Maxwell, 2012, 8th ed.), p. 635, [15-026].
192 HC (06.11.1875) (1875) 1 CPD 35.

the price exceeded the amount set by s. 17 Statute of Frauds for the conclusion of parole sale of goods contracts, it fell within the exception, since the buyer had accepted and actually received part of the goods. Lord Coleridge CJ held that 'treating them as not being *fructus industriales*, the proposition is that where the thing sold is to derive no benefit from the land, and is to be taken away immediately, the contract is not for an interest in land'[193] and Brett J. also that 'if the thing, not being *fructus industriales*, is to be delivered immediately, whether the seller is to deliver it or the buyer is to enter and take it himself, then the buyer is to derive no benefit from the land, and consequently the contract is not for an interest in the land, but relates solely to the thing sold itself.'[194]

d.   Effect of the duality

Prior to the enactment of the Sale of Goods Act, and also that of the Law of Property Act 1925, the Statute of Frauds provided uniformity of purpose. That purpose was the degree of formality for the formation of a contract. The subsequent codifications gave rise to the possibility of two different definitions of land and goods for the purposes of each new Act. The most developed ideas on the consequences of transactions being both contracts for sale of goods and contracts for an interest in land is given in *Sutton and Shannon on Contracts*. The view is there taken that 'If the provisions of both statutes apply then both statutes must be satisfied; and the fact that a wide definition of goods is given in the one Act cannot operate to restrict the meaning of an "interest in land" in the other, or to overrule cases decided thereunder or under the statute which it replaces.'[195]

The problem with this view is that the legal purposes of both statutes are, in fact, the same. The Law of Property Act, providing rules for the law of real property, and the Sale of Goods Act, providing rules for the law of (tangible) personal property, are functionally the same and merely provide two streams of alternative rules. This is not the case, for instance, between statutes on points of tax law, such as capital allowances or income tax regimes, where the distinction of personalty and realty may serve a different purpose from a statute on the law of execution and may therefore allow for the same transaction to be qualified as realty for the one and personalty for the other. Such examples would be "specific function"-driven definitions of land and goods, whereas the definitions in the Sale of Goods Act and s. 2, Law of Property (Miscellaneous Provisions) Act, are co-ordinatory definitions sorting out which transactions fall within the one or the other area of law.

---

193 (1875) 1 CPD 35, 40.
194 (1875) 1 CPD 35, 43.
195 Diamond et al., *Sutton and Shannon on Contracts* (London, Butterworths, 1970, 7th ed.), p. 244.

The difficulty of qualifying the same transaction as both personalty and realty *for the same purposes* can be illustrated by a few examples. For instance, the passing of property under the Sale of Goods Act occurs when the goods are identified or ascertained or at a later time intended by the parties, whereas the passing of property in land, or of an interest in land, depends upon a conveyance and, in the modern system of land law, upon registration of the conveyance. Since the passing of the risk depends, as a default rule, in English law upon the passing of property, should the parts of land sold for severance be destroyed by natural disaster, the risk cannot lie at the same time upon the seller under the rules of the law of realty and upon the buyer under the law of personalty.

The same applies to the formalities for the validity of the contract; how can the same contract be valid between the parties[196] under the law of the sale of goods, since parole contracts are valid under s. 4 SGA 1979, yet invalid between the parties under the law of real property, s. 2 LP(MP)A 1989? The contract can only be, at least as between the two parties themselves, either valid or invalid. Furthermore, the proponents of the dual regime recognise that prior to the enactment of the SGA, 1893, the question was always whether the contract was for the sale of land or goods, never both.[197]

Sealy writes in *Benjamin's Sale of Goods* that 'the extended definition given to the term "goods" by the Act may not prevent the contract from being considered to be a contract relating to land for other purposes, e. g., it may need to be evidenced in writing under s. 40, Law of Property Act 1925 [now s. 2, LP(MP)A 1989]'.[198] This view is, however, not strictly speaking one of duality of characterisation, but rather of the precedence of the LP(MP)A 1989 in relation to formalities of contract. In this respect, LP(MP)A 1989 is simply "[an]other Act" to which the freedom of form provided for in s. 4, SGA 1979, is subject. In this sense, the distinction of realty/personalty adopted in s. 2 LP(MP)A 1989 continues the distinction between sections 4 and 17 of the Statute of Frauds 1677 for the specific purpose of determining the applicable formalities for concluding a contract of sale, whilst the definition of goods/not goods [i.e. realty and intangible personalty] adopted in s. 61 SGA 1979 serves the wider purpose of channelling the two systems of property, of personalty and realty.

---

196 This considers the question upon the same function. An example of a differing function would be the validity of the transaction, on the one hand, between the parties and, on the other hand, as against third parties, For examples of the latter, Chapter 4. Nursery plants, German Christmas trees and transplantation.

197 *Sutton and Shannon on Contracts* (1970), p. 242: 'Difficulty was always experienced in deciding whether a contract of sale under which something was to be severed from the land and taken away, as e.g., growing crops or a building which was to be demolished, was a disposition of an interest in land within s. 4 of the Statute of Frauds, now s. 40 of the Law of Property Act, 1925, or was a contract of sale of goods.'

198 Sealy in Guest et al., Benjamin's Sale of Goods (1974), [88].

In support of the proposition of the duality of classification that 'inconvenient as the result may be, there is no necessary impossibility about it,' Megarry and Wade cite *Sims* v. *Thomas*[199] and *in re Baldwin, ex parte Foss*[200].[201] These two decisions do ostensibly appear to support this proposition since it was held that the same property could be movable for the purposes of one Act and not movable for the purposes of another. Movable property or personalty encompasses in English law generally both choses in possession (tangible movables) and choses in action (intangible movables), such as debts. It was held in *Sims* v. *Thomas* that personal estate in the then Insolvent Debtor's Act did not include intangible personalty, such as the conditional bond in question, on analogy with the Statute of Elizabeth[202] whereby intangible movable property could not be seized in execution by the debtor's creditors as 'goods and chattels.' In *ex parte Foss*, it was held that for the purposes of the reputed ownership clause of the Bankruptcy Law Consolidation Act 1849, that the right of copyright, or right of publishing a newspaper, fells under the term "goods and chattels", with the result that the assignment of the right without any corresponding change in the register set up for such rights and the continued use of the premises by the mortgagor to publish could not be set up against the mortgagor's general creditors.[203] However, rather than being authority for the proposition that contracts of sale for parts of land to be severed must satisfy requirements of two Acts of Parliament treating the *same point of law*, it is submitted here that the better view is that both cases demonstrate that where *a different function* is served by the distinction – execution levy, on the one hand, bankruptcy laws, on the other hand – the different function can justify a divergence in definition.

e.   Academic accounts of English law

Even the doctrinal accounts of the rules themselves differ as between the different authors. Differences appear in terms of which rules attach to what property. Other accounts differ in terms of the circumstances under which each characterisation is satisfied. Some rules are even seen as alternatives to one another, awaiting a definitive decision of the courts, whilst other authors consider the rules as equally valid albeit merely adding to the overall complexity of the law.

---

199 (1840) 12 A&E 536.
200 (1858) 2 De G&J 230.
201 Megarry & Wade, *Law of Real Property* (1984), p. 575, fn. 77.
202 Fraudulent Conveyances Act 1571 (13 Eliz 1, c. 5).
203 (1858) 2 De G&J 230, 239; 44 E.R. 977, 980, *per* Turner LJ: 'I feel no doubt, therefore that the property in these newspapers must be considered as goods and chattels within the meaning of the Bankruptcy Act'.

A general pattern can be distinguished of, on the one hand, certain parts of land which when sold for severance are always sales of goods and, on the other hand, other parts of land which are sold are sales of goods only when the seller is to sever. This distinction normally places *fructus industriales* within the first rule and everything else within the second. Nevertheless, Goode places fixtures, timber and all types of crop under the first rule and 'minerals, soil, underground water, sand and gravel, and the like' under the scope of the second rule.[204] This is, however, an isolated opinion, which does not appear to have a textual justification upon the statute. Although Blackburn wrote that in *Evans* v. *Roberts* Bayley J. said that 'growing crops were mere goods, and might be recovered under a count for goods sold'[205] Bayley J. nevertheless stressed in that case that 'the vendor was to raise the potatoes from the ground at the request of the vendee.'[206]

According to *Sutton & Shannon on Contracts*, if the contract confers present possession of the parts of land to be severed and such parts are either not ripe for severance under the contract or there is no immediate obligation to sever, then the contract is one for a disposition of an interest in land.[207] According to Megarry, all contracts concerning *fructus naturales* are for an interest in land, unless the *fructus naturales* are to be severed by the seller or the buyer is obliged to sever them as soon as possible.[208] For Megarry, sales of fixtures are always sales for an interest in land unless sold by a tenant entitled to remove them.[209] In *The Law of Real Property*, Megarry & Wade added to the last condition that the contract must provide 'to sever them at once, so that they will not remain part of the land for any long time after purchase.'[210] For Goode, if it is the buyer who is to sever but, having paid the price, is free to extract or not, or the buyer is to have an interest in the materials *in*

---

204 Goode, *Commercial Law* (London, Penguin, 1982), p. 155: 'If the transferor is to extract and to supply at a price, the transaction is usually one of sale' although this only refers to 'the physical content of land – minerals, soil, underground water, sand and gravel, and the like' but not fixtures, timber and crops.

205 Blackburn, Treatise On the Effects of the Sale of personal property (1910, 3rd ed.), pp. 13–14.

206 *Evans* v. *Roberts* (1826) 5 B&C 829, 831; 108 ER 309, 310.

207 *Sutton and Shannon on Contracts* (1970), p. 243: 'it is submitted that the true distinction to be drawn is … between cases in which it is intended to confer present possession of the crops or trees, etc., on the land when there is either no immediate obligation to sever or no possibility of severing, because the time of maturity has not yet arrived, and cases in which by the terms of the contract no property or interest is to pass until severance, and entry on the land is given solely for the purposes of severance.'

208 Megarry, *A Manual of the Law of Real Property* (London, Stevens & Sons, 1962, 3rd ed.), p. 354: '*Fructus naturales* are to be treated as land within the statute unless either they are to be severed by the vendor and not the purchaser or else the contract binds the purchaser to sever them as soon as possible.'

209 Megarry, *idem.*: 'A contract for the sale of fixtures together with the land to which they are attached falls within s. 40, and the same applies to a sale of fixtures separately from the land to a stranger, either by the landlord or, it seems, the tenant.'

210 Megarry & Wade, *The Law of Real Property* (1984, 5th ed.), p. 574.

situ the transaction is a disposition of an interest in land, namely, the grant of a profit à prendre.[211] As a solution to the irreconcilability of the authorities, Hudson proposes two alternative tests, the first being the time when title is intended to pass. The second and preferred test is whether the parts of land sold are ripe for severance at the time of the conclusion of the contract.[212]

For one author, the cases holding that contracts for the sale of growing crops are, in fact, contracts for the disposition of an interest in land 'are to be explained on the ground that by the terms of the contract the property was intended to pass at once, thereby conferring on the purchaser either a right to possession of the land or an interest in things attached to the land while they are still attached, which is the same thing as conferring an interest in the land itself.'[213] In determining whether this is the case, the test is 'whether, in order to effect the intention of the parties, it is necessary to give the buyer an interest in the land.' However, '[i]t is only where the intention of the parties, as expressed in the contract, cannot be given effect to without the purchaser having an interest in the land that a contract for the sale of a growing crop will be construed as passing an interest in the land.' The author thus concludes that, as a general rule, such contracts, provided that they provide for severance, are contracts of sale because in most cases all that is necessarily implied by the contract of sale in relation to the land is a licence. Whether, according to the same author, title passes is another question.[214]

According to Guest et al., it is unclear whether a contract for another to enter upon land and take away minerals, other products of the land capable of forming the subject-matter of a profit à prendre, or other parts of the land can ever be a sale of goods. On the one hand, they assert that the language of the Sale of Goods Act, i.e. things forming part of the land, 'is clearly wide enough to include the soil itself and mineral products.'[215] On the other hand, they assert that 'there seems to be a reluctance among commentators to extend the analogy of *fructus naturales* so far' and that a possible line of distinction could be between contracts for definite quantities to be severed by the other party, in which case the contract would be a sale of goods, and contracts for indefinite quantities, in which case the contract would be for an interest in land.[216] Guest et al conclude that 'the judgments as a

---

211 Goode, *Commercial Law* (London, Penguin, 1982), p. 155.

212 Hudson, 'Goods or Land?' (1958) 22 *Conv* 137, 139: 'The second test is to ask, are the crops intended to obtain further benefit from remaining in the soil after the making of the contract'.

213 Anon, 'Growing crops – the passing of property before severance' (1943) 93 *The Law Journal* (LJ) 259.

214 For the purpose of determining third party rights and the allocation of the risk *inter partes.*

215 Guest et al (ed.), *Benjamin's Sale of Goods* (1974), [90].

216 Sealy in Guest et al (ed.), *Benjamin's Sale of Goods* (1974), [90].

whole give no clear indication of the point at which, or the grounds on which, [the] analogy [of a contract which gives a man a right to enter upon land with liberty to dig from the earth *in situ*, so much gravel or brick earth or coal on payment of a price per ton] is to give way to the wording of the [Sale of Goods] Act.'[217]

Amos & Ferard contrast the case in which parts of land, such as fixtures,[218] are sold with the land from cases in which they are sold separately. In the former case, the formalities of s. 4 of the Statute of Frauds 1677 always apply, whilst in the latter case, 'the subject of the contract is in the view of the parties a bare chattel.'[219] On the basis of the distinction between *fructus industriales* (emblements) and *fructus naturales*, the authors propose that where the seller has a limited-interest in the land whereby the fixtures would ordinarily pass to the seller's executors as personalty and has therefore a right of severance, the requirement of writing does not apply.[220] On the other hand, when sold by an absolute owner, or tenant for life, of the land and to whose heirs the fixtures would pass as part and parcel of the land, the authors submit that the sale of the fixtures would require the formality of writing. An exception to the latter rule, is, again on analogy with *fructus naturales*, made where the fixtures are agreed to be severed immediately. The otherwise applicable rule therefore only applies where title is to pass in the fixtures before severance and the fixtures are to remain fixed to the land for 'any considerable period' before severance.[221]

Furthermore, the statement of the law in *Sutton & Shannon on Contracts* is supposed to apply regardless of whether the parts of land for severance are *fructus industriales* or *fructus naturales*[222] and, if title is not to pass until severance, regardless of whether the buyer or seller is to sever.[223] For Goode, there is also no distinction to be made between *fructus naturales* and *industriales*, rather between *fructus* and other parts of land, thus all sales of lands' renewable resources are considered to be sales of goods.[224] Nevertheless, the leading view is

---

217 Ibidem.
218 Generally things attached to a building but, in a broader sense, any construction built on land; cf. Gray, *Elements of Land Law*, [1.52].
219 Amos & Ferard on the Law of Fixtures (1883, 3rd ed.), p. 329.
220 Idem., p. 330; *Petrie* v. *Dawson* Assizes (19.08.1845) 2 C&K 138; 175 ER 58.
221 Idem., p. 331.
222 *Sutton and Shannon on Contracts* (1970), p. 243: 'it is submitted that the true distinction to be drawn is not between *fructus naturales* and *fructus industriales*...'
223 Idem., p. 242: 'If by the terms of the contract no property or interest is the crops is to pass until severance takes place the contract is for the sale of goods... and it should make no difference whether the severance and removal are to be done by the seller or the buyer.'
224 Goode, *Commercial Law* (London, Penguin, 1982), p. 155: 'a sale of fixtures or timber to be severed before sale or pursuant to the sale contract is a sale of goods. So also is a sale of crops to be severed, whether they be industrial growing or *fructus naturales*.'

that any contract for the severance of *fructus industriales* is a sale of goods.[225] In line with the guiding principle of his interpretation of the case-law to keep as many transactions outside the scope of formal requirements, Hudson writes that 'despite the doubts expressed by Sutton & Shannon, it would be held that a contract for the sale of standing *fructus industriales* is always a contract for the sale of goods.'[226]

f   Synthesis of the various statements of the law

From the preceding discussion, the most immediate impression of English law, especially when compared with the relative simplicity of French law and the following account of German law, is one of excessive complexity and great difference in opinion. In order to synthesise the variance of opinion, the following propositions of law can be summarised. It is, on the one hand, argued that all parts of land agreed to be severed under a contract of sale are goods for the purposes of the Sale of Goods Act. This is the literal interpretation of s. 61, SGA 1979. Such contracts are therefore not subject to the formality of writing.

On the other hand, it is argued that for the purposes of the formal requirement of writing the previous common law position has been maintained. Under the leading contours of the rules developed by the courts, punctuated by a number of rules of more limited approval, under a contract of sale:

(a) *fructus industriales* are goods
(b) *fructus naturales* are land unless,
    (i)   the seller is to sever,
    (ii) the buyer is to sever (immediately/as soon as possible/without time for maturity)
    (iii) (or the buyer is under an obligation to sever)
(c) Other parts of land (fixtures, minerals, buildings etc.) agreed to be severed are land, unless
    (i)   the seller is to sever
    (ii) (or the buyer is under an obligation to sever)

---

225 Guest, *Anson's Law of Contract* (Oxford, Clarendon Press, 1969, 23rd ed.), p. 73: 'The law seems to be that *fructus industriales* are always goods and any agreement for their sale need not be evidenced by writing.' Ontario Law Reform Commission, *Report on sale of goods* (1979), vol. 1., p. 57–58: 'Under the Statute of Frauds, [*fructus industriales*] were treated as chattels and not as part of the land or an interest in land, and agreement for the sale of such crops, whether mature or immature, and whether the property in them was purportedly transferred before or after severance, was not governed by section 4.'

226 Hudson, 'Goods or Land?' (1958) 22 *Conv* 137, 139.

Certain pressure points nevertheless relate to each proposition. For instance, for Sutton & Shannon rule (b) applies to *fructus industriales*. On the other hand, for Goode, *fructus naturales* fall under rule (a). Rule (b)(iii) is supported by Sutton & Shannon. For some, rule (b) applies to other parts of realty to the exclusion of rule (c). Rule (c)(ii) is supported by Goode.

g.   Brief comparative overview of Anglo-American jurisdictions

The difficulty and complexity encountered in English law regarding the characterisation of parts of land agreed to be severed under a contract of sale is not limited to the jurisdictional borders of England and Wales. The rules of the Statute of Frauds were carried over across to the Anglo-American jurisdictions.

For example, in Ontario, a jurisdiction of Common Law Canada, the definition of the Sale of Goods Act 1893 was adopted in 1920 and remained untouched when the legislation was amended in 1990.[227] The Ontarian definition of realty does not differ substantially from the legislation of English law[228] and the Statute of Frauds' distinctions and requirements of writing still apply.[229] Although the Ontario Law Reform Commission wrote that '[i]t is obvious that the ambiguous definition of goods in *The Sale of Goods Act* needs clarification in its application to things attached to land,' their recommendations were not take up in the 1990 amendment and the uncertainly therefore still persists.

---

227 Sale of Goods Act, SO 1920, c. 40. Sale of Goods Act, RSO 1990, s. 1 [Definitions and interpretation] '"goods" means all chattels personal, other than things in action and money, and includes emblements, industrial growing crops, and things attached to or forming part of the land that are agreed to be severed before sale or under the contract of sale.'

228 The Conveyancing and Law of Property Act, RSO 1970, c. 85, s. 1(1)(b): 'messuages, tenements, hereditaments, whether corporeal or incorporeal, and any undivided share in land'; The Registry Act, RSO 1970, c. 409, s. 1(d): '"land" means land, tenements, hereditaments and appurtenances and any estate or interest therein'; Registry Act, RSO 1990, c. 20, s. 1 'In this Act… "land" means land, tenements, hereditaments and appurtenances and any estate or interest therein'; Land Registration Reform Act, RSO 1970, c. 4 (definition of land same as Registry Act). Conveyancing and Law of Property Act, RSO 1990, c. 34, s. 1 (unamended), however, cf. s. 9: 'A partition of land, an exchange of land, an assignment of a chattel interest in land, and a surrender in writing of land not being an interest that might by law have been created without writing, are void at law, unless made by deed' (although probably relates to fixtures).

229 Statute of Frauds, RSO 1990, c. 19, s. 1(1): 'Every estate or interest of freehold and every uncertain interest of, in, to or out of any messuages, lands, tenements or hereditaments shall be made or created by a writing signed by the parties making or creating the same, or their agents thereunto lawfully authorized in writing, and, if not so made or created, has the force and effect of an estate at will only, and shall not be deemed or taken to have any other or greater force or effect.'; s. 4: 'No action shall be brought … to charge any person upon any contract or sale of lands, tenements or hereditaments, or any interest in or concerning them, unless the agreement upon which the action is brought, or some memorandum or note thereof is in writing and signed by the party to be charged therewith …'

The picture does not appear to be much different in Australia. In New South Wales, for example, the definition of goods 'includes emblements and things attached to or forming part of the land which are agreed to be severed before sale or under the contract of sale.'[230] Similarly, s. 54A, Conveyancing Act 1919 reproduces the wording of s. 4, Statute of Frauds.[231]

Section 4 of the Statute of Frauds was also taken up by most states of the United States. There was subsequently divergence amongst the states as to whether contracts for the severance of timber, for example, were sales of goods or of interests in land.[232] One judge thus said 'Can trees growing on land be sold without a writing? Scarcely a legal question on which there has been more elaborate discussion and more differing opinion and decision.'[233] The first proposal for a Uniform Sales Act effectively copied Chalmer's definition of goods as 'the term includes emblements, industrial growing crops, and things attached to or forming part of the land which are agreed to be severed before sale or under the contract of sale.'[234]

Nevertheless, as amended in 1972, the Uniform Commercial Code effectively provided that sales of growing crops and standing timber, as opposed to minerals,[235] were contracts for the sale of goods and that title can pass before severance provided that the crops or timber are identified.[236] It is further specified

---

230 s. 5, Sale of Goods Act (New South Wales) 1923.

231 s. 54A, Conveyancing Act 1919: '(1) No action or proceedings may be brought upon any contract for the sale or other disposition of land or any interest in land, unless the agreement upon which such action or proceedings is brought, or some memorandum or note thereof, is in writing, and signed by the party to be charged or by some other person thereunto lawfully authorised by the party to be charged.'

232 As an interest in land: Arkansas (*Griffith* v. *Ayer-Lord Tie Co.* (07.07.1913) 159 SW 218, 109 Ark. 223); Georgia (*Coody* v. *Gress Lumber Co.* (08.07.1899) 82 Ga. 793, 10 S.E. 218); Indiana (*Hostetter* v. *Auman* (09.03.1889) 119 Ind. 7; 20 N.E. 506); Ohio (*Hirth* v. *Graham* (24.01.1893) 50 Ohio St. 57; 33 N.E. 90). As a contract of sale for goods: Connecticut (*Bostwick* v. *Leach* (1809) 3 Day (Conn.) 476); Kentucky (*Cain* v. *McGuire* (09.12.1852) 13 B.Mon. 340; 52 Ky. 340); Maryland (*Whittington* v. *Hall* (15.11.1911) 116 Md. 467; 82 A. 163); Massachusetts (*Claflin* v. *Carpenter* (1842) 4 Metcalf 580; 45 Mass. 580); Maine (*Erskine* v. *Plummer* (1831) 7 Greenl. 447; 7 Me. 447).

233 *Fluharty* v. *Mills* (30.03.1901) 49 W.Va. 446; 38 S.E. 521, 522 per Brannon J. See, Davis, 'Sale or contract for sale of standing timber as within provisions of statute of frauds respecting sale or contract of sale of real property' (1949) 7 *American Law Reports* (2nd ed.) 517.

234 s. 76, Uniform Sales Act 1906.

235 § 2-107 (1), Uniform Commercial Code: 'A contract for the sale of minerals or the like (including oil and gas) or a structure or its materials to be removed from realty is a contract for the sale of goods within this Article if they are to be severed by the seller but until severance a purported present sale thereof which is not effective as a transfer of an interest in land is effective only as a contract to sell.'

236 § 2-107 (2), Uniform Commercial Code: 'A contract for the sale apart from the land of growing crops or other things attached to realty and capable of severance without material harm thereto but not [minerals] or of timber to be cut is a contract for the sale of goods

that such a contract of sale for goods only affects third parties with rights in the realty if the contract is registered, thereby constituting notice.[237] This position corresponds exactly to French law, if not with greater coherency in that it specifically provides for a system of registration. As a result, whilst contracts for the sale of standing timber are not required, in principle,[238] to be made in writing for the validity of the contract as between the parties, vis-à-vis third parties entitled to the realty such a contract would need to be in writing and registered. The adoption of the Uniform Commercial Code has, however, not been altogether unproblematic. For instance, whilst such contracts for the sale of standing timber are apparently capable of registration under Article 9, UCC,[239] and thereby held to bind third parties in some states,[240] other states have not held such registered contracts binding *erga omnes*.[241]

3. German law

Whilst the distinction of land and goods is applied regarding formalities for the conclusion of contracts in German law, the characterisation of standing timber as land or goods is irrelevant to the question of whether the formalities for the conclusion of a contract over land apply to standing timber. As set out in the chapter on tax law, sales of standing timber need not fall within the binary classification of land and goods but fall instead with a third category. Any sales contract over standing timber is not a sale of land or goods but merely the sale of the right to fell and appropriate, the latter element constituting the sale of *future* goods. The same applies to crops sold prior to harvest.

---

within this Article whether the subject matter is to be severed by the buyer or by the seller even though it forms part of the realty at the time of contracting, and the parties can by identification effect a present sale before severance.'

237 § 2-107 (3), Uniform Commercial Code: 'The provisions of this section are subject to any third party rights provided by the law relating to realty records, and the contract for sale may be executed and recorded as a document transferring an interest in land and shall then constitute notice to third parties of the buyer's rights under the contract for sale.'

238 Subject to § 2-201, Uniform Commercial Code, which maintains the principle of s. 17 Statute of Frauds for contract for a price of $500 or more.

239 § 9-102, Uniform Commercial Code: 'The term ["goods"] includes (i) fixtures, (ii) standing timber that is to be cut and removed under a conveyance or contract for sale, (iii) the unborn young of animals, (iv) crops grown, growing, or to be grown, even if the crops are produced on trees, vines, or bushes [etc.].'

240 New York: *Fischer* v. *Zepa Consulting A.G.*, (09.07.1999) 263 A.D.2d 946, 695 N.Y.S.2d 456, 41 U.C.C. Rep. Serv. 2d 772 (4th Dep't 1999), order confirmed in, 95 N.Y.2d 66, 710 N.Y.S.2d 830, 732 N.E.2d 937, 41 U.C.C. Rep. Serv. 2d 774 (2000).

241 South Carolina: *Epstein* v. *Coastal Timber Co.*, (11.07.2011) 393 S.C. 276, 711 S.E.2d 912, 75 U.C.C. Rep. Serv. 2d 85. Held prior mortgagee not bound.

There are two equally applicable legal characterisations of a contract whereby a person entitled to sever parts of land, in particular a landowner, but also a limited rights user of land such as a tenant, allows another to appropriate parts of land. On the one hand, it is termed a contract literally of permission (to appropriate) – *Gestattungsvertrag*[242] – or, using the English terminology of real property law, a contractual licence. In this sense, the sale of standing timber for instance has been stated to confer an *Abholzungsrecht*, the right to fell timber. This is a contractual licence to enter land, sever and ultimately appropriate the resulting goods. When the permission is given in exchange for a price, the alternative analysis of a sale of future goods is also applicable and referred to in the literature. Landsberg, for instance, writes of the timber buyer as the buyer of future property.[243]

Both analyses rely upon § 956 BGB as a textual basis. In performance of his obligations under the sales contract, the owner of the forest permits (*gestattet*) the buyer to appropriate the standing trees (*die Bäume sich anzueignen*).[244] Integral parts of land, such as standing trees, do not become goods until physically severed. Since the trees only come into legal existence once separated from the land, when standing they can only be future goods.

This transaction appears merely to entail the simple application of otherwise general principles of German private law set out in the BGB. For title to be transferred in movable property that property must generally be physically delivered, which implies that parts of land such as standing trees must first be felled before title in them can be transferred to a person other than the landowner. The

---

242 The previous addition in parentheses of 'to appropriate' as in *Erzeugnisse oder sonstige Bestandteile sich anzueignen* is implied.

243 Landsberg, 'Kauf von Holz auf dem Stamme' [1899] *Juristische Monatsschrift für Posen und Westpreußen* 177, 180: '...Holzkäufer (so wird man ihn als Käufer künftiger Sachen auch fernerhin noch nennen dürfen)....'; Wirtgen, *Der Kaufvertrag über Bäume auf dem Stamme* (1931), p. 9: 'Der Vertrag bezieht sich nicht auf das Grundstück selbst, sondern auf die künftig beweglichen Bestandteile.' Salier, *Verkauf von Bäumen auf dem Stamm* (1903), p. 4: 'Weder also nach gemeinem noch nach bürgerlichem Recht sind Bäume auf dem Stamm selbständige Sachen. Als solche kommen sie nur für die Zukunft in Betracht, in welcher sie von der Muttersache getrennt sein werden: *separata corpora*, nicht mehr Bestandteile.'

244 Landsberg, 'Kauf von Holz auf dem Stamme' [1899] *Juristische Monatsschrift für Posen und Westpreußen* 177, 180: 'Dieser "Gestattungsvertrag" kann sich auch darstellen als ein Kauf künftiger beweglicher Sachen, nämlich der durch Trennung zu rechtlicher Sonderexistenz gelangenden Erzeugnisse und sonstigen Bestandteile eines Grundstücks... Dem Holzkäufer gestattet gemäß der übernommenen Vertragspflicht der Waldeigentümer, die Bäume (Erzeugnisse der Sache, des Grundstücks) sich anzueignen.' Jickeli & Stieper in Staudinger (2011), § 93, [25]: 'Eine Übereignung künftiger Sachen kann auch in der Aneignungsgestattung nach § 956 gesehen werden, aufgrund welcher sich ein Dritter wesentliche Bestandteile der Sache aneignen darf.'

acquisition of title in parts of land upon severance under a contract of sale is, however, governed by specific rules laid down in § 956 BGB et seq.[245]

The analysis of the sale of future goods has received both judicial and doctrinal approval. For instance, in a decision treating the effects of a term for the reservation of title in standing timber in 1909, the Reichsgericht characterised the question of law in terms of 'the sale of parts of land which will only come into being in the future (separately from the land).'[246] Similarly, after considering the possible objects of such a sales contract, namely what the rights arising under the contract refer to, such as possession of land, a right etc., Wirtgen concludes that the 'contract concerns nothing other than a sales contract for future goods, subject to a condition precedent, but otherwise to which the provisions on contracts for sales of goods apply.'[247]

It follows from the characterisation of the contract as for the sale of future goods that the contract need not satisfy the requirements of form for the transfer of land. For example, Wirtgen explains that the contract does not relate to immovable property but rather to parts of land which will be movable property in the future.[248] This is because a contract over immovable property capable of having an immediate effect in the law of property can only mean a contract over the land itself.[249] Present sales contracts under which parts of land are to be separated can only have effect in the law of property at a future date, namely the physical separation of the parts from the land. 'Since the contract does not relate to the land itself, but rather parts of land which will exist as movable property

---

245 Wirtgen, Der Kaufvertrag über Bäume auf dem Stamm (1931), pp. 2–3.

246 *A v. R* RG (17.12.1909, VII 132.09) (1909) 72 RGZ 309, 312: 'Vorliegend handelt es sich um den Verkauf von Holz auf dem Stamm, von Sachbestandteilen, die erst zukünftig durch Trennung vom Grund und Boden selbständige Sachen werden sollen'.

247 Wirtgen, *Der Kaufvertrag über Bäume auf dem Stamm* (1931), p. 9: 'Die bisherigen Ausführungen in diesem Abschnitt haben gezeigt, daß es sich beim Kauf von Holz auf dem Stamme um nichts anderes handelt als um einen Kaufvertrag, der künftige bewegliche Sachen zum Gegenstand hat, daher aufschiebend bedingt ist, im übrigen aber den Kaufvorschriften des BGB unterliegt.'

248 Wirtgen, *Der Kaufvertrag über Bäume auf dem Stamm* (1931), p. 9: 'Daß sich der Vertrag nicht auf eine gegenwärtige bewegliche Sache bezieht, ist daraus zu folgen, daß sich die Kaufverpflichtung auf eine unbewegliche Sache oder deren Bestandteil erstreckt. Die Annahme, es handele sich um einen Vertrag über eine unbewegliche Sache, widerspricht dem Gesetze.'

249 See further, Chapter 8. Ownership of parts of land as immovable property separate from land itself & personal servitudes. A singular attenuation of this principle is provided by the concept of segmental possession (*Teilbesitz*), see, for example, Chapter 3: Allocation of the risk. A. [Transfer of segmental possession (*Teilbesitz*)], despite the fact that a contract of lease over a segment of land, for example, operates in effect if not in nature as a real right of use in land this doctrine does not directly put the principle of *Sonderrechtsfähigkeit* into question, since possession is not a real right.

only in the future, the requirements of form provided for in § 311b BGB (prior to 2002, § 313 BGB[250]) do not apply.'[251]

Although without adopting the analysis of a gift of future movable property, a recent decision of the Bundesgerichtshof nevertheless confirms by necessary implication the proposition that a contract for the appropriation of standing timber need not satisfy the requirements of form for a disposition of land. According to the Bundesgerichtshof, the fact that the subject-matter of the contract was delimited but unspecified, i.e. standing timber, rather than a specific amount of timber, meant that a right to fell and appropriate standing timber had been gifted, rather than, for example, future movable property, i.e. felled timber.[252] The contract had only been made in writing, not the otherwise applicable form of authentication before a notary, which would have been necessary had the contract concerned a disposition of the land.[253]

C.   Conclusions

1.   Relevancy and application of the distinction

From the present chapter, it can be concluded, at the highest level of abstraction, that the distinction of movable and immovable objects of commerce is not always drawn for the same legal purpose. For instance, the distinction applies in England and Germany for the purposes of distinguishing two sets of formal requirements for the validity of a sales contract. It is, however, only relevant in determining the applicable rule for a sales contract for the severance of standing trees, this year's crop and nursery plants in England. In Germany, the doctrine of future property (*zukünftige Sachen*)[254] allows such contracts to escape the form of writing

---

250 Gesetz zur Modernisierung des Schuldrechts (26.11.2001, BGBl. I. 3138).
251 Wirtgen, Der Kaufvertrag über Bäume auf dem Stamm (1931), p. 9: 'Der Vertrag bezieht sich nicht auf das Grundstück selbst, sondern auf die künftig beweglichen Bestandteile. Aus diesem Grund bedarf der Kaufvertrag auch nicht der Formvorschrift des § 313 BGB.' cf. Pufe, *Der Kaufvertrag von Holz auf dem Stamme und seine Erfüllung, insbesondere im Konkurse des Verkäufers* (Breslau, 1928), p. 4.
252 BGH (19.07.2005, X ZR 92/03): [2005] NJW-RR 1718, 1719: '[Gegenstand] ... war nicht die Übereignung einer bestimmten Menge Holz, sondern die Gestattung, auf den Waldgrundstücken [des Schenkers] Holz einzuschlagen und sich anzueignen.'
253 Ring, G., Grziwotz, H., & Keukenschrijver, A., *NK-BGB – Sachenrecht* (Nomos, Baden-Baden, 2013, 3rd edition), § 956, [4].
254 The term "sale of future property" or *emptio rei speratae* is unfortunately used with two distinct meanings. In German law the term "future property" means an entity of property which presently does not form the subject-matter of a real right, whether physically existing (i.e. standing timber) or to come into existence (i.e. next year's crop presently unsown) (Wirtgen, *Der Kaufvertrag über Bäume auf dem Stamm* (1931), 10–11). In French doctrine

without resorting to the classification of standing timber or houses sold for demolition as movable objects of commerce. In England, on the other hand, there is great variance in the opinions expressed in legal scholarship and, whilst the courts have tended towards opening up sales contracts for the severance of standing trees, this year's crop and nursery plants from the formality of writing, that tendency has not been fully confirmed.

In France, the distinction is not even applied to the formal validity of such a contract of sale. The distinction of movable and immovable objects of commerce is therefore neither relevant to formalities for the conclusion of sales contracts in general, nor sales contracts specifically for the transformation of parts of land, such as standing trees, this year's crop and nursery plants, eventually into goods. A distinction is, however, drawn for both purposes in relation to contracts of gift. Here, although differing views have been expressed, the better view, as espoused by Fréjaville, and one which is consistent with the distinction of objects of commerce drawn for sales contracts between formal validity and third party effect, is that *inter partes* the requirement of writing is not needed. From a comparison of the different solutions, it can be concluded that when the present purpose of determining whether the contract of sale requires the form of writing is applied, the principle of party autonomy applies. That principle lies both behind the characterisation of standing trees, this year's crop and nursery plants sold in English law as movable objects of commerce, in the national terminology as a "chattel personal", as well as behind the characterisation of the subject-matter of the sales contract as future property in German law.

2.   Profit à prendre and usufruct/life-interest analyses

A key distinction which is not always made in statements of the law, particularly in English and French law, is that between contracts for the severance and sale of parts of land, on the one hand, and, on the other, third party rights in land authorising the severance and appropriation of parts of land. In the latter case, such rights have as their object the plot of land as a whole but enable the right-holder to take away a certain type of product of the land (such as wood, fish, sand etc.), or a certain quantity thereof over a particular period of time (x no. of trees/ year). In the case of the English law profit à prendre or French and German law equivalents in the law of servitudes or usufruct, such rights are limited to *fructus*

---

and under the English Sale of Goods Act, its sense is ordinarily restricted solely to property to come into existence (Fréjaville, *La mobilisation par anticipation*, p. 167–168; s. 5 (Existing or future goods) and s. 61 (1) "future goods" and "goods" SGA 1979. Gow, 'When are trees timber?' (1962) *SLT* 13, 16). Hence presently-growing standing timber would be future in property German law but not in English and French law.

naturales and cannot exist over *fructus industriales*, given that the latter is planted annually. Profits cannot exist over *fructus naturales* which have been ascertained (that tree, that fish), they give an entitlement to an unascertained abstract quantity. As far as the right of usufruct is concerned, it confers possession of land up to a life-time, entitling the usufructuary to the fruits of the land during that time. In all the legal systems under consideration contracts for limited rights in land, such as certain servitudes and profits and usufructs and life-interests, all require the compliance with the formalities for contracts transferring ownership of the land, whether it be written form or notarization.

A contract of sale of goods, on the other hand, can confer a contractual licence to enter land only, effectively for the purpose of taking delivery of the goods sold. Rights arising thereunder relate specifically to the object sold, not to the land. Although there is some overlap and all grants of a profit can appear as sales contracts, not all sale of goods contracts can be analysed as grants of profits, nor will they operate to grant a profit. For instance, to take an example from the French legal literature, in considering the sale of successive crops of land over a number of years and the sale of minerals to be extracted from a quarry already in operation to be movable regarding the crop and minerals to be extracted of the current year, but immovable regarding that of the remaining years, Vazeille and Coin-Delisle are, in fact, regarding the transaction as operating to grant a usufruct for future years' severance, entailing possession of the land and the right to appropriate its fruits. The same reasoning would apply in German law if the contract were regarded as intended to govern the grant of a life interest in the land, which incidentally sanctions the severance of the fruits of the land. As a contract for an interest in the land, such a contract would need to be notarized.

As far as the discussion of English law is concerned, a number of statements can relate only to profits to the exclusion of sale of goods contracts. Obviously, the requirement of writing is necessary for contracts for the grant of profits but that the same requirement must be carried over to contracts for the sale of parts of land for severance is far from obvious.

Chapter 4.
A conceptual framework for the application of the distinction outside of property law

In the previous chapter, requirements of form for sales contracts in land were considered in respect of contracts for the severance of parts of land, in particular in respect of standing timber. The distinction of land and goods was found to bear different degrees of relevance, ranging from irrelevant to partially relevant and to conclusive. That was the case of German law, French law and English law, respectively. Given the significant differences in the use – and even non-use – of the distinction, the great variation in doctrinal constructions expressed – even in national law – a conceptual framework is necessary to present the comparative findings clearly.

The present chapter therefore sets out a conceptual framework for the application of the distinction outside of property law in order to analyse diverging views on a correct statement of national law regarding the distinction of land and goods on the basis of the preceeding chapter. A number of considerations are interwoven in an overall picture of the law. This is done in two parts. First, a number of policy considerations are extrapolated from the national law discourse (A), followed by a breaking down of the findings in terms of systemics, purpose, policy and factual distinctions (B).

A.   Policy considerations and *ratio legis*

In support of the various statements of the law in English and French law, a number of policy considerations are given as to whether or not contracts for the severance of parts of land should be subject to stricter formalities which apply to contracts in respect of land. The essence of the conflicting policy considerations centre around the fact that a part of land, subject as such to all rights existing over the land as a whole (ownership, security rights, rights of enjoyment etc.), is about to be detached from that legal matrix and, in a new life as goods, subjected to a new range of third party rights. What are therefore the reasons militating for and against a requirement relating specifically to contracts for land?

The policy considerations can be framed in terms of three opposing couplets: solemnity/expediency; ordinary/extraordinary; immediacy/long-term. These policy considerations must also be set against the wider question of whether to adhere strictly to the position in property law or whether, when applied for the purposes of formalities for the formation of a contract, divergence may be admitted to the distinction. The former approach results in a uniform distinction of land and goods, the latter in different distinctions of land and goods depending on the field of law to which it is applied.

1.   Expediency/Solemnity

Greater solemnity in the conclusion of contracts serves the purpose of ensuring that the contracting parties take seriously the obligations which they create. The formality of writing and notarization also provides long-lasting evidence of the particulars of the agreement and such a record is a necessary condition to any system of registration. Registration and publication themselves are inherently linked to notice to and enforceability against third parties. As seen above, the hesitations in French law relate primarily to whether a gift of a part of land to be severed must be published so that the transaction can be enforced against third parties with rights in the land. This underlines the application of the greater formality to contracts for the severance of parts of land.

Opposing the need for solemnity is (greater[255]) freedom of form in the interests of commercial expediency. Commercial expediency is itself a key component of party autonomy – that the parties to the contract are best placed to determine the elements of their agreement as a result of which formal restrictions should be kept to a minimum. Time and time again, the legitimacy of the theory of mobilisation by anticipation in French law is based on the intention of the parties,[256] tempered only when third parties are concerned.[257] This view is also

---

255 As far as French law is concerned.

256 CA Paris (12.04.1851): [1853] 2 *Journal du Palais* 184: Considérant qu'il résulte des faits, circonstances et documents, de la cause, que la vente de la coupe de bois dont il s'agit faite à Meurisse était mobilière, puisque dans l'intention des parties cette coupe devait se faire soit immédiatement, soit à la volonté de l'acheteur. *Gontard & Gravier* v. *ville de Neufchâtel* (Cour de cassation): 'Attendu, en effet, que si la cession de ce droit d'extraction constitue, non un bail mais une vente mobilière, le caractère assigné à cet acte dérive de la nature de l'objet du contrat envisagée au temps de la réalisation de ce contrat et au point de vue de l'intention des parties contractantes.'. *Avril* v. *Vidal-Engaurran* (Cour d'Aix): 'ce caractère mobilier ne saurait exister que dans les rapports des parties entres elles.' (Cour de cassation): 'le caractère [mobilier] est assigné à l'acte à raison de la nature de l'objet du contrat, considéré au jour de la réalisation de ce contrat, et au point de vue de l'intention des parties contractantes' A.-J.-P., *Le principe de la relativité des conventions en droit privé français*

reflected in the traditional English law treatise on fixtures, where Amos & Ferard assert that in a contract for the severance of a fixture, 'the subject of the contract is in the view of the parties a bare chattel.'[258] Similarly, one of the only guiding principles extracted from the case-law in English law is said to be 'to confine the operation of [the Statute of Frauds] within as narrow a field as possible'[259] so as to exclude as many transactions concerning the severance of parts of land from the requirement of formality, in the interests of commercial expediency.

2.   Ordinary/Extraordinary

One aspect of the English law characterisation of contracts for the severance and sale of parts of land where points of view converge overwhelmingly is that for the sale of emblements (*fructus industriales*). Here the very nature of annually-planted agricultural crops is that they will, in the ordinary course of events, reach maturity and be harvested as goods. Similarly, where the landowning-seller contracts to sever the parts of land sold himself, there is no need for the protection of third parties because the landowning-seller is the person to transform a part of his land into goods. In French law, this is the point at which divergence creeps in, to a certain degree, to the legal discussion regarding gifts of parts of land severed in the ordinary course of the management of land. It is there argued that the pendulum should swing in favour of the donee, as against a third party, as there is no element of secrecy in a disposition of something related to the normal exploitation of the land.

Contrariwise, it is asserted that a change in the substance of the thing through the operation of a gift of goods contract must result in publication if it is to be enforceable against third parties. By definition, a change in the substance of something is an extraordinary event where a sudden change in affairs could be more easily cloaked in secret. This is the view underlying the distinction asserted by Megarry that sales of fixtures, which appear to form a part of buildings, are always contracts for the sale of an interest in land whereas when sold by a tenant

---

(Strasbourg, Dalloz, 1938) (Thesis), [147]: 'La théorie de la mobilisation par anticipation est une conséquence de « l'influence de la volonté des parties sur la condition juridique des biens »'. *Compain* v. *Gillet* Cass. civ. (25.01.1886): [1886] 1 S 269; 5 D 39: 'le caractère mobilier ou immobilier des biens se détermine avant tout par le point de vue auquel les ont considérés les parties contractantes'.

257 *Epoux Pelloux* v. *UFITH SA* Cass. civ³ (26.06.1991): 'La nature, immobilière ou mobilière, d'un bien est définie par la loi et la convention des parties ne peut avoir d'incidence à cet égard' [1992] 2 JCP 21825, case-note Barbiéri; [1993] D 93, case-note Freij-Dalloz; [1993] D (Somm.) 291, case-note Pérochon; Zénati, [1992] RTD civ. 144.

258 Amos & Ferard on the Law of Fixtures (1883, 3rd ed.), p. 329.

259 Hudson, 'Goods or Land?' (1958) 22 *Conv* 137, 138.

entitled to remove them, given that such a tenant may in the ordinary course of events remove them, the contract need not be made in writing.[260]

3.   Immediacy/Long-term

Another couplet on which the formal requirement for contracts in land has been advocated is dependent on whether the contractual activity is immediate or of a long-term nature. Where the latter, it must necessarily involve a certain degree of occupation on the land.[261] Thus, in English law, 'where the thing sold is to derive no benefit from the land, and is to be taken away immediately, the contract is not for an interest in land.'[262]

On the other hand, long-term activity seems to militate in favour of a different approach. According to *Sutton & Shannon on Contracts*, when there is no immediate obligation to sever, then the contract is one for a disposition of an interest in land.[263] According to Megarry, all contracts concerning *fructus naturales* are for an interest in land, unless the *fructus naturales* are to be severed by the seller or the buyer is obliged to sever them as soon as possible.[264] In *The Law of Real Property*, Megarry & Wade added to the last condition that the contract must provide 'to sever them at once, so that they will not remain part of the land for any long time after purchase.' Similarly, for Goode, where the buyer is free to extract or not, such a contract should be subject to the formal requirement of writing.[265] In French law too, for the gift of property which is immovable by destination and the delivery is to take place at a much later date, Coin-Delisle considered publication necessary in terms of third party enforceability.[266] Vazeille also consid-

---

260 Megarry, *idem.*: 'A contract for the sale of fixtures together with the land to which they are attached falls within s. 40, and the same applies to a sale of fixtures separately from the land to a stranger, either by the landlord or, it seems, the tenant.'

261 cf. the discussion of usufructs and life-interests in the next section.

262 (1875) 1 CPD 35, 40.

263 *Sutton and Shannon on Contracts* (1970), p. 243: 'it is submitted that the true distinction to be drawn is ... between cases in which it is intended to confer present possession of the crops or trees, etc., on the land when there is either no immediate obligation to sever or no possibility of severing, because the time of maturity has not yet arrived, and cases in which by the terms of the contract no property or interest is to pass until severance, and entry on the land is given solely for the purposes of severance.'

264 Megarry, *A Manual of the Law of Real Property* (London, Stevens & Sons, 1962, 3rd ed.), p. 354: '*Fructus naturales* are to be treated as land within the statute unless either they are to be severed by the vendor and not the purchaser or else the contract binds the purchaser to sever them as soon as possible.'

265 Goode, *Commercial Law* (London, Penguin, 1982), p. 155.

266 Coin-Delisle, *Donations et Testamens* (1844), p. 226, Art. 936, [16]: 's'il se doit écouler un temps plus ou moins long avant [la] livraison [d'immeubles par destination donnés à titre gratuit], il faudrait [la] faire transcrire; car au moment de la donation, ils avaient la qualité

ered that the sale of successive crops of land over a number of years and the sale of minerals to be extracted from a quarry already in operation would be movable regarding the crop and minerals to be extracted of the current year, but immovable regarding that of the remaining years. In English law again, the long-term effect on land is at play when it is argued that a contract whereby a young crop is disposed of, but the buyer is to tend to it, harvest it and which confers upon the seller an immediate right of re-entry upon a certain date, irrespective of the harvest's progress would pass an interest in the land.[267]

4. German law: third party protection and commercial expediency

In German law, the simple reason why parts of land sold for severance need not satisfy the notarization requirement for contracts in land is that land may only be sold whole – a part of land is not a plot of land. The underlying reason is that its implicit[268] statutory distinction of land and goods is premised on what may be the subject matter of third party rights.[269] Thus, in terms of third party rights, a part of land has no legal existence – it is an integral part of the plot of land of which it forms a part. A contract for sale is premised on the transfer of ownership of the object sold and, as far as parts of land such as standing timber are concerned, ownership can be transferred only once a tree has been felled and thereby transformed into something capable of sustaining the third party right of ownership. Any sales contract is therefore one for future goods, not for a presently-existing plot of land. Given that there is no potential for a sale of future property to prejudice third parties, there is no reason to subject it to formalities by which third parties could have notice of it or an added degree of solemnity. The contract with a forest-owner for timber is no different from that with a goldsmith for jewellery, both are contracts for future goods. As a result, full range may be given to commercial expediency.

---

d'immeubles, et ils la conservent à l'égard des tiers qui ne doivent jamais être trompés par une libéralité secrète.'

267 Anon, Growing Crops – the passing of property before severance' (1949) 93 The Law Journal 259. That view being advocated despite the fact that the subject matter of the contract is nevertheless one of fructus industriales.

268 No article of the BGB specifically sets out the distinction of corporeal property into land and movable property. It is, for instance, merely implied in Articles 90–103 on the distinctions of different forms of property. Elsewhere different rules are given depending on whether the property is a plot of land or movable property (e.g., rules specific to the loss and acquisition of ownership of land (§§ 925–928) and of movable property (§§ 929–936) or § 946 and § 947).

269 § 90 ('Sachen im Sinne des Gesetzes sind nur körperliche Gegenstände') read in conjunction with § 903 ('Der Eigentümer einer Sache…') BGB. Corporeal things only (either land or movables) can form the subject-matter of ownership, which is the archetypal third party right.

B.   Systemics and purpose

Statements of the law on what things of the natural world are land or goods tend to focus exclusively on physical proximity, in a broad sense. How attached is the thing to the land? In other words, what damage would be incurred in its removal? These questions are almost completely absent from the expositions of the law given in this chapter, certainly as far as the dominant outcome: contracts for the felling of standing timber need not satisfy the higher formalities to which contracts in land are subject.

It is submitted here that the reason why the property law rules on what is land or goods are almost irrelevant lies in the fact that the distinction of land and goods is being borrowed by another area of law *for another purpose*, in the present case that of contract law. A conceptual framework is therefore needed which is broader than a simple equation based on (i) the distinction land/goods, (ii) the property law rules and (iii) factual circumstances. Such a conceptual framework must take account of the purpose for which the distinction of land and goods has been borrowed.

1.   A conceptual framework

From a comparative law perspective, the relevant elements of a comprehensive conceptual framework must be even broader. Such a framework must take account of the fact, first of all, that a particular legal distinction borrowed in one legal system from one field to another may not even be applicable in another legal system. This was the case in the previous chapter in respect of formal requirements for the formation of a contract: the distinction of land and goods is applicable in English and French law but not in German law. In German law, the applicable distinction is between land and everything else.

Furthermore, every point of law posits a particular legal requirement. As far as the previous chapter is concerned, the applicable requirement in respect of land is writing for English law and notarization in German law. However, in French law, it is publication in respect of land and an unpublished signed description in respect of goods.

Moreover, a legal distinction determining a particular requirement may not relate to the same legal construct in different legal systems. That is the case where the requirements of writing and of notarization in English and German law respectively apply to contracts in land. The requirement of publication of the contract or a signed description of the goods in French law applies to gratuitous contracts but not to contracts of sale.

The natural corollary of any legal requirement is the resulting consequence of non-compliance with it. The effect of non-compliance with a requirement is also inherently related to the legal construct at hand. In this chapter, the main focus has been limited to the validity of a contract, whether it be of sale or of a gift. However, it would be inaccurate not to refer to the possibility that non-compliance with the requirement of publication would, in French law, lead to the impossibility of enforceability against third parties. That possibility is, however, strictly-speaking limited to third party enforceability, which is the primary preoccupation of property law.

Equally important are any factual permutations which determine whether something falls under one or the other of the categories formed by the distinction in question, namely land/goods in English and French law and land/not land in German law. Key factual circumstances include whether the contract concerns *fructus naturales*, *fructus industriales* (emblements), which of the contracting parties is to sever the parts of land, identification of the objects sold or gifted, etc. These factual permutations have a bearing on the characterisation of something as land or goods, where applicable, and/or on which of the requirements applies (writing, notarization etc.).

Lastly, underlying such factual distinctions and the outcome itself, the policy considerations or *ratio legis* must also be identified. To avoid repetition, these have been set out fully in the previous chapter.

Once all of these elements have been broken down it is possible to follow a particular line of reasoning within one legal system and compare those elements systematically.

Contracts for the severance of parts of land	English law	French law	German law
Legal distinction	land/goods	land/goods	land/not land
Requirement	writing/parole	publication/unpublished signed description	notarization/parole
Legal construct	sales contracts/ profit à prendre	gratuitous contracts (gift)	contracts (sales/ gifts)
Effect of compliance with the requirement	contractual validity	contractual validity/third party enforcement (*opposabilité*)	contractual validity
Ratio legis/ policy considerations	solemnity/expediency immediacy/long-term ordinary/extra-ordinary	solemnity(notice)/ expediency immediacy/long-term ordinary/extra-ordinary	expediency future goods

(Continued)

Contracts for the severance of parts of land	English law	French law	German law
Factual permutations	*fructus industriales, f. naturales,* other parts of land	*fructus industriales, f. naturales*	all parts of land (*Bestandteile*)

To take German law, given that the legal requirement in question connected to the legal construct of contract and that the legal systemics preclude the existence of third party rights overs parts of land, there is no need to provide for added formality in the lapse of time between the conclusion of the contract and severance from the land.

Turning to French law, if the elements of the horizontal row in the above table are limited specifically to one effect of compliance, i.e. contractual validity, the situation is actually not far removed from German law. Contracts concluded for the severance of parts of land are valid between the parties without being subject to the additional legal requirement applicable to contracts for land. One difference, however, is clear in the national legal framework. French law also provides for a legal requirement specifically directed at tangible movable property, that is to say goods. It is also clearer to isolate the policy considerations relating to that requirement. If the introduction of such a requirement were hypothetically introduced into German law, then it too would in all probability require such contracts to adhere to it, since the greater solemnity to a contract of gift serves primarily the incidence of the contract between the parties. A signed description identifies the object of the gift with greater precision, preventing a reticent donor from substituting one object for another. To let gifts of future goods escape the formalities for presently-existing goods would defeat the ratio legis of the underlying requirement.

2.   English law

Where national law appears complex or a wide range of views are expressed, this conceptual framework is most useful. That is the case of English law. It is perhaps also one of the chief sins in the literature to assume that the distinction of land and goods is a unitary one, applying indiscriminately regardless of the point of law at issue. The continued uncertainty, for instance, in English law on this point affects the discourse over a number of related questions, particularly the nature of the legal transaction itself and the transfer of title. Once the considerations of legal construct and the effect of non-compliance are isolated, namely a contract of sale and contractual validity, it is clear that the overwhelming tendency is to favour commercial expediency. Having concluded that commercial expediency is the prevailing ratio legis, it is obvious why the requirement of writing has been whittled down in successive judicial decisions and legislative reforms.

There is also a natural incongruity between enforceability against third parties and contractual validity. Thus, in French law, even where the greater formality of publication is discussed in connection with contracts of gift for the severance of parts of land, that greater formality is coupled with the enforceability of rights arising under the contract vis-à-vis third parties. In German law, where the question of third party enforceability is set apart from freedom of contract, the requirement of notarization for contracts in land also has no bearing on the validity of a contract for the severance of a part of land. It was previously clear in English law, under the Statute of Frauds, that the distinction of land and goods was precisely limited to a mere requirement of form for the purposes of contractual validity, and therefore to the exclusion of third party enforceability. However, the branching off of that distinction, with the rule on when a contract is considered one for goods and therefore not subject to the formal requirement of writing incorporated into the Sale of Goods Act and the rule on when a contract is for an interest in land (and therefore subject to the requirement of writing) ultimately to the Law of Property Act, seems to have muddled the legal purpose at issue. This is because both statutes deal with issues of contract and property. From a comparative perspective, this muddling of purpose is wrong.

This does not mean that the English law in this area is wrong, but merely that certain interpretations of it are inconsistent, and should therefore be corrected in the interest of legal certainty.

One obvious systemically-consistent interpretation would be to restrict the requirement of writing to contracts for the grant of a profit à prendre – a limited real right in land, leaving all contracts for the sales of goods open to conclusion by parole in respect of all types of parts of land (*fructus*, fixtures etc.). The policy considerations of solemnity and long-term activity would then be indicators of whether a profit was intended to be granted. This would furthermore be consistent with the law on the creation of profits, whereby the requirement of writing is a precondition to third party enforceability by way of registration but, if there is partial performance, not an impediment to enforceability *inter partes*.

Another interpretation of the existing statutory framework and case-law would be to consider that, on a better construction, the definition drafted by Chalmers in the Sale of Goods Act operated reform of the position at common law, simplifying it and ultimately abolishing the requirement of writing for all 'emblements, industrial growing crops, and things attached to or forming part of the land which are agreed to be severed before sale or under the contract of sale'. Such reform would, however, also operate to apply issues governed by the Sale of Goods Act, such as the passing of the risk and title transfer, to such contracts.

This would in fact bring English law back to a number of very early courts decisions whereby 'if the tenant in tail sells the trees to another, now they are a chattel in the vendee, and his executors shall have them, and in such case *fictione juris* they are severed from the land'.[270]

A more conservative interpretation would be to carve out the definition of goods in the Sale of Goods Act for the specific purpose of the requirement of writing. In effect, this would entail a codicil to the definition of goods meaning that, provided that the requirement of writing (in the Law of Property Act) was satisfied, such a contract would be validly constituted and therefore capable of falling within the scope of the Sale of Goods Act for other purposes (transfer of the risk, title etc.). Whilst adhering to the idea that Chalmers was effecting a statutory restatement of the common law rules, this interpretation does nevertheless run counter to the express wording of that consolidatory[271] (or codificatory[272]) statute, which lays down that 'a contract of sale may be made in writing (either with or without seal), or by word of mouth, or partly in writing and partly by word of mouth, or may be implied from the conduct of the parties'.[273]

In any event, what is conceptually impossible is for property to be goods the under Sale of Goods Act and land under the Law of Property Act *for the same legal function*, i. e. for a contract to be valid *inter partes* according to the one Act and invalid for the other, provided of course that the same legal construct is at issue[274]. That conceptual impossibility is most clearly discernible once account is taken of the legal purpose behind the legal requirements at issue, rather than limiting consideration of the correct outcome merely to factual permutations, such as the nature of the object (i. e. *fructus industriales* or *fructus naturales*), or which of the contracting parties is to effect severance.

In any of the above interpretations, there is a question of third party enforceability which is still ultimately not covered by the Law of Property Act or the Sale of Goods Act, that is to say falling outside of the scope of the leading statute on rights in land and that on rights in goods. This is the co-ordinatory function of the distinction of land and goods of funnelling the rules on third party enforceability either within the scope of the corresponding rules concerning rights in land or those concerning rights in goods. This is due to the irrefutable rule of law that, for certain purposes, and *a minima* when land is transferred as a whole without any specific direction, all parts of land, whether emblements, *fructus naturales*, fixtures or other, are regarded as forming part of the whole of an

---

270 *Liford's case* (1615) 77 ER 1206, 11 Co. Rep. 46b.
271 1979 wording.
272 1893 wording.
273 s. 4, Sale of Goods Act 1893, now Sale of Goods Act 1979.
274 cf. following section.

individual plot of land.[275] It is therefore entirely possible for a dispute to arise between one party who claims the objects at issue as land (i. e. a mortgagee) and another who claims them as goods (a purchaser under the sale of goods contract, or even creditors of the latter). It is, however, arguably here – with respect of the co-ordinary function of the distinction of land and goods – that the policy considerations of solemnity, extraordinary and long-term activity would be relevant to the outcome of such a dispute, not in relation to the requirement of writing for the purpose of the validity of a contract. That point of law does, however, appear to have been conclusively dealt with in the early decisions of the common law, in favour of giving priority to the holder of rights in the land, unless given prior notice of the sales contract.[276]

C.   Conclusion

The present chapter has set out a conceptual framework for analysing diverging views on a correct statement of national law regarding the distinction of land and goods on the basis of the preceeding chapter. A number of considerations are interwoven in an overall picture of the law. The proposed framework in-corporates systemics and purpose, first by breaking down the abstract legal distinction in question (land/goods) into that distinction itself and the corre-sponding legal requirement (writing/publication/description etc.), then the function of the former in terms of the legal construct concerned (contract of sale/ gift) and the effect of non-compliance in the system of national law (invalidity/ third party unenforceability), which allows for the contextualisation of the un-derlying policy considerations (solemnity/expediency etc.) and any related fac-tual distinctions (*fructus industriales/naturales* etc.) to be taken into account independently.

---

275 s. 205(1)(ix) LPA 1925: '"Land" includes land of any tenure, and mines and minerals, whether or not held apart from the surface, buildings or parts of buildings (whether the division is horizontal, vertical or made in any other way) and other corporeal heredita-ments…'

276 *Herlakenden's case*, KB (1589) 4 Co. Rep. 62a; 76 ER 1025; *Liford's case* (1615) 11 Co. Rep. 46b; 77 ER 1206; *Stukeley* v. *Butler* (1615) Hob 168; 80 ER 316.

Chapter 5.
Nursery plants, German Christmas trees and transplantation

Chapter 2 concerned the use of the distinction of land and goods, ultimately derived from property law, in a particular area of tax law, the levying of a tax on acquisitions of land. The distinction was drawn in all three legal systems under consideration. It homes in on the question of whether sales contracts for the severance of parts of land, such as that of standing timber or unharvested crops, are subject to land acquisition taxes. The key finding was that the imposition of the tax was in the vast majority of outcomes determined solely by the strict position of property law. Only in exceptional cases was the distinction as drawn in property law adapted for the specific purposes of tax law. In Chapter 3, a question of law was considered which demonstrated greater variety in the use of the distinction of land and goods, or even its irrelevance, according to the national systems under consideration. Chapter 4 developed a conceptual framework for analysing the distinction of land and goods from a comparative perspective. That framework distinguished the multiple facets of legal purpose and certain factual permutations having an influence on the outcome of a particular case. Those chapters effectively kept considerations of legal systemics constant, such as the imposition of a certain tax and requirements of form.

The present chapter keeps certain factual permutations constant in order to identify variations in the distinction of land and goods in terms of legal purpose. Those specific factual permutations are nursery plants, Christmas trees and other "transplantations". Does such living vegetation constitute goods or land in English, French and German law? In what legal constructs does their classification as goods or land arise?

A.   France

1.   Doctrinal discussion

All French authors make an exception from the rule of *superficies solo cedit* in the case of plants planted by a lessee of land. Such plants are movable and this rule applies with the same force to the plants grown by the tenant-nurseryman. However, where the nurseryman also owns the land, the authors diverge. On one interpretation, such trees never become immovable by nature. According to Marcadé, writing in 1844, nursery plants are 'only momentarily, transiently attached to land as if stored in a warehouse'[277] and will only become immovable by nature 'when planted with the intention of leaving them in the soil permanently; thus only then will tree and soil form an intentionally indivisible whole.'[278] This does not, however, prevent Marcadé from qualifying the trees on other grounds as immovable. He writes that such plants are actually immovable by destination.

In the case where young trees are transplanted to another nursery for sale, Duranton and Demolombe reject Marcadé's characterisation of such nursery plants as immovable by destination. The reason given is because these plants are not placed in the other soil permanently (*à perpétuelle demeure*), but rather are only stored momentarily and provisionally.[279] Duranton and Demolombe thus conceive of nursery plants which require no further growth as finished products – they are not intended to remain on the land much longer. Marcadé's view is, however, based upon the idea that the plants are necessary for the exploitation of the land as a nursery. In the latter sense, it would not be necessary for the plants to remain on the land in perpetuity, under the second head of immobilisation by destination, but rather to be seen as stock necessary for the exploitation of the land as a nursery, i. e. the first limb of the test for immobilisation by destination.

In contrast to Marcadé's reading of nursery trees as movable by nature, but immobilised by destination, other treatises, on the other hand, continue to qualify nursery trees as immovable by nature in application of the general rule of *superficies solo cedit*. This is, for instance, the view expressed by Duranton, Aubry & Rau, Pothier and Demolombe. These authors diverge, however, in their account of when and in what circumstances nursery plants become movable. The

---

277 Marcadé, *Eléments du droit civil français* (2ⁿᵈ ed., Paris, 1844), vol. 2, art. 521, p. 365: 'les arbres d'une pépinière sont meubles; car ils ne sont là que momentanément, passagèrement et comme en dépôt.'

278 Marcadé, *Eléments du droit civil français* (2ⁿᵈ ed., Paris, 1844), vol. 2, art. 521, p. 365: 'C'est dans le terrain où on les plantera avec volonté de les y laisser, qu'ils deviendront immeubles, du moment même de la plantation; alors seulement le sol et l'arbre feront un seul tout intentionnellement indivisible.'

279 Demolombe, vol. 9, [148].

earliest author, Pothier, who was commenting upon the French law pre-codification but whose views were particularly influential on the drafts of the later Code civil, made what seems to be the broadest exception. According to Pothier,

> 'the rule of [*quae sata sunt, solo cedere intelligentur*] suffers another exception for the trees of nurseries, which are transplanted from the soil which produced them to another soil where they are placed as in storage to be nourished and fortified until uprooted for sale. These trees retain their movable character which they acquired from being uprooted from the soil which gave them life and are not reputed to form part of the land in which they are transplanted since they were not planted there permanently (*à perpétuelle demeure*) and remain there only for storage until such time at which they will be removed to be sold.'[280]

It is this account of the law and another passage to similar effect which form the basis of the later authors' characterisation of nursery plants. The essential elements of this exception are, first, transplantation from one nursery to another, which is the moment when the plants first lose their immovable character and, second, the temporary depositing of such plants, despite nourishment and further growth, in another soil before being finally removed and sold.

The tendency of later authors has been to restrict the terms of Pothier's exception for plants moved to another plot for sale. Duranton, whose opinion is also adopted by Demolombe,[281] does not admit this exception where the plants are moved to another plot for further growth (*pour s'y fortifier*). For Duranton, the transplantation exception should only apply where 'the plants have been uprooted at a very advanced stage in their development and are only deposited in the new soil for storage.'[282] However, even Duranton later restricted, or at the least clarified, his original account, by adding 'and are to be sold immediately or at the first occasion.'[283] Aubry & Rau, for their part, do not distinguish in general between those plants which have been grown on the same plot and those which are transplanted to another part, be it for their continued nourishment or further

---

280 Pothier, R. J., *De la communauté* (Paris: Debure, 1770), [46]: ']: 'Suivant la règle, que nous venons d'exposer, les arbres des pépinières, qui tiennent encore à la terre qui les a produits des pépins qui y ont été semés, sont censés faire partie de cette terre, et ne faire qu'un seul et même tout avec elle. Mais, lorsqu'ils ont été arrachés et séparés, ils deviennent une chose meuble, distinguée de cette terre. Ils conservent même cette qualité de chose meubles, lorsqu'ils sont haubinés, c'est-à-dire, transplantés dans une autre, où ils sont mis en dépôt, pour s'y fortifier quelque temps, jusqu'à ce qu'on les en arrache pour les vendre ; car n'étant que comme en dépôt dans cette terre, ils n'en font pas partie …'.

281 Demolombe, vol. 9 (4th ed., 1870), [148].

282 Duranton, vol. 4 (2nd ed., 1828), [44]: 'Nous n'adoptons cette modification que pour le cas où les plants ont été arrachés étant déjà très-avancés, et pour rester seulement en dépôt dans le nouveau lieux.'

283 Duranton, vol. 4 (4th ed., 1844), [44]: 'Nous n'adoptons cette modification que pour le cas où les plants ont été arrachés étant déjà très-avancés, et pour rester seulement en dépôt dans le nouveau lieux, *et être vendus de suite ou à la première occasion*.' [author's emphasis].

growth.[284] Their exception applies to 'trees which are only momentarily deposited in another soil until their sale or transplanted.'[285] Despite the clear allusion to sale, the lack of a reference to tree nurseries may imply that Aubry & Rau's account of the rule applies to all plants irrespective of whether in a nursery or not provided that they are momentarily transplanted.

According to Laurent, even Pothier's reference to transplantation for future sale is not strictly in conformity with the Code, nor the fact that they are not planted permanently (*à perpétuelle demeure*). For Laurent, it is the connection with the soil (*incorporation*) which is conclusive of property's character as movable or immovable not the intention of the owner.[286] Despite making the point that the material connection is conclusive for the category of immovables by nature, Laurent nonetheless immediately excepts both 'uprooted plants to be sold which are provisionally deposited in the soil before delivery' as well as plants sold whilst still standing, which are movable 'by virtue of the contract'.[287]

For Demolombe and Duranton the plants of nurseries are analogous to vegetables and other annual crops. Since crops are destined to be removed upon harvest, yet are immovable until removed, the same must apply to nursery plants. Marcadé, however, distinguishes between crops and nursery plants because the latter are removed from the soil entirely to be reunited with another soil still in the same form. Crops, on the other hand, the severance of which is necessitated by their very nature (as comestibles), undergo a change in nature; they can never be reunited with the soil in the same way again. Though true of many industrial crops, such as wheat, where the steam is removed and therefore the crop is 'dead', tuberous crops like the potato could be reintroduced into the soil and grown. However, given that in most cases even the potato harvest is destined to be sold and consumed, Marcadé's argument must still hold in terms of objective intention.

Normally, as is recognised by all authors, there is no difference in legal regime between immovables by nature and those by destination once the conditions for their immobilisation under either of these two heads is satisfied. As a result, much of the debate upon whether something should be classified as land by nature or destination is academic or, in the words of Marcadé, merely '*pour la*

---

284 Aubry & Rau, vol.2, § 164, [1°], p. 11: 'Il n'y pas non plus à distinguer entre les arbres qui se trouvent encore dans le sol qui les a produits, et ceux qui, après avoir été arrachés, ont été transplantés dans un autre fonds, ne fût-ce que pour s'y nourrir et s'y fortifier.'

285 Aubry & Rau, vol.2, § 164, [1°], p. 11: 'Mais les arbres qui n'auraient été que momentanément déposés dans un fonds, jusqu'à leur vente ou leur transplantation, ne sont point à considérer comme immeubles.'

286 Laurent, *Principes de droit civil français* (1871), vol. 5, [420], p. 527.

287 Idem.

rectitude des idées.[288] Nevertheless, two situations can be given in which the authors would appear to attribute different effects to the two categories. Once already immobilised, the first is their mobilisation by the mere conclusion of a sales contract or the granting of security rights separate from the land without the handing over of possession. The second situation is in the process of immobilisation, depending upon whether the nurseryman plants his own plants or those of another. Upon closer analysis, in actual fact, only in the second situation does the characterisation of the plants as immovable by nature or by destination make a difference to the rights of third parties over the land.

Duranton and a number of other authors[289] appear to attribute different consequences in legal regime to the two sorts of immovable. Thus, Duranton writes that 'since there can be differences, in law, between these diverse types of immovable realty, it is important not to confuse the two';[290] property by way of destination only maintains its immovable character as long as the 'destination' continues so that, once ended, the property in question returns to its movable state. Thus, once movable again, the mortgagee has no claim to the property in application of Article 2119 Code civil: *'les meubles n'ont pas de suite par hypothèque.'* However, as an example, Duranton names mirrors forming part of wood panelling, which in general also fall under a mortgage on the land, but which, having been detached, then pass into the hands of a third party acquirer. Mirrors cannot in such circumstances be claimed by the mortagagee who then seizes the land.[291] As Marcadé points out, great trees, exquisite wainscoting of a house and minerals, though indisputably immovable by nature, will, once separated by the mortgagor and delivered to a third party, become movable and beyond the reach of the mortgagee.[292]

It is considered to be a rule that the immobilisation of movable property placed on land for its better exploitation is brought to an end when the former

---

288 Marcadé, Explication théorique et pratique du code civil, vol. 2, [351].
289 Delvincourt, *Cours de Code Napoléon*, p. 142–143: 'Il faut observer, au surplus, que les objets meubles, destinés par le propriétaire au service du fonds, n'acquièrent la qualité d'immeubles qu'à raison de l'emploi qui en est fait par le propriétaire, et qu'ils ne la conservent qu'étant que cet emploi n'est pas changé par le propriétaire lui-même.'
290 Duranton, *Cours de droit français* (4th ed., Paris, 1844), vol. 4, [15].
291 Delvincourt, *Cours de Code Napoléon*, p. 521 (note 11 to p. 142): 'Ainsi, l'hypothèque sur un fonds frappe bien sur tout ce qui est censé immeuble, d'après les règles posées ci-dessus; mais il y a cette différence entre le fonds lui-même, qui est immeuble par sa nature, et les objets qui ne sont immeubles que par destination, et comme accessoires du fonds, que le premier ne peut perdre sa qualité d'immeuble qu'en périssant tout-à-fait; d'où il résulte que l'hypothèque le suit toujours, dans quelque main qu'il se trouve; les seconds, au contraire, n'étant immeubles qu'à raison de ce qu'ils sont accessoires du fonds, cessent d'être sujets à l'hypothèque, du moment qu'ils sont passés en mains-tierces, séparément du fonds.'
292 Marcadé, Explication théorique et pratique du code civil, vol. 2, [351].

movables are sold separately from the land.[293] This is certainly the case as between the two contracting parties.[294] Nevertheless, as regards third parties, such as a mortgagee of the land, the objects sold separately are still immovable until the purchaser takes possession in good faith of the "goods" in which title has passed under the contract.[295] For example, in *Caisse commercial du Quesnoy* v. *Syndicat Valin*, a farmer who had mortgaged his land later sold the animals used for working the land and the buyer took possession of the animals.[296] The mortgagee had full knowledge of the sale having allowed its own prior seizure of the animals to be lifted. The Cour d'appel de Douai held that the mortgagee could not claim the animals from the purchaser, nor their price from the mortgagee. Where immovables by destination are sold and delivery is made, they are without doubt movable.

The same principle has been applied where immovables, though sold, are not removed from the land. For example, in *Hesnard et veuve Legrand* v. *Anciens établissements Duperron*, the owner of a pharmaceutical factory granted a mortgage over the land and, without any suggestion of fraud, subsequently created a company in whose assets the factory machinery was transferred and to whom the factory itself was leased.[297] The company also later gave the machinery to another in pledge. The question before the courts was whether the mortgagee or the pledgee should have priority over the machines. The Cour de cassation quashed the judgment of the Cour d'appel for having preferred the claim of the company (and the pledgee claiming under it), and instead preferred the mortgagee, since the corporate buyer of the plant continued to possess it in fact and use it in the same way that the mortgagor who had originally placed it in the

---

293 Dalloz, *Rep. de législation, de doctrine et de jurisprudence* (1847), biens, [129], citing: *Mourier* v. *Carrichon* Grenoble (19.12.1815) and *Enregistrement* v. *Japy* Cass. Civ. (19.11. 1823). Also, *Johnston* v. *Firbac* Bourges, (31.01.1843), cited in *Jurisprudence générale* (1847), biens, [132]; Demolombe, [322]-[323]; Aubry & Rau, p. 20.
294 *Simon et Bondaux* v. *Enregistrement* Cass. (27.06.1882): [1883] 1 S 382; 1 P 965: where a factory owner sells the machinery to a company which he also rents the factory to, for tax purposes the sale is considered as of a good, even though the machinery is not removed from the land.
295 *Hesnard et veuve Legrand* v. *Anicens établissements Duperrou* Cass. Civ. (01.05.1906): [1909] 1 D 345: 'Lorsque le propriétaire d'un immeuble hypothéqué a cédé à des tiers des objets mobiliers placés dans l'immeuble pour son service et son exploitation, ces tiers ne peuvent paralyser l'action du créancier hypothécaire en invoquant la règle « en fait de meubles, possession vaut titre », que si les objets ont été détachés de l'immeuble et possédés par eux séparément'. Terré & Simler, *Droit civil, Les Biens* (6th ed., Dalloz, Paris, 2002), [33]: 'la volonté de désaffectation est insuffisante à faire perdre la qualité d'immeuble par destination s'il n'y a pas soit séparation effective entre l'immeuble par nature et l'immeuble par destination, soit aliénation de l'un et de l'autre.'
296 CA Douai (16.12.1886): [1888] 2 S 115.
297 Civ. (01.05.1906): [1909] 1 D 345.

factory.[298] Where immovables by destination are sold but not delivered, they remain immovable.

In conclusion, even authors who assert that contracts for the sale of immovables by destination separately from the land effect the "mobilisation" of the subject-matter of the contract also support the solution of allowing third parties holding real rights in the land to claim immovables by destination where they have not been removed from the land in execution of a contract of sale or non-possessory pledge.[299] As a result, returning to the example of nusery plants, should a nurseryman purport to pledge the trees of the nursery as security without handing over the trees to the pledgee the trees will still form part of the mortgagee's security if the mortgagee seizes the land.[300] This is the case irrespective of whether the trees are by nature or destination immovable; in both cases they are immovable.

This confusion seems to result from the very definition of property immovable by destination itself. *Immeubles par destination* are actually movables according to their physical nature but which the law considers to be land.[301] The temptation is to the return to the physical classification of the object, ignoring its legal classification, and then attribute consequences as if the object were actually movable in law. Without more, this reasoning is flawed. Once an object of the physical world, considered to be movable, is legally reputed immovable for whatever reason, arguments based on its physical characteristic as movable or immovable can no longer affect its legal characterisation as they do not negate the reasons behind the original characterisation of a physically movable thing as immovable in law. The real reason for the mobilisation of an immovable is a combination of considerations of a legal nature, such as party autonomy, the protection of third parties and the added value of keeping two things together.

---

298 [1909] 1 D 345, 347: 'ils n'ont cessé de posséder ce mobilier, matériellement, sans aucun changement apporté au mode d'exploitation de l'immeuble, dans l'état où il avait été placé par le propriétaire de hypothéqué […]; qu'au regard de ces derniers, leur possession est donc inefficace'.

299 Duranton, vol. 19. (4th ed., 1844), [283]: 'Dans le cas de vente de livraison des [immeubles par destination], [les créanciers hypothécaires] ne peuvent donc les faire réintégrer, à moins toutefois qu'il n'y ait eu collusion de la part de l'acheteur.'

300 Otherwise in Germany.

301 Sauvalle, *De la distinction entre les immeubles par nature et les immeubles par destination et spécialement de l'outillage immobilier* (Giard & Briere, 1902, Paris) (Thesis), p. 54–55; Malaurie, *Les Biens* (Paris: Defrénois, 4th ed., 2010), [137]: 'Les immeubles par destination sont des biens qui, physiquement, sont des meubles, mais que le droit considère fictivement comme des immeubles parce qu'ils sont l'accessoire d'un fonds et qu'il est opportun de maintenir ce lien entre le fonds et ses accessoires'; Terré, *Les Biens* (6th ed., Dalloz, Paris, 2002), [34]: Il s'agit des choses mobilières considérées fictivement comme des immeubles en raison du lien qui les unit à un immeuble par nature dont ils constituent l'accessoire'.

The classification of nursery trees is nevertheless decisive as a cause of immobilisation. For example, in a situation whereby a nurseryman who had no more space on his land were to lend some young trees to a neighbouring nurseryman with a larger plot of land and the mortgagee of the neighbour were then to seize that land, the characterisation of the trees determines whether the trees can be the object of rights separately from the land. If qualified as immovable by nature, the mortgage's rights would extend to the saplings lent; yet, if not, the trees would not have been immobilised by destination because the trees lent were not owned by the second nurseryman, despite being necessary for the exploitation of the land. In the latter case, the original nurseryman could have the plants lent excluded from the seizure of the land.

2.   Case-law

The facts which formed the basis of a decision given by the Cour de cassation provide judicial application of almost all of the principles discussed in doctrine. In *Faillite Sénéclauze* v. *Sénéclauze* a nursery business was operated on three plots of land, two of which were owned by the nurseryman, one of which was rented.[302] The nursery included seedlings and particular tree, bush and plant nurseries grown in the open air as well as in greenhouses, including some which were in plant-pots. The nurseryman died and, in the judicial sale by public auction which followed, one of the coheirs made the highest bid for the land of one of his late father's plots as well as for the whole nursery business extending over all three plots of land. The other plot owned by the deceased was destined by the heirs to be sold to another. The coheir, as highest bidder, who continued the nursery business, went bankrupt without having paid the price in full. This is important because, in French law, the highest bidder in an auction who becomes the owner of the land by virtue of the sales contract, goes into possession of the land but if he does not honour the conditions of the sale, particularly by not paying the full price, is retrospectively declared to have never owned the land. The bankrupt coheir was thus declared to have possessed the land in bad faith from the date of the auction. The coheirs also had a charge on the land which they had duly registered (*privilège de copartageant*). The trustee in bankruptcy sold the land and the business at a second public auction, but the highest bid was lower than the price of the original price at the first auction.

One of the coheirs brought an action against her brother and his trustee in bankruptcy claiming that all the nursery trees, shrubs and plants attached to the land of all three plots, being of an immovable nature, fell within the ambit of her

---

302 Civ. Cass. (05. 07. 1880): [1880] 1 D 321; [1881] 1 S 105; [1881] 1 P 238.

charge over the immovable property sold. This would have the result, first, that the coheirs' charge would also extend to the value of the plants still standing on the plot not sold to their brother (as well as the plants growing on the land originally leased to their father). A number of plants, trees and shrubs had also been sold in the ordinary course of business by the bankrupt, as well as subsequently by the trustee in bankruptcy, in the period from the time of the declaration of bankruptcy until the forced sale of the nursery at auction. The claimant argued that, since they were part of the land over which she had a charge, the proceeds of the sale of the nursery plants also fell under the charge. Given the particular facts of the case, the courts were faced with the characterisation of the plants of the nursery as goods or parts of land, first, as part of leased land, second, as part of land first sold but then declared to have been always owned by the unpaid sellers and, third, as part of land which although never sold, had been intended to be sold at a later date. Each of those situations will now be treat individually.

In respect of leased land, the nursery plants were held to be regarded as goods at both first and second instance. This point was considered to be 'without interest' and was therefore not included in the report of the case.[303] The unanimity surrounding this characterisation should, however, be compared with a decision of the court of appeal of Rouen from 1839 which held that only six years after planting could trees in a nursery be seized by the general creditors of the nurseryman.[304] Both the court of first instance and the court of appeal considered the trees of the nursery as *fructus industriales* despite the term of maturity being every six or seven years rather than annually. This decision does seem inconsistent with the notion that plants planted by a lessee are, 'in all circumstances,' movable,[305] since the seizure was limited to those trees which had reached maturity. Since all movable property can be seized by execution-creditors including the attachment of crops ready for harvesting (*saisie-brandon*[306] – attachment of fruits), all of the trees in the lessee's nursery, whether ripe or not, should have been capable of seizure.

In contrast to other authors who extend the ambit of the *saisie-brandon* to periodical products of the land,[307] Chaveau criticises this decision as 'completely arbitrary'[308] for extending the attachment of fruits to periodical products of land,

303 [1880] 1 D 321, 322.

304 *Legendre* v. *Debras* CA Rouen (01.03.1839): 2 S 421.

305 See, Aubry & Rau.

306 Etymology: Chaveau, 'Des meubles par anticipation' [1893] Rev crit 574, 613 [49].

307 Demolombe (4th ed., 1870), vol. 9, [138]: 'à tous les fruits, à tous les produits périodiques quelconques de la terre, et même aux bois taillis ou bois de haute futaie mis en coupes réglées.'

308 Chaveau, 'Des meubles par anticipation' [1893] Rev crit 574, 615, [51], fn 1.

whose severance from the land in the first case 'if not imperatively dictated by the laws of nature, then nevertheless demanded by the rules of good husbandry'[309] whereas in the second case the severance is 'uncertain, conditional and ambulatory…[depending] in reality upon the whim of the owner'.[310] Chaveau thus considered the nursery trees as immovable (even in the case where the debtor is the lessee of land). However, a principled criticism would be to point out that the whole nursery business should have been capable of seizure to the extent that the lessee created the nursery and the land was not leased as a nursery, which would normally mean susceptible to seizure in execution of a debt. To take Demolombe's reasoning as a classic exposition of the nature of the lessee-farmer's right in land, the object of the farmer's right is not the land but the fruits to be had from it in their future state. The lessee's right to the fruits is therefore movable, a right in respect of goods. It would, however, seem logical to follow this premiss with the conclusion that the general creditors should be able to seize nursery trees. This internal contradiction seems only capable of reconciliation if the plants of a lessee are considered in many, and in fact most but not all, circumstances as goods. In other circumstances, the lessee's plants remain parts of land.

In *Faillite Sénéclauze* v. *Sénéclauze*, both the court of appeal and the Cour de cassation considered that the charge of the coheirs over the land extended to the various plants growing on the nursery. The Cour de cassation held that 'although all the plants and bushes of a nursery, even when not attached to the ground at all, can be considered as immovable provided that they form part of the land to which they have been incorporated for its exploitation, this is no longer the case when, by the wishes of the owner, the land on which they have been planted is owned separately from the business exploiting the land.'[311] Unless differences in the distinction of land and goods are drawn between private law and tax law, this decision must be seen as putting into question a decision by the Minister of Finances,[312] cited by Championnière & Rigaud,[313] according to which 'trees planted in a nursery are movable or immovable according to whether or not they

309 Chaveau, 'Des meubles par anticipation' [1893] Rev crit 574, 615, [50]: 'si elle n'est pas imposée aussi impérieusement que pour les fruits et récoltes par une nécessité de nature, elle est cependant réclamée par les règles d'une bonne administration'.
310 614 [49]: 'La séparation des fruits et récoltes [à l'opposé des produits (périodiques)] n'a rien d'incertain, de conditionnel, d'aléatoire; elle ne dépend pas en réalité du bon plaisir du propriétaire'.
311 'Attendu que si tous les arbres, plantés et arbustes qui composent une pépinière, lors même qu'ils ne sont point adhérents au sol, peuvent être considérés comme immeubles tant qu'ils fond partie de l'établissement immobilier auquel ils ont été incorporés pour son service et son exploitation, il n'en est plus de même lorsque, par la volonté du propriétaire, le sol sur lequel ils ont été placés forme une propriété distincte de l'établissement lui-même'.
312 Ministre des finances (10.06.1810): JE 3881.
313 Championnière & Rigaud, *Droits d'enregistrement*, vol. 4, [3166].

were previously uprooted or not and are destined to be sold or not.'[314] Despite any difference in classification for the purposes of private law or tax law, the decision in *Faillite Sénéclauze* v. *Sénéclauze* seems to reject any distinction on the past history of the nursery plants (whether planted as seeds in the nursery or transplanted from another plot etc.) and, to this extent, prefers the straightforward opinion of Marcadé that all nursery plants are immovable. Although the facts of the case allude to a 'vast horticultural business composed of seedlings, nurseries of trees, bushes and plants cultivated in the open air, in plant pots and in greenhouses' in which it is likely that the oft mentioned exception of transplanted plants would probably have been applicable, the court made no distinction between the plants. Instead, for the case that a nursery and the land are owned by the same person, the Cour de cassation restricted the movable characterisation of the plants grown there for those which were legitimately[315] uprooted.[316] This rejection of the majority opinion expressed in the commentaries could, however, be due to the particular circumstances of the case.

In relation to the plot of land which was not sold, but whose plants were sold as part of the sale of the business, the Cour de cassation held that the nursery plants are no longer immovable 'when, by the wishes of the owner, the land on which they have been planted is owned separately from the business exploiting the land.'[317] Assuming this to be a correct application of the law, this would seem to support Marcadé's interpretation that all plantations in a nursery are legally by nature movable although when assigned to the use and exploitation of the land they become immovable by destination. Had the Cour de cassation, for example, considered some plants to be immovable by nature, then the separate disposition of land and business would have made no difference to their classification, since concurrent ownership of land and movable is not a necessary condition of immobilisation by way of incorporation. Nevertheless, there is another explanation not mentioned in the case-note commentary. The disposition of the nursery business separately from the land could be seen to have mobilised the trees in

---

314 'Les arbres plantés en pépinière sont meubles ou immeubles, suivant qu'ils ont été ou non précédement arrachés, et qu'ils sont destinés ou non à être vendus.'

315 The mortgagor has a right to the fruits of the land in the normal course of business provided that the value of the land is not affected. *Argumentum e contrario*, had the nurseryman sold all of the plants on the land to another, this would not be in the normal course of business and the mortgagee would not be bound by the sale. The exception for nursery plants therefore appears not to be as wide as in Germany.

316 'Que [l'arrêt attaqué] a ainsi attribué la qualité d'immeubles à des objets qui, par l'exercice légitime des droits du propriétaire, avaient été détachés de l'établissement immobilier dont ils avaient fait partie, et avaient ainsi perdu cette qualité… En quoi il a violé les articles [524 et 528] de la loi.'

317 '…il n'en est plus de même lorsque, par la volonté du propriétaire, le sol sur lequel ils ont été placés forme une propriété distincte de l'établissement lui-même.'

anticipation of their future severance. The doctrine of mobilisation in anticipation of severance applies, if not indistinguishably between immovables by nature and by destination, then particularly to immovables by nature. Given these alternative analyses, the case cannot be used to support a conclusive characterisation of nursery trees in French law.

There are, however, reasons for doubting the correctness of the Cour de cassation's application of the law in *Faillite Sénéclauze* v. *Sénéclauze*. The quashed reasoning of the Court of appeal of Lyon is, on a purely logical basis, flawless. The fact that the coheir who bought the nursery business was not able to satisfy the conditions stipulated by the auction meant that the sale was resolved. Therefore ownership of the nursery had in law never been separated from the sellers' ownership of the land. As a result, there is no strict legal basis for affirming that the nursery trees had ever become movable, even by way of anticipated severance. Nevertheless, the particular facts of the case justify the decision of the Cour de cassation. Although in terms of strict property law ownership of the plants never left that of the land, the doctrine of *non concedit venire contra factum propriam* should apply against the other coheirs. Having intended to sell the land separately from the nursery business, which means considering the plants as movable, they cannot then be heard to assert their otherwise applicable legal rights by which the plants are immovable. It is submitted that therein lies the reason for the different decisions of the Cour d'appel and the Cour de cassation. It would also follow that, had there been a real mortgagee distinguishable from the person of the seller, the contrary would have been decided. In such a case, the sale of the nursery business would have exceeded the general management rights of a mortgagor and, not being party to the sales contract, the third party would have been allowed to rely on the immovable characterisation of the nursery plants.

Nursery plants	Legal distinction	Rule	Legal construct	Legal consequence	Ratio legis/ policy considerations	Relevant factual distinctions
French law	L(im.p.n./ im.p.d) /G(m.p.n/ m.p.a.)	Subject-matter of third party rights	- insolvency - attachment by judgment creditors	L/G[a)]	- only momentarily and provisionally stored in land - objective intention (operation of a nusery business on the land)	- nursery plants/*fructus industriales?* - notice of sales contract - placed in pots/ planted - ownership of land & nursery business ≠'earmarked for sale' =prior transplantation + removal as living plants
		Transactional (contract) law	Land acquisition tax	= G		
			Rescission of contract/judicial sale	= G		

[a)] Not conclusive.

B.   Germany

1.   Legislative framework

§ 94 BGB provides that everything firmly attached to land becomes an integral part thereof, including buildings, (natural) products of the land for as long as they are still attached to the land, and that seeds and plants become integral parts of the land once sown and planted. Such *wesentliche Bestandteile* ('integral or essential parts') of the land cannot form the subject-matter third party rights other than as third party rights in the land to which they are attached. This is a legislative statement of the general principle of *superficies solo cedit.*

Nevertheless, § 95 BGB sets out an exception to the rule of *superficies solo cedit* where certain things are attached to the ground only temporarily. Such temporary fixtures are only apparent component parts (*Scheinbestandteil*). They are therefore goods and, as a result, rights can exist in those objects in their severed, movable form separately from rights in the land despite the fact that they are generally, in a physical sense, firmly attached to the land (or another part thereof).

§ 95 BGB is primarily and specifically aimed at governing additions to land made by a contractual tenant or limited real right holder – since both a contractual tenant and a usufructuary have rights in the land which are temporally limited, all of their additions to the land are presumed to be parts of the land only temporarily. However, the majority of legal scholars consider that additions made by the landowner, who has an absolute third party right not limited in time, may also affix goods to the land for a temporary purpose, thereby preventing their accession to the land.[318] This view is based on the consideration that the first draft of the BGB had originally limited the rule to things attached temporarily 'by a person other than the landowner' but that limitation was then jettisoned in the rule as enachted by being worded in the passive voice, thereby opening up the benefit of the rule to landowners too.

Given the wording of § 94 BGB, which refers specifically to the sowing of seeds and setting into the soil of plants, it is perhaps surprising that plants in commercial tree nurseries and Christmas trees in plantations have throughout the lifespan of the BGB been regarded, under the exception in § 95 BGB, as goods.

---

318 Staudinger (2011) § 95, [13].

2.   Case-law illustrations

Two early decisions of the Reichsgericht illustrate the interplay of §§ 94 and 95 BGB as applied to standing timber and tree nurrseries.

As illustration of the rule of *superficies solo cedit*, in 1905, the Reichsgericht heard the case of *Vermögensverwaltungsstelle für Offiziere und Beamte* v. Z, in which there had been a sale of standing trees first, then of the land, to two different persons.[319] The buyer of the trees had been assured by the landowner that a notice of the sale of the trees would be entered into the land register (*Grundbuch*), and was so entered. However, the seller of the trees then sold his plot of land to another who refused to allow the buyer of the standing timber to fell it. Upholding the decision of the lower *Kammergericht*, the *Reichsgericht* held that, under the BGB, standing timber forms an integral part of the land, incapable of forming the subject-matter of a third party right, so that a landowner can only bind himself in personam to fell or let another fell and remove standing trees. Trees only become movable once physically severed from the land.

The reason why such a case came before the highest German civil court, despite express legislative wording clearly in favour of one of the parties, presumably lies in the decision's temporal proximity to the enactment of the BGB, which departed on this point significantly from the previous law in force in certain parts of Germany. Such an entry of notice would, for instance, have been valid under the Prussian Code (*Allgemeines Landrecht für die Preußischen Staaten*). The analysis employed by the Reichsgericht to this particular set of circumstances has, however, never been called into question.[320] Dealing as it does with a fundamental, yet basic, point of German property law, undoubtedly no future decision will arise on similar facts. It can therefore be safely concluded that the decision would be the same today.

Not so, as far as nursery plants are concerned. It has also been the prevailing interpretation throughout the life of the BGB that the temporary attachment exception of § 95 BGB applies to the plants of a tree nursery.[321] Only two years later from the decision in *Vermögensverwaltungsstelle für Offiziere und Beamte* v. Z, in 1907, the *Reichsgericht* held that the plants, shrubbery and trees of a tree

---

319 *Vermögensverwaltungsstelle für Offiziere und Beamte* v. Z, Reichsgericht, II. Zivilsenat (24.03.1905): 60 *RGZ* 317, 319.

320 *Münchener Kommentar zum BGB* (2013): § 93 Wesentliche Bestandteile einer Sache (Stresemann), [16]; § 883 Voraussetzungen und Wirkung der Vormerkung (Kohler), [18]; *Staudingers Kommentar zum Bürgerlichen Gesetzbuch mit Einführungsgesetz und Nebengesetzen* (2011), § 93 (Jickeli/Stieper), [25].

321 Beitzke et al. (ed.), *Staudingers Kommentar zum BGB* (München: Schweitzer, 1925), § 94, [4], § 95, [3]; Hoffmann et al. 1913, Busch, § 95 [2].

nursery, although firmly connected to the soil for their own nourishment, were only temporarily attached to the land until their future sale.[322]

The case arose upon the seizure of a two-sixths share of land and the forced sale of that share. The purchasers of the shares claimed that, as a result of becoming co-owners of the land, they had also acquired the same proportional share in the plants of the tree nursery operated by the other landowners on the ground that those plants were integral parts of the land. The Reichsgericht nevertheless confirmed the interpretation of the court of appeal, according to which 'the litigious parts of the garden centre were from the very beginning earmarked for sale and that they were only connected with the soil for a certain time, namely until becoming saleworthy'.[323]

The application of the rule of temporality for nursery plants was re-affirmed in another decision of the Reichsgericht in 1922. Here, in *Akt.-Gesellschaft Wollwäscherei und Kämmerei* v. *R*,[324] it was held that the tenants of land on which they operated a nursery business were able to claim damages from a factory on neighbouring land which had replaced its older, lower chimneys with higher ones resulting in damage to the plants grown on the adjacent plot of land.

The Reichsgericht introduced, however, a factual distinction which, although present in scholarly writings, was not referred to in the grounds for the decision in 1907. The court was at pains to distinguish, on the one hand, 'those plants which [the tenant] does not yet own, and which he will acquire only through their severance; for these are part and parcel of the land'[325] from 'those plants, on the other hand, over which he had already acquired ownership before planting them on the land leased – such as seedlings, which he tended in tree nurseries, greenhouses, boxes etc., replanted into the soil of the land leased and keeps there until saleworthy –'[326]. The tenant retained ownership of the seedlings transplanted into the soil of the land because – and here the court restates its previous case-law prior to the enactment of the BGB – they, being from the very beginning earmarked for sale, are connected with the soil for a temporary purpose only.'[327]

---

322 *T und Gen.* v. *R und Gen.* Reichsgericht (27.04.1907): 66 RGZ 88, 89.

323 66 RGZ 88, 89: 'die streitigen Baumschulbestände [waren] von vornherein für den Verkauf bestimmt, und [waren] im Grund und Boden nur für eine gewisse Zeit, nämlich so lange bleiben sollten, bis sie verkaufsfähig geworden waren…'.

324 Reichsgericht, V. Zivilsenat (04.10.1922, V 611/21): 105 RGZ 213.

325 105 RGZ 213, 215: '…die Pflanzen, die noch nicht sein Eigentum geworden sind, an denen er gemäß § 956 BGB est mit der Trennung das Eigentum erlangt; denn diese sind Bestandteile des Grundstücks'.

326 105 RGZ 213, 215: 'Diejenigen Gewächse anderseits, an denen er schon vor der Einpflanzung in das Pachtgrundstück das Eigentum erworben hatte – indem er etwa die jungen Pflanzen in Baumschulen, Treibhäusern, Kästen usw. zog und sie sodann in das Pachtgrundstück pflanzte und dort bis zur Verkaufsfähigkiet behielt –'.

327 105 RGZ 213, 215: '…weil sie, als von vornherein für den Verkauf bestimmt, nur zu einem vorübergehenden Zwecke mit dem Grund und Boden verbunden sind'.

Plants of the first type are integral parts of land under § 94 BGB, those of the second type are goods under § 95 BGB.

In terms of the lessee's entitlement to a remedy in tort, however, there was no practical difference from the damage incurred by the lessee affecting the transplanted plants over which he had acquired ownership and those which he had sown but had not yet displaced. Claims regarding both types of plants were successful, merely that the underlying reasoning changed depending on their characterisation as or as goods integral parts of land. According to the wording of § 823 BGB, in the former case, his 'ownership' had been infringed; in the latter case, his possession of the land was infringed, such possession being covered by the wording 'another right'.[328] The distinction of land and goods therefore played no role here in the outcome regarding the existence of a claim in tort for interference with another's property. The Reichsgericht's classification of the plants was, in a sense, academic. It was relevant only to the underlying systemics and legal technique: interference with another's goods, on the one hand; interference with possession in land, on the other.

Similarly, in a court of appeal decision from 1992 in which, following the crash landing of a military plane on training into a forest of trees intended to be sold as Christmas trees, damages were awarded on the basis of a trespass to goods.[329] The court distingished, on the one hand, the general rule for the assessment of damages for damage to trees forming part of the integral parts of land as 'calculated on the basis of the reduction in value of the land', which was to be appraised according to factors such as 'the cost for the acquisition and planting of young plants, the husbandry costs during the time of their growth, the risk of poor growth, interest on the capital laid out acquisition and husbandry'[330]. However, that rule did not apply to 'plants, the cultivation of which serves the purpose of removal as Christmas trees and nursery plants,'[331] which, as *Schein-*

---

328 *Akt.-Gesellschaft Wollwäscherei und Kämmerei* v. R Reichsgericht, V. Zivilsenat (04.10.1922, V 611/21): 105 RGZ 213, 218: 'Verletzt ist einmal, soweit der Kläger Eigentümer der Pflanzen (§ 95 BGB) ist, sein Eigentum an diesen. Weiter ist er nach den Feststellungen des Vorderrichters in seinem Besetz an den Pachtgrundstücken geschädigt, und dieser Besetz, insbesondere eines Mieters oder Pächters, ist in Sinne des § 823(1) BGB den dort geschützten "Rechten" anzuschließen'.

329 OLG Hamm (28.02.1992): NJW-RR 1438.

330 Idem: 'Bei der Beschädigung von Gehölzen ist für die Ermittlung des zu ersetzenden Schadens grundsätzlich auf die verursachte Wertminderung des Grundstücks abzustellen. Die Schadensersatzpflicht beschränkt sich auf eine nach wirtschaftlich vernünftigen Anhaltspunkten vorzunehmende Schätzung. Solche Anhaltspunkte sind die Kosten für den Erwerb und die Anpflanzung junger Bäume, die höheren Pflegekosten während der Anwachszeit sowie die Bewertung des Anwachsrisikos und die Aufzinsung des Kapitaleinsatzes zur Anschaffung und Pflege.'

331 NJW-RR 1438, 1439: 'Dies gilt aber nicht für Gehölze, deren Anzucht der Entnahme als Weihnachtsbäume und Verkaufspflanzen dient'.

bestandteile under § 95 BGB, were properly characterised as goods and therefore the amount of damages was to be calculated 'according to the market value of those individual plants at the time of the tortious interference'. For those trees which were already ripe for felling as Christmas trees their market value would therefore include the profit to be made on their sale.

The factual distinction of whether the trees from the Christamas tree plantation had been grown on the plot from seed or whether young 3–4 year-old trees had been acquired and replanted is not mentioned in the case note. It would appear that a common method of production in Europe, and specifically Germany, is for the seed to be sown in tree nurseries, after three or four years the young trees to be uprooted and sold to a Christmas tree farmer who replants the trees and harvests them between four and eight years later.[332] The other method is, however, to sow the seeds onto a plantation directly and harvest eight to twelve years later. Given its relative novelty and that the market for the sale of 'living Christmas trees'[333] is still a very small percentage of the 50 million Christmass trees sold annually in Europe,[334] it can be assumed with a high degree of certainty that the Christmas trees in the 1992-case were to be cut down for sale.

3.   Systemics: transplantation and Christmas trees

From a consideration of the application in German law of the distinction of land and goods to nursery plants a number of factors can be brought together. First of all, nursery plants are *a priori* regarded as integral parts of the land from which they grow but may, in certain factual circumstances, can regarded as individual objects of third party rights in the form of goods prior to severance from the soil. Here the distinction of land and goods serves its primary purpose of determining what is covered by third party dealings with land or conversely with goods (when such plants are considered individually). Thus, when integral parts of land, seizure of the land comprises the plants growing from it, when not integral parts of land (and therefore goods), seizure of the land would not include such plants, but a retention of ownerhsip clause could cover them and be valid as against third parties.

The coordinatory function of the distinction of land and goods is also at play. Any real-world damage specifically to nursery plants will lead either to an interference with possession – if the land is possessed by a limited rights holder – or

---

332 https://web.archive.org/web/20071125213649/http://www.weihnachtsbaumversand.de/Wiss enswertes%3A_%3A35.html.

333 https://en.wikipedia.org/wiki/Christmas_tree.

334 https://en.wikipedia.org/wiki/Christmas_tree_production.

ownership – if the owner is in direct possession of the land – of the land in those cases where nursery plants are integral parts of the land. The same real-world damage will, on the other hand, lead to interference with goods where § 95 BGB applies to nursery plants. In some instances, the resulting remedy will not change despite a different characterisation. That will not always be the case, however, as shown by the 1992 Christmas tree case, where the fact that the damaged trees were regarded as goods allowed the plantation owner to claim the full market price for those trees which had reached maturity.

As far as the *ratio legis* is concerned, the application of the present distinction is justified by the tempory purpose of the connection to the soil. It is certainly the prevailing view that the subjective intention (*innerer Wille*) of the person planting the trees, or their seeds, is decisive where that intention is readily and objectively recognisable (*mit dem nach außen in Erscheinung tretenden Sachverhalt vereinbar*).[335] Similarly, it is clear that the ultimate aim of the trees' planting is their future severance.[336] Excluding 10-year old Christmas trees, the plants of a nursery are earmarked for removal from the land in connection with their future sale (*zum Verkauf bestimmt*).

Having set out this overal picture of the consideration of nursery plants (and Christmas trees) in terms the function of the distinction of land and goods, the relevant rule relating to the distinction and its consequences, the relevant legal constructs, their *rationes legum* and the factual distinctions drawn, there does appear to be a certain degree of tension, in particular, between the *ratio legis* and factual distinction.

The recurrent judicial statement of law is 'earmarked for sale' (*zum Verkauf bestimmt*). It is submitted that this is not, however, a factual distinction but a policy consideration, allowing for greater inflection of the rule of § 94 in favour of application of § 95 BGB, or, at most, a factual consideration supporting temporality of purpose. Here, the view is taken that the conclusive factual distinctions in relation to the application of §§ 94 and 95 BGB to nursery plants are two in number: (i) prior transplantation and (ii) future transplantation. The first is, to a certain extent, borne out in the older case-law, especially the decision from

---

335 Staudinger (2011), § 95, [6]: 'Für die Bestimmung des vorübergehenden Zwecks ist nach ganz herrschender Meinung die innere Willensrichtung des Einfügenden maßgeblich, soweit diese mit dem nach außen in Erscheinung tretenden Sachverhalt vereinbar ist'; Säcker & Rixecker (2012), § 95 [3]: 'Maßgeblich ist nicht die Beschaffenheit der verbundenen Sache oder die Verkehrsanschauung, sondern der innere Wille des Einfügenden im Zeitpunkt der Verbindung der Sache. Dieser muss allerdings mit dem nach außen in Erscheinung tretendem Sachverhalt in Einklang zu bringen sein.'
336 Staudinger (2011) § 95, [5]: 'eine als dauernd bezweckte Verbindung liegt demgegenüber vor, wenn ein Endpunkt begrifflich nicht feststeht'.

Nursery plants and Christmas trees	Legal distinction	Rule	Legal construct	Legal consequence	Ratio legis/ policy considerations	Relevant factual permutations
German law	Integral parts of-land/goods	Subject-matter of third party rights	3rd party dealings with land or plants individually (e.g. scope of seizure of land)	=if L(w.B[a]) ≠if G[b]	temporality[c] + intention (OR +limited right of use in land (i.e. contractual lease) OR, if absolute right (owner) + *Verkehrsanschauung*)	≠'earmarked for sale' =prior transplantation +/- removal as living plants
		Rules of coordination resulting from different legal characterisations (e.g. compensation for harm suffered)	E.g.: tort law: damage caused by another	n/a market value incl. profit	particular protection for tree nursery businesses	

[a] *w.B.*=Wesentlicher Bestandteil (integral part) of L=land.
[b] G=goods.
[c] i.e. § 95 BGB.

1922 where those plants which were regarded as goods had specifically been planted into the soil when already seedlings.

The second factual distinction which is not expressly refered to in the case-law – other than as a consequence of being earmarked for sale – is that those replanted plants will be removed from their temporary location in the nusery to be definitively planted on land possessed by the ultimate purchaser. Presumably for reasons of space, the modern commentaries refer only to the fact that the plants of a nursery are earmarked for sale to be bought, and therefore retain their character of goods when replanted into the soil of the nursery. The older commentaries, by contrast, expressly add that the plants of a tree nursery are goods when they are left in the land only until they are ripe for sale *and are to be sold as living plants.*[337] This is also the view advocated in the *travaux préparatories* leading to the enactment of the BGB, according to which the rule in § 95 BGB was intended to apply, inter alia, to the plants of a tree nursery which are affixed to the land for a temporary purpose only.[338] It was also expressly explained that to exclude such an application would unfairly deprive the nursery business of its ownership of the plants as against, for instance, a transferee of the land.[339] On this basis, German law has effectively adopted the view of Pothier whereby nursery plants retain their characterisation as goods after severance if re-planted in the nursery as if merely stored in a warehouse.

Not to take account of these two factual distinctions would appear to undermine the relationship between § 94 and § 95 BGB. For instance, one version of the *ratio legis* for § 95 BGB is the weight given to the subjective intention (*innerer Wille*) of the person affixing something to land as decisive where that intention is readily and objectively recognisable (*mit dem nach außen in Erscheinung tretenden Sachverhalt vereinbar*).[340] To rely only on the criterion of 'earmarking for sale' as indicative of a temporary purpose would ultimately lead to consequences greatly departing from the letter of the BGB and, in effect, invert the relationship

---

337 Hoffmann et al., *Das bürgerliche Gesetzbuch: mit besonderer Berücksichtigung der Recht- sprechung des Reichsgerichts* (Nürnberg: Sebald, 1910); Busch et al., *Idem* (1923), § 95 [2]: 'auch die Pflanzenbestände einer Baumschule, die nur solange im Boden bleiben sollen, bis sie verkaufsfähig geworden sind, und die als lebende Pflanzen verkauft werden sollen'.

338 Achilles et al. (1897), p. 11: 'Der § 785 Halbsatz 1 passe im Uebrigen auch auf Pflanzungen, die zu einem vorübergehenden Zwecke gemacht seien, wie Baumschulen, Pflanzgärten.'

339 Achilles et al. (1897), p. 11–12.

340 Staudinger (2011), § 95, [6]: 'Für die Bestimmung des vorübergehenden Zwecks ist nach ganz herrschender Meinung die innere Willensrichtung des Einfügenden maßgeblich, soweit diese mit dem nach außen in Erscheinung tretenden Sachverhalt vereinbar ist'; Säcker & Rixecker (2012), § 95 [3]: 'Maßgeblich ist nicht die Beschaffenheit der verbundenen Sache oder die Verkehrsanschauung, sondern der innere Wille des Einfügenden im Zeitpunkt der Verbindung der Sache. Dieser muss allerdings mit dem nach außen in Erscheinung tretendem Sachverhalt in Einklang zu bringen sein.'

of general of accession in § 94 BGB to exception of temporary attachment in § 95 BGB.

Specifically taking the Christmas tree plantation further, whilst such a plantation is certainly an outward manifestation of the temporality of the attachment of the trees to their soil, it equally blurs the distinction between a permanent and temporary purpose. Every tree in a commercially-operated forest plantation is, upon maturity, earmarked for future severance and therefore planted with an end-point in sight, their felling.[341] Such operations will frequently be outwardly observable, with fences marking the boundaries of the operations. Outward appearance may even be more obvious where individual trees are marked out for felling. Although such a characterisation is, from a comparative perspective,[342] perfectly plausible, it would directly contradict previous case-law and the policiy considerations underlying the relationship between § 94 and § 95 BGB.

This view is also supported by the *travaux préparatoires* for the BGB. During the second reading of the bill for a Civil Code, a further sub-paragraph was proposed for what is now § 95 BGB which would have excluded plants from being counted as temporarily attached to land.[343] In support of jettisoning that proposition, it was argued that the application of the rule to plants actually detracts from the clarity of the rule in § 94 BGB that plants are integral parts of land once planted,[344] since it could lead to the implication that the plants from seeds sown by a tenant (*Pächter*) would only be temporarily attached to land.[345] Secondly, it was also decided that the article could not be applied to the cultivation of the land, since such plants are to be connected to the land for their entire existence, i. e. they are permanently planted in the land until reaped or felled.[346]

It is therefore submitted that, when the distinction of land and goods, its purpose and underlying ratio legis are properly set out, the apparent extension of the nursery plants exception to Christmas tree plantations in the case-law is

---

341 Staudinger (2011) § 95, [5]: 'eine als dauernd bezweckte Verbindung liegt demgegenüber vor, wenn ein Endpunkt begrifflich nicht feststeht'.
342 Weil, Terré & Simler (1985), [29]: 'on tient compte [en matière de mobilisation par anticipation] de la volonté des parties qui imprime à un bien dès à présent le caractère qu'il n'aura, en fait, que dans l'avenir'; [30], fn. 75: 'Par cette prise en possession [soit du commencement de l'abattage, soit du martelage] jointe à sa bonne foi, l'acquéreur du meuble par anticipation réalise l'acquisition d'une propriété parfaite vis-à-vis des tiers'.
343 Achilles et al. (1897), p. 9.
344 Achilles et al. (1897), p. 9: 'Der § 785 sei in der Anwendung auf [Pflanzen] geeignet, die Bedeutung des § 784 zu verdunkeln.'
345 Achilles et al.1897, p. 9–10: '[Der Paragraph] könne zu dem Mißverständnisse führen, als sei eine von einem Pächter gemachte Pflanzung als seine befugter Weise zu einem vorübergehenden Zwecke bewirkte Verbindung der Pflanzen mit dem Grundstück anzusehen.'
346 Achilles et al. (1897), p. 11: 'Eine Pflanzung zu vorübergehendem Zwecke liege nicht vor bei der Feldbestellung des Pächters, da dieser die Aussaat für die ganze Dauer ihrer Existenz mit dem Grundstücke verbinde.'

based on a misapprehension of the law as it stands. On a proper construction, "Christmas trees" on a plantation are integral parts of the land unless transported as saplins from elsewhere and earmarked for sale as living trees. That does not apply to plantations at the end of the production chain, to be felled at a future date. Only young Christmass trees which will be uprooted to grow to maturity elsewhere and which were grown from saplings originally grown elsewhere (in boxes/greenhouses) should be regarded as goods.

C.   England

Nursery plants certainly fall *a priori* within the general rule of *superficies solo cedit*. When in the ground they accede to the freehold. Nevertheless, the legal position of nurserymen and third party rights in their plantation has received little attention in England, neither specifically nor as the application of the general principles of the classification of property as land or goods. This has led to conflicting views on their legal classification.[347] The characterisation of nursery trees will therefore be considered first of all doctrinally followed by consideration of the precedents organised into contractual and third party constellations.

1.   Superficies solo cedit

As part of the land, nursery plants could linguistically fall into one of two sub-categories, *fructus naturales* or *fructus industriales* (the latter also being termed emblements). From a literal reading of the two terms natural and industrial fruits, it might have been thought that the distinction is determined by whether the vegetation is produced by the industry of man or the fate of mother nature. This definition is often used to introduce the origins of the two terms, and in this sense it would seem more appropriate to qualify nursery plants as *fructus industriales*, since they are planted and tended to by the industry of the nurseryman and are to be removed from the land once ripe.

However, the true legal criterion used to distinguish *fructus naturales* from *fructus industriales* is whether the plant is cultivated annually to be reaped as a crop (i. e. annual profit). All other vegetation is *fructus naturales*. The plant must be amortised in a literal sense in the year after sowing.[348] In the case of *Grave* v.

---

347 Amos & Ferard, *Law of fixtures* (1883), p. 266 (nursery plants are emblements) *contra* Grady, *Law of fixtures* (1845), p. 84, [173] (nursery plants are not emblements).
348 *Grave* v. *Weld* (1833) 5 B. & Ad 105; 110 ER 731.

Weld, Chief Justice Denman thus said 'the plaintiff insisted that the tenant was entitled to the crop of any vegetable of that nature, whether produced annually or not, which was growing at the time of the transfer of the tenant's interest; the defendant contended that he was entitled to a crop of that species only which ordinarily repays the labour by which it is produced, within the year in which that labour is bestowed, though the crop may, in extraordinary seasons, be delayed beyond that period. And the latter proposition we consider to be the law.' As applied to the business of a nursery, whereas *fructus industriales* are crops which are to be mortally severed from the land once fully matured and sold as chattels having grown their whole lives in one particular field, the plants of nurseries are only temporarily attached to the land until they are strong enough to be sold and taken away to be either transplanted to another plot of land or to continue their existence in a plant pot. The nature of plants grown in nurseries are therefore destined to a more long-lasting living existence than the transient connection of growing crops to land and are consequentially as a rule *fructus naturales*.[349] The conclusion that nursery plants are not 'industrial fruits' is more easily grasped from the synonymous term of English law, emblements which originally meant to sow wheat.[350]

2.   View of Amos & Ferard

Despite the preceding preliminary conclusion drawn from the primary distinguishing factor between *fructus industriales* and *naturales* that nursery plants are *fructus naturales*, Amos & Ferard seem to treat them as *fructus industriales*. For example, in discussing the very distinction of *fructus naturales* from *industriales*, that 'in general, trees and the fruit and produce of them, from their intimate connection with the soil, follow the nature of their principle ... But corn and other products of the earth which are produced annually by labour and industry, having been sown with the intention of being afterwards separated from the realty, are held to partake of a personal nature,'[351] Amos & Ferard add to this traditional definition that 'Trees removable by a nurseryman belong to his

---

349 Cf. the trees of a managed forest in France are *fructus naturales*, *Berruyer et Dubosc.* v. *Ligneau-Grandcour* Cass. Civ. (21.07.1818): 1 S 375, 376: (*les bois taillis sont des fruits naturels*).

350 Old French, *emblaer*; modern French *emblaver*: to sow land with wheat (*blé*); compare Latin: *imbladare*.

351 Amos & Ferard (1883), p. 266; See *Duppa* v. *Mayo*, 395, Case-note Williams: 'In such a case where the things are fructus industriales, then, although they are still to derive benefit from the land after the sale in order to become fit for delivery, nevertheless it is merely a sale of goods [for the purposes of the Statute of Frauds].'

executors.'[352] Since *fructus industriales* pass to the executors as goods (person-alty) whereas *fructus naturales* pass to the heir as land (realty), this seems to suggest that they considered that the exception made for industrial crops also applies to nursery plants.'

The earlier authorities cited by Amos & Ferard do not conform to the view proposed by the two later authors. For instance, *Liford's case* is cited, yet *Liford's case* does not once mention nursery plants, but rather dealt with a freeholder's disposition of his entire interest in the land save the trees, which was held to operate a conveyance of the whole estate in the land with property in the trees being kept only as chattels and only for certain purposes. Those purposes were the relationship of buyer and seller as well as heir and executor: trees sold passing to the executor of the buyer in the event that he died before their felling. This does not mean that where a freeholder sells standing trees and then dies, irrespective of the buyer's monetary claim in the estate, that the *seller*'s executor would get title to the trees. Rather the trees would pass to the heir as part of the land. Thus, it was held in Liford's case that 'The trees, notwithstanding the exception, remain parcel of the inheritance of the land; and are not chattels, nor shall go to executors, but shall descend to the heir.'[353]

Similarly, the other authority cited by Amos & Ferard is also contrary to the proposition that nursery trees are goods at common law. In Comyn's *Digest of the Laws of England* it is actually written that 'things, which give no annual profit, are not comprehended under emblements: as, if he sow the land with acorns.'[354] The original passage in which this appears is to be found in Coke on Littleton and it follows the very distinction between *fructus naturales* and *industriales*. It is thus expressly stated that trees planted by a lessee, disseisor or owner who dies are claimable by the lessor, the rightful owner and the heir respectively, despite the industry of the plantor 'because [the plants] yield no present annual profit.'[355]

3.   Reconciliation with Elwes v. Maw

This view is generally supported by the otherwise formerly-applicable drastic consequences of allowing nursery plants to pass to the executor.[356] This would have meant that the executor could remove all nursery trees on land which passed

---

352 Idem.
353 *Liford's case* (1615), 11 Co. Rep. 46b, 50a, 77 ER 1206, 1214.
354 Vol. 2, (1824, 5th ed.), Title: Biens (H), 272.
355 Coke on Littleton, 55. b: "But if he plant young fruit trees, or young Oaks, Ashes, Elmes etc., or sowe the ground with Acornes, etc., there the lessor may put him out notwithstanding...."
356 In modern English law, no distinction is made between real and personal property for the purposes of intestate succession.

to the heir. However, the purpose to which the land had been put, a nursery-ground, would then be destroyed. To this extent, an exception for nursery plants on analogy with emblements would run contrary to Lord Ellenborough's dictum in *Elwes* v. *Maw*, where it was held that the exception to the rule of *superficies solo cedit* that applies to trade fixtures did not apply to agricultural fixtures.[357] The exception granting the executor the emblements is probably based upon the fact that their harvest does not affect the value of the land. The argument of removal affecting the value of the land has no weight when applied to nursery plants which have matured in the year and are ready for sale.[358] This argument does not, however, appear to have received judicial approval.

Where the deceased nurseryman did not have an estate in the land, but merely a leasehold interest, this might have led to the curiosity, or absurdity, that the right to possession of the land would pass to the executor, since a lease is qualified as a chattel real, whereas the nursery plants themselves would pass to the nurseryman's heir. Although the distinction between realty and personalty is no longer of practical significance for the purposes of the law of inheritance (since all the property of the deceased now passes to statutory heirs in the case of intestate succession) it is submitted that in such a case the nursery plants would have passed to the executor, however, not on the basis of their characterisation as personalty. It is submitted that they would pass to the executor on the basis of the executor's interest in the land. For example, in the Scottish case of *Bain* v. *Brand*, a dispute arose between the heir and executor over the machinery which the deceased had installed in a colliery which he had leased whose term still had time left on his death. In contradistinction to England where a lease in land was movable property (personalty), in Scots law a lease is immovable property (heritable). The executor of the deceased argued that although the lease indis-putably devolved to the heir, he as executor ought to have the machinery affixed to the land as movable property; as between the landlord and the deceased lessee, the machinery was movable since the latter had a right to sever it, a character-isation which the executor could now rely on. The House of Lords rejected this argument and unanimously held that the machinery should descend with the soil to the heir. In the words of Lord Selborne, 'This is a right which, on the death of the lessee before any severance has taken place, passes to his successor in the estate: in England, to his executor, because there his executor succeeds to the

---

357 *Elwes* v. *Maw* KB (13.11.1802): (1802) 3 East 37, 53; 102 ER 510, 516.
358 Cf. French law, especially *Legendre* v. *Debras* CA Rouen (01.03.1839): 2 S 421 where the court extended the French equivalent to an English writ of fieri facias to nursery trees of six years growth, being ready for sale *contra*, in England, *Rodwell* v. *Phillips*, HC (Exch. of Pleas) (31.01.1842): 9 M & W 501, 505; 152 ER 212, 214 per Lord Abinger at 505: 'Growing fruit would not pass to an executor, but to the heir; it could not be taken by a tenant for life, or levied in execution under a writ of fi. fa. by the sheriff.'

lease; in Scotland, to his heir, because a lease for years is heritable in Scotland.'[359] Thus, as the machinery passed to the heir of a lessee in Scotland where the lease is realty, in England where the lease is personalty nursery plants would have passed to the executor to whom the remaining term on the lease devolved.

4.   Bilateral relationships: removal during the currency of the landlord-tenant relationship

Amos & Ferard submit that 'nurserymen are entitled to sell and remove trees, shrubs, and other produce of their grounds, planted by them with an express view to sale; and this on the ground of their carrying on a species of trade.' This statement of the law cannot, however, be used to qualify nursery plants as personalty in relation to third parties. This is because all of the modern authorities cited by Amos & Ferard in favour of this proposition discuss the law almost exclusively from the perspective of contractual relations between landlord and tenant. Nursery plants are, first, fructus naturales, and, second, trade fixtures: the nurseryman has a right to their removal, but – as is the case of the law on fixtures – until such a time they are regarded as part and parcel of the land.

For instance, the case cited of *Penton* v. *Robart* was one in which it was held that a lessee remaining in possession of land after the determination of his term who removed buildings which he erected during the term was liable in trespass to land but not *de bonis asportatis*.[360] Lord Kenyon CJ expressly drew the analogy with the legal position of greenhouses erected by nurserymen,

> 'Shall it be said that the great gardeners and nurserymen in the neighbourhood of this metropolis, who expend thousands of pounds in the erection of green-houses and hot-houses, &c. are obliged to leave all these things upon the premises, when it is notorious that they are even permitted to remove trees, or such as are likely to become such, by the thousand, in the necessary course of their trade. If it were otherwise, the very object of their holding would be defeated. This is a description of property divided from the realty.'[361]

Similarly, in *Elwes* v. *Maw*,[362] despite Lord Ellenborough CJ's express rejection of an agricultural tenant's right to remove agricultural fixtures, Lawrence J. intimated that 'if ground were let expressly for nursery ground, it might be con-

---

359 *Bain* v. *Brand* 16.03.1876 Privy Council: (1876) 1 AC 762, 779.
360 King's Bench (23.11.1801) 2 East 88; 102 ER 302.
361 2 East 88, 90; 102 ER 302, 303.
362 KB (13.11.1802) 102 ER 510, (1802) 3 East 37.

sidered as implied in the terms of the contract that it was to be used for taking up young trees, &c. as is usual in such cases.'[363]

In *Wyndham* v. *Way* the tenancy agreement between lessor and lessee excepted all trees from the lease on a plot of land in an area where 'almost every farm consists in greater or less part of orchards.'[364] The lessee lopped young apple trees, which though for the benefit of future years meant that the following year, by which time the lessee's interest would have expired, the trees would produce no apples. In defence to the lessor's action of trespass, the lessee argued that the exception of the trees only referred to the timber trees and not nursery trees. There are actually two points of law to this defence. The first is whether apple trees can be excepted in the lease of an orchard, which would otherwise eliminate all purpose in the lease of the land. The other point is whether, despite the exclusion of apple trees in the orchards, the farmer might not lop the nursery trees, remove them and sell them, it being 'customary for the farmers to be their own nurserymen' and that during the term the lessor had used some to replenish the orchards whilst sold others, 'without question made' by the lessor. The leading judgment of Lord Mansfield CJ is based solely on the interpretation of the exception of all trees from the lease and the absurdity that the 'landlord might have entered and taken away these trees, and the fruit of them; and that the tenant would have had no right to take from them a single apple.'[365] However, in the course of argument the nurseryman defence was withdrawn in response to Heath J's ruling that the point was not justified 'unless the tenant were a nurseryman, and made it his trade.'[366] Consequently, the headnote of the law report reads that 'a farmer who raises young fruit trees on the demised land, for filling up his lessor's orchards, is not entitled to sell them. Otherwise of a nurseryman by trade.' Although a correct statement of the law between lessor and lessee, it is clear that the proposition is specifically directed to the relationship of lessor-lessee and does not provide an answer to third party rights in the nursery plants such as, for instance, where the nurseryman assigns the remaining term to one and sells the plants to another, the buyer of the nursery plants not having removed the plants before the assignee took possession.[367]

---

363 (1802) 3 East 37, 45; 102 ER 510, 513.
364 (27.04.1812): 4 Taunt 316, idem; 128 ER 351, idem.; 13 Rev Rep 607.
365 4 Taunt 316, 318; 128 ER 351, 352.
366 4 Taunt 316, 316; 128 ER 351, 351.
367 See also *Bullen* v. *Denning* KB (01.01.1826) 5 Barnwell and Cresswell 842; 108 ER 313: the exclusion in lease of timber trees and other trees but not the annual fruits therefore was held not to apply to apple trees planted and subsequently cut down by the tenant. See 'Note to *Bullen* v. *Denning*' (1827) 5 Property Lawyer 89.

In *Lee* v. *Risdon* the lessor had sold to the lessee the fixtures attached to the house that was leased.[368] Relying upon the fact that the lessee had taken possession of the premises, the lessor-seller contended that the lessee-buyer had received delivery of the fixtures sold and, given that the buyer had not paid, brought an action in assumpsit against him to recover the price. The court held that there had been no delivery of the fixtures as goods since they had not been severed from the land. In explaining the law, Gibbs CJ also referred to the example of the nurseryman's plants:

> 'many of these articles, though originally goods and chattels, yet when affixed by a tenant to the freehold, cease to be goods and chattels by becoming part of the freehold; and though it is in his power to reduce them to the state of goods and chattels again by severing them during his term, yet until they are severed, they are a part of the freehold, as wainscots screwed to the wall, trees in a nursery ground, which when severed are chattels, but standing, are part of the freehold, certain grates, and the like. And unless the lessee uses during the term his continuing privilege to sever them, he cannot afterwards do it; and it never, I believe, was heard of, that trover could be afterwards brought.'[369]

Although this statement can only be obiter, since it was not necessary to dispose of the case at issue, it is consistent with another authority actually decided in such circumstances.

Finally in relation to way-going crops, namely crops which are still in the ground upon the determination of a tenancy and to which the tenant ordinarily has a right of removal, in *Watherell* v. *Howells* the away-going tenant removed strawberry plants which he himself had paid for at the beginning of the tenancy.[370] It was held that the sale of the plants at the beginning of the tenancy was merely 'because people, rather than suffer mischief from another, would sometimes pay [another] a sum of money to observe the law'.[371] As a result, the 'the taking up [of] strawberry roots was not necessarily in itself an injury to the inheritance for which an action would lie; but if the defendant in this instance ploughed up the beds before they were exhausted, and without having any reasonable object in view, he had certainly prejudiced the plaintiff's reversionary estate.'[372]

---

368 Common Pleas (22.11.1816): 7 Taunton 189, 129 ER 76.
369 129 ER 76, 77; 7 Taunton 189, 191.
370 (26.02.1808): 1 Camp. 228; 170 ER 939.
371 Idem.
372 Idem.

5.   Third party situations

There is one case which has been decided in a third party situation. In *Oakley* v. *Monck* a life tenant leased his land to a nurseryman for a number of years under terms that at the end of the tenancy the lessor would pay for any plants left by the lessee on the land. The term came to an end and the tenant for life refused to make a fresh lease on the same terms, but allowed the lessee to 'go on from year to year'. The life tenant then died and whilst his successor in title continued to receive rent from the original lessee, the succeeding life tenant served notice on the lessee and refused to pay for the plants growing on the land. It is even 'stated that the effects on the premises were subject to a bill of sale' given by the lessee to another third party.[373]

The judgment of the court of first instance, which held that the successor in title was absolutely entitled to the plants growing on the land, was upheld upon appeal. Amos & Ferard write that 'Blackburn J. expressed an opinion that [the litigious term] did not deprive the tenant of his right of removing the fruit trees and shrubs, to which he was entitled as a nurseryman.'[374] At another point, Amos & Ferard cite the very same judgment of Blackburn J, as he then was, in support of the proposition that 'It is now clearly settled that nurserymen are entitled to sell and remove trees, shrubs and the other produce of their grounds, planted by them with an express view to sale; and this on the ground of their carrying on a species of trade.'[375] This citation of the learned judge in support of the proposition probably refers to the following lines:

> 'A person who holds a nursery ground as tenant, has a right at the expiration of his tenancy, to remove fruit trees and shrubs planted by him, and which then in fact form part of his stock in trade; but this does not entitle him to cut down or remove plants which would only be destroyed by such a process, and would after it be of no use to him for the purpose of his trade; such mere waste as this is not allowed to him by the rule.'[376]

The importance of that statement must, however, be relativised for two reasons. The words cited could mean, on the one hand, that since the fruit trees were left to grow they had become established and their removal would only mean their destruction, but that if the trees had been young enough then the lessee could have taken them *in all events*. However, equally the same statement, on the other hand, may also be read as a mere clarification of the lessee nurseryman's personal right of removal of fruit trees whilst in possession of the land. Whilst in possession, a nurserymen may remove his stock-in-trade, young trees capable of

---

373 (1865–1866) LR 1 Exch 159, 161.
374 Amos & Ferard, p. 161.
375 Amos & Ferard, p. 101.
376 *Oakley* v. *Monck* (1865–1866) LR 1 Exch 159, 167, per Blackburn J.

transplantation, but not fruit trees which are established and incapable of removal. In the first interpretation, a lessee would be able to reclaim the young trees both during and after the expiration of the lease not only as against the original lessor, but also any successor in title to the reversion. This is the reading of Amos & Ferard. Under the second interpretation, a lessee would still be able to reclaim the young trees during term of the lease, but not after its expiration of the lease, neither against any successor in title to the reversion nor the original lessor himself.

The first interpretation is, however, inconsistent with the facts of the case. It is clear that 'The plaintiff is a nurseryman, and the demised premises were intended to be, and always have been, used by the plaintiff as a nursery-ground.'[377] The nurseryman does not appear to have allowed any young fruit trees to establish themselves in order to sell their fruit. Moreover, although only described as 'fruit trees and shrubs' or 'stock', it does not appear at all that any of the plants were not capable of being transplanted, especially given that such 'stock' was actually sold on auction by the successor in title.[378] If the removal of the fruit trees in question would have brought about their destruction, then no-one would have bought them separately from the land.

Second, there are also discrepancies in the various law reports of this case. In the corresponding part of his speech as reported in the Law Times Reports, Blackburn J. is instead supposed to have said, 'A nurseryman has no right to cut down fruit-trees, which are fixtures, and that is no harder upon him than the same rule is upon other tenants. There was an agreement that Oakley should be paid for his fruit-trees, &c., at the end of the term, if he chose to leave them; that did not prevent him from moving them if he had chosen so to do.'[379] The discrepancy probably relates to the dual nature of the fixtures. As fixtures the plants are part of the land and their removal would constitute the tortious action of waste but for the exception engrafted onto the rule of *superficies solo cedit* that during his term, and for a reasonably time thereafter if the tenancy is periodic, the lessee can remove them as stock-in-trade. If, however, the plants are not removed whilst the lessee is entitled to remove them, they pass with the reversion of the land to the lessor. This is consistent with the thrust of Willes J's judgment, with which Blackburn J. concurred,[380] according to which 'It is impossible to read the case, without feeling that there may be a hardship inflicted on the plaintiff, and that property which she might have removed under the ordinary rule as to

377 (1865–1866) LR 1 Exch 159,160.
378 (1865–1866) LR 1 Exch 159, 161.
379 14 LT Rep NS 20, 23.
380 14 LT Rep NS 20, 23; (1865–1866) LR 1 Exch 159, 166.

trade fixtures, may have been converted into money, which the defendant retains, in consequence of her not having taken that course at the proper time.'[381]

Given the two reasons of the re-contextualisation of Blackburn J's statement to the facts of the case as decided and the discrepancies between the law reports, it is submitted that the precedent of *Oakley* v. *Monck* is more probably such that as soon as a nurseryman's interest in land expires his right to remove plants from the nursery is also extinguished. Nursery plants are, at least on the basis of this case, not to be considered as mere chattels. At best the proposition of Amos & Ferard is based upon *obiter dictum*; at worst a dissenting judgment from a learned judge who was of the same opinion as the majority. This account of the law is consistent with the case of *Gough* v. *Wood & Co.* where a boiler was installed under hire-purchase agreement on a nurseryman's land as mortgagor in possession and it was held removable by the supplier before mortgagee's entry, but not afterwards. In support of the decision, Kay LJ said, 'until prevented by the mortgagee taking possession, [the nurseryman] might remove and sell the young trees that he was cultivating for that purpose, though they, while growing, were a part of the land.'[382]

6.   Conclusion

The most reasonable conclusion to be drawn from doctrinal discussions and the case-law is that nursery plants are to fall within the same category of property as trade fixtures. This means that during the term of the businessman's interest in the land, he has a right to remove such fixtures. Where the interest is of an uncertain duration, such as a (renewable) periodic tenancy, if the lessor gives notice to quit the nurseryman will have a reasonable time in which to remove the nursery plants. If, however, the nurseryman has not removed young trees by the determination of an interest certain in the land, though such trees may be been sold to another with a contractual right to enter the land and remove them, the lessor will have the better right to the plants as part of the realty and the lessor's reversionary interest in it. If the market growers legislation is applicable to the case of nurserymen, the lessee may have a claim against the lessor for the value of the plants, but this claim is only of a personal nature and does not change the characterisation of the trees in third party relations as part of the land.

---

381 (1865–1866) LR 1 Exch 159, 163; 14 LT Rep NS 20, 23.
382 [1894] 1 QB 713, 722.

Nursery plants	Legal distinction	Rule	Legal construct	Legal consequence	*Ratio legis*/ policy considerations	Relevant factual distinctions
English law	L (part thereof) /G	Subject-matter of third party rights	Successor in law to land	= L	Priority to real rights in land	– nursery plants/ *fructus industriales?*
		Transfer by operation of law	Former law on intestate succession	= G	Removal does not affect value of land	– nursery plants
		Transfer by sale	Contract for sale concluded by limited rights user of land	= G	Right of removal of limited rightholder (e.g. lessee)	
		Removal (default rule of contract)	At end of lease	= G	Protection of investment	
			After end of lease/Law of waste	= L	Protection of value of land	

Chapter 6.
The distinction of land and goods in EU law

To date, the Court of Justice of the European Union (CJEU) has ruled on the distinction of land and goods exclusively in relation to the VAT Directive.[383] In that directive, as amended and consolidated over the years, transactions relating to goods (movable property) are subject to value-added tax (VAT), whereas the 'leasing' of land (immovable property) is expressly exempt.

Despite the notion of goods being a key legal term, it is not defined in the directive. One reason for this could be that the notion of goods is so basic that it was not apparent to the framers of that directive that a definition was needed. Another reason may lie in the fact that tax legislation rarely defines goods or land, such legislation being premised on its definition in private law. Regardless of the real reason, due to the transposition of that directive into all legal systems of the European Union, each with its own notion of the distinction of land and goods, in order to ensure a uniform application of VAT, it was inevitable that rules would need to be developed for determining whether property must be regarded as goods or land for the purposes of that directive. In the absence of legislative intervention, the CJEU has stepped into the void in a number of cases spanning several decades.[384] This chapter sets outthe relevant provisions of the VAT Directive (A), followed by an analysis of the factual permutations considered by the CJEU in its case-law and the outcome of its decisions (B). It then catalogues the grounds given for the decisions in those cases (C) before highlighting a number of policy considerations apparent from the CJEU's reasoning. A summary of findings (E) is then followed by an analysis of what appears to be the underlying purpose for which the distinction of land and goods is drawn in the VAT Directive (F) in order to propose a recalibration of the criteria for

---

383 Council Directive 2006/112/EC of 28 November 2006 on the common system of value added tax (OJ 2006 L 347, p. 1).

384 Most of those decisions have been analysed in Ramaekers, 'Classification of objects by the European Court of Justice: movable immovables and tangible intangibles' [2014] ELR 4, who considers that the incoherent and inconsistent approach in the case-law of the CJEU justifies legislative intervention in the form of an optional instrument.

determining, in the light of the CJEU's case-law, when something must be regarded as land or goods.

A. The relevant provisions of the VAT Directive

VAT is charged on transactions in goods and services. In order to achieve the necessary level-playing field in matters of taxation for the purpose of creating an internal market across the EU Member States, the rules on VAT were harmonised. VAT is thus the natural corollary to the land acquisition tax considered in Chapter 2. It can be said as a consequential rule of thumb that the taxation of goods is a matter of EU law whilst that of land remains the prerogative of the national law of the Member States.

Specifically, Article 1(2) provides that 'VAT entails the application to goods and services of a general tax on consumption exactly proportional to the price of the goods and services' and 'supply of goods' is defined as 'the transfer of the right to dispose of tangible property as owner'. In the exemptions from VAT, Article 135(1)(j), (k) and (l) lists 'the supply of a building or parts thereof, and of the land on which it stands', 'the supply of land which has not been built on' and 'the leasing or letting of immovable property', respectively. As a result, sales and leases of land are exempt from VAT whereas the sale and hiring of goods is subject to VAT. Other than Article 12(2), which defines a building as 'any structure fixed to or in the ground',[385] the directive gives no further clues as to what is meant by goods or 'immovable property', i.e. land.

In 2013, an implementing regulation was enacted pursuant to Article 397 of the VAT Directive.[386] One of its purposes was to provide a definition of 'immovable property'.[387] Thus, Article 13b was added to a consolidated version of the general regulation implementing measures in respect of the VAT Directive.[388] In order to ensure a 'smooth transition' due to the fact that 'the introduction of that concept [of immovable property] could have a considerable impact on the legislation and administrative practices in Member States',[389] that 'definition' did not enter into force until 1 January 2017. The definition is a non-exhaustive list of

---

385 In respect of 'estate agent transactions'.
386 For a recent critique of such implementing acts, see Englisch, "'Detailing' EU Legislation through Implementing Acts', [2021] 1 Yearbook of European Law, p. 1.
387 Council Implementing Regulation (EU) No 1042/2013 of 7 October 2013 amending Implementing Regulation (EU) No 282/2011 as regards the place of supply of services (OJ 2013 L 284, p. 1).
388 Council Implementing Regulation (EU) No 282/2011 of 15 March 2011 laying down implementing measures for Directive 2006/112/EC on the common system of value added tax (OJ 2011 L 77, p. 1).
389 Recital 18 to Implementing Regulation No 1042/2013.

what constitutes immovable property. Given that the Commission's 'Detailed explanation of the proposal' considers that its definition '… is largely based on the case-law of the [CJEU]',[390] the definition will be considered in the light of the evolution of the rules described below.

B. Factual permutations and outcomes

Whilst the vast majority of the CJEU's decisions on the exemption in Article 135 (1)(l) relate to the definition of 'leasing or letting', namely the nature of the legal relationship or, in other words, the constitutive rights and obligations of such a relationship,[391] in several judgments it has ruled on what constitutes 'immovable property' for the purposes of that provision. In Case C-60/96, the CJEU held that tents, caravans or mobile homes were goods and therefore the rent received when leased was therefore incapable of falling within the exemption for the leasing of immovable property and also liable to VAT. In Case C-315/00, the CJEU held that a prefabricated building for the temporary housing of asylum seekers intended to be dismantled and reassembled elsewhere at the end of the lease was immovable property. In Case C-428/02, the CJEU held that water-based mooring berths for pleasure boats are immovable property but that the 'parking exception' from the 'letting of immovable property VAT exemption' also applies to boats so that the leasing of mooring berths for boats is subject to VAT. In Case C-532/11, the CJEU held that a houseboat, without a system of propulsion, permanently attached alongside a riverbank used exclusively for the permanent operation of a restaurant-discotheque was immovable property but that such a boat did not fall within the parking exception and was therefore exempt from VAT. Two further decisions have emerged recently. In Case C-17/18, the CJEU held, in respect of capital equipment and inventory items, namely equipment and kitchen appliances, included in the lease of a restaurant, first, that certain items had been incorporated as 'integral parts' of the kitchen, and therefore of the land. Second, it held that the remaining items of catering equipment were accessories to the land and, as such, were also covered by the exemption for immovable property. In Case C-215/19, the most recent decision delivered on 2 July 2020, the CJEU held

---

390 Proposal for a Council Regulation amending Implementing Regulation (EU) No 282/2011 as regards the place of supply of services (COM/2012/0763 final).
391 E.g., Case C-270/09, [46]: 'the fundamental characteristic of the concept of 'letting of immovable property' for the purposes of Article 13B(b) of the Sixth Directive lies in conferring on the other party to the contract, for an agreed period and for payment, the right to occupy property as if that person were the owner and to exclude any other person from enjoyment of such a right'.

that 'equipment cabinets in a computing centre for holding customers' servers' were goods.[392]

C.   Reasoning

In interpreting EU law, the CJEU generally follows two mutually-exclusive interpretative approaches. In most situations, particularly where there is a legislative text governing a certain point of law, it follows an 'autonomous' approach.[393] The autonomous approach is to exclude any particular national law account of a concept and develop a distinct EU concept, based on the wording, purpose and scheme of the legislation at issue.[394] This approach attempts to avoid potential inconsistencies which could arise from variations in the national laws of the Member States. The other approach, generally used less frequently and if so particularly in the absence of a legislative text or in respect of well-established rules of law such as proportionality or legal certainty, is the 'common principles' approach. In this second approach, the CJEU applies a rule which is common to the traditions of all Member States.[395] Whilst laudable, this approach – if generalised – would entail the employment of significant resources of comparative law analysis and would always leave decisions of the CJEU liable to criticism if a minority of the Member States' traditions were found to adopt a different rule. The 'common principles' approach is thus applied parsimoniously, mainly in a constitutional or procedural context.

It is therefore unsurprising that in its case-law on the distinction of land and goods the CJEU has followed the 'autonomous' approach, according to which it has its 'own independent meaning in [EU] law'[396] and 'cannot be determined by the interpretation given by the civil law of a Member State'.[397] The definitions of Member States' civil law cannot be decisive in determining whether, for the purposes of interpreting EU law, property is land or goods. This approach, whilst perfectly understandable for practical reasons, and one which given that the cases

---

392 Case C-215/19, [48] and Operative Part 1.
393 'Les termes d'une disposition de droit de l'Union qui ne comporte aucun renvoi exprès au droit des États membres, pour déterminer son sens et sa portée, doivent normalement trouver une interprétation autonome, qui doit être recherchée en tenant compte du contexte de la disposition et de l'objectif poursuivi par la réglementation en cause'.
394 Case C-315/00, [27].
395 E.g., Case C-98/91, [9] and Case C-340/08, [64]: 'un texte du droit dérivé de l'Union, tel que ce règlement, doit être interprété, dans la mesure du possible, dans le sens de sa conformité, notamment, avec les principes généraux du droit de l'Union, et, plus particulièrement, avec le principe de la sécurité juridique'.
396 C-428/02, [27]; C-532/11, [17].
397 Case C-315/00, [26]; C-532/11, [17].

have all arisen in respect of the VAT Directive can give full expression to the specificities of the particular tax regime in which the distinction of land and goods is used, ignores a key component of the use of the distinction in tax law, as fully exemplified in Chapter 2. Its use is parasitic. The distinction is generally carried over wholesale from its definition in property/private law. Even where tweaks are made to take account of the specificities of tax law, the terminology and reasoning is couched in the language of property law. The task faced by the CJEU in this area is thus formidable: develop case-law rules on the distinction of land and goods for the purposes of VAT without any definition in EU law of the distinction for property law-related purposes.

In terms of its wording, purpose and scheme-based interpretative approach, the CJEU notes that the VAT Directive does not define the term 'immovable property'[398]. The purpose of the wording 'immovable property' is stated to be to distinguish land from goods.[399] As far as the scheme of the VAT Directive is concerned, the CJEU considers that there is 'no reason to treat [the terms immovable property/land] differently' depending on whether a building and its land is sold (Article 135(1)(j) and (k)) or leased (Article 135(l)), so that 'any structure fixed to or in the ground' must also be regarded as immovable for the purposes of Article 135(l).

In Case C-60/96, given that the French Government – against which the action for failure to fulfil its obligations had been brought by the European Commission – eventually accepted that tents, caravans or mobile homes were in fact goods, the CJEU did not state the rules by which it considered those items to be goods. The first rules were stated in Case C-315/00. The CJEU held, as regards the rules of accession *strictu sensu*, that goods are 'either mobile ... or easily moved' whereas land is 'not mobile; nor can [it] easily be moved'.[400] The judgment in Case C-428/02 did not further specify the definition of accession to or severance from land but rather to the spatial conception of land. Land is an area which 'is clearly delimited and cannot be moved' when covered with water.[401] In Case C-532/11, whilst sticking to the physical criteria of fixed attachment and immobility, the Court added permanency of location to its rules for determining whether something was land.[402]

---

398   Cases C-315/00, [28]; C-428/02, [28].

399   Case C-315/00, [29].

400   Case C-315/00, [31] and [32].

401   Case C-428/02, [34].

402   Case C-532/11, operative part 1: 'the concept of the leasing or letting of immovable property includes the leasing of a houseboat, including the space and the landing stage contiguous therewith, which is fixed by attachments which are not easily removable to the bank and bed of a river, stays in a demarcated and identifiable location in the river water and is exclusively used, according to the terms of the leasing contract, for the permanent operation of a restaurant-discotheque at that location.'

In Case C-17/18, in the first case following the entry into force of the implementing regulation, the CJEU found that 'some of the movable property, such as the equipment and kitchen appliances, are incorporated in that immovable property and must, at this stage, be considered to be an integral part of that property'.[403] It is far from clear how modern-day kitchen appliances, presumably such as ovens and dishwashers, are not easily removable, although they would certainly be intended to remain in place for the duration of the lease and for its operation as a restaurant. They can also be seen as 'completing' a kitchen. However, even a cursory glance at national case law on whether built-in kitchens accede to the land or continue to exist as goods reveals the potential for great disparities in factual assessment, which runs contrary to the express purpose of the clarification of the definition of land and goods in the implementing rules. Thus, kitchens have infamously been held by the courts to be integral parts of land in the north of Germany but goods in the south.[404]

In the most recent judgment concerning the exemption from VAT for immovable property in Case C-215/19, delivered on 2 July 2020, the CJEU relied on both the rule of physical attachment and that of permanency of location in considering that 'equipment cabinets in a computing centre for holding customers' servers' did not fall within the VAT exemption for land. First, it relied on the fact that they were only screwed into the floor and could therefore be moved easily, as a result of which it considered that they were not 'permanently installed' (FR: *installé à demeure*; DE: *auf Dauer ... installiert*).[405] Interestingly, it would appear that the criterion of physical attachment is being used as indicative of permanency of location, which is nevertheless a subjective criterion. Second, the CJEU considered that the building could not be regarded as incomplete without the equipment cabinets.[406]

On the point of integral parts which 'complete' a building or structure, the judgments in Cases C-17/18 and C-215/19 would appear to be at odds with one another. It is true that the enumerative list in Article 13b(c) of the implementing regulation of 'doors, windows, roofs, staircases and lifts' without which a building is incomplete is limited to the structural integrity of a building. In that

---

403 Case C-17/18, [39].

404 BGH (21.05.1953): NJW [1953] 1180 (kitchens are integral parts of a house); OLG Düsseldorf (19.01.1994): NJW-RR [1994] 1039 (kitchens are goods which are only accessories to a house).

405 Case C-215/19, [48]: '... d'autre part, ces baies de brassage, étant simplement vissées au sol et pouvant donc être déplacées sans destruction ou modification de l'immeuble, ne sont pas non plus installées « à demeure »'.

406 Case C-215/19, idem: '... d'une part, les baies de brassage ne font nullement partie intégrante de l'immeuble dans lequel elles sont installées, dès lors que ce dernier ne serait pas considéré, en leur absence, comme étant structurellement « incomplet »' (EN translation not available at the time of writing).

sense, no IT equipment cabinet could be regarded as structurally integral to a building. However, in considering easily removable kitchen appliances to be incorporated as integral parts of a building operated as a restaurant, clearly a more purposive notion of the 'completion' of a building has been applied. It could equally be argued that IT equipment installed in a building specifically fitted out for the operation of a data centre becomes an integral part of the use to which the building has been put, and without which it would not be a data centre. Whether such definitions of immovable property as those introduced by the implementing regulation will lead to the uniform tax treatment of supplies of services connected with immovable property, as stated in recitals 12 and 18 to that implementing regulation, is therefore questionable.

In addition to regarding kitchen appliances as integral parts of land, in Case C-17/18, the CJEU also applied a theory of accessories to the notion of immovable property.[407] The CJEU had, of course, already developed a general theory of accessories in relation to transactions some of the sub-elements of which may be tax-exempt, or subject to different rates of tax, so that the predominant element of a transaction be taken into account for the purposes of the imposition of VAT.[408] In regarding catering equipment as accessories to the lease of a building permanently operated as a restaurant, it is not obvious from the CJEU's reasoning whether such equipment was regarded as an accessory of the land or whether its hiring was regarded as an accessory to the lease of the land.[409] Such alternative perspectives demonstrate that the distinction of land and goods is not neutral but always involves a specific underlying legal framework.

The Court has thus, on the whole, and in particular in its 'organic' case-law purely based on the interpretation of the VAT Directive itself, adopted a naturalistic approach the distinction of land and goods.[410] As stated by Advocate General Jacobs in his Opinion in Case C-315/00, 'The question whether … objects are in legal terms immovable property may in principle be answered either by objective criteria … or by subjective criteria'.[411] What Advocate General Jacobs was referring to was physical attachment, on the one hand, and intention, on the other. On that view, the CJEU's case-law would seem to prefer objective to subjective criteria. It is submitted, however, that it is more helpful to distinguish

---

407 Case C-17/18, [32].
408 judgment of 27 June 2013, *RR Donnelley Global Turnkey Solutions Poland*, C-155/12, EU: C:2013:434.
409 Case C-17/18, [39].
410 No better characterisation of the test which the CJEU has developed can be found that in its own reasoning: '"immovable", the decisive element in defining the concept of "immovable property" for the purposes of the Sixth Directive' (C-428/02, [23]). Everything is land which cannot be moved.
411 Opinion in Case C-315/00, [33].

between physical attachment, objective intention and subjective intention, only the latter of which the CJEU has explicitly rejected.

As far as physical considerations are concerned, 'buildings with a concrete base erected on concrete foundations sunk into the ground,'[412] that is to say, things strongly fixed to parts of land are regarded as immovable. A different formulation of the same rule is difficulty of removal, which in modern times is essentially a question of cost.[413] In the prefabricated buildings case, the CJEU considered that recourse to eight persons over ten days was an indicator of difficulty of removal rather than ease of removal.[414] Similarly, in its newer case-law – whilst on the basis of guidelines put on a statutory footing – IT cabinets for storing servers are certainly easily removed and were regarded as goods. However, that rule would not cover easily removable kitchen appliances.

As far as intention is concerned, the CJEU held in its early case-law that 'Nor is the term of the lease decisive for the purpose of determining whether the buildings at issue are movable or immovable property.'[415] Thus, the distinction of land and goods in EU VAT law does not turn on the subjective intention of contracting parties. That position is not necessarily consistent with subsequent decisions.[416] Objective intention, on the other hand, is decisive. In conjunction with other physical means of attachment, slight though they be, the intention to operate a houseboat as a club-restaurant, plain for all to see, the permanency of intention of which was also demonstrated by its connection to basic utilities, meant that the houseboat had become part of that land to which it was fastened.[417]

Lastly, another potential consideration has been rejected in that the underlying legal relationship is regarded as irrelevant. Thus, the CJEU held, in the

---

412 Case C-315/00, [32].
413 Case C-532/11, [23].
414 Case C-315/00, [32]: 'They can be dismantled on expiry of the lease for subsequent re-use but by having recourse to eight persons over ten days.'
415 Case C-315/00, [33]: 'Those immobilisation measures cannot be removed easily, that is to say without effort and considerable cost'. The judgment does not mention how many buildings were concerned by the removal.
416 Case C-532/11, [24]: 'By the terms of the leasing contract which is concluded for a duration of five years and which shows no wish of the parties to confer an occasional and temporary character to the use made of the houseboat, the latter is used exclusively for the permanent operation of a restaurant discotheque.'
417 C-532/11, [25]: 'Taking account of the houseboat's link with the elements that constitute its site and of the fact that it is fixed to those elements, which render it, in practice, a part of that space taken as a whole, and taking into account also the contract which allocates the houseboat exclusively and permanently to the operation, on that site, of a restaurant-discotheque, and taking account of the fact that the latter is connected to the various mains, it must be held that the whole constituted by the houseboat and the elements which compose the site where it is moored must be regarded as immovable property'.

prefabricated buildings case, that 'Whether the lessor makes available to the lessee both the building and the land on which it is erected or merely the building which he has erected on the lessee's land is irrelevant'.[418]

D.   Policy considerations

It is perhaps useful to note that the exemptions from the VAT Directive are to be interpreted strictly.[419] This rule can be seen in the light of the division of powers of taxation whereby the payment of VAT on transactions in goods fall within the ambit of EU law whereas the payment of land acquisition tax on land is a question of national law. However, given the supremacy of EU law, the CJEU considers itself to be the ultimate arbiter of where EU law begins and ends.[420] The strict interpretation of exemptions from VAT ultimately means that, in a borderline case in the distinction of land and goods, the pendulum should swing in favour of characterisation of property as goods, so as not to be excluded from VAT.

One policy consideration alleged to militate against the use of subjective criteria in determining whether something is land or goods for the purposes of VAT is legal certainty.[421] This consideration is also claimed to militate against criteria which would involve complex assessments, such as that of inseverability.[422] As far as tax is concerned, simplicity would therefore appear to be of paramount importance.

Another little-mentioned policy consideration is fair competition and the economic definition of the relevant market. For instance, in the houseboat case, the question was put as to whether the houseboat used as a stationary restaurant ought to be assimilated to boat-restaurants which cruise along a river during the course of a meal or the general market for traditional restaurants in buildings built on dry land. The CJEU noted that '... having regard to the objective envisaged by the contracting parties and the function allocated by them to the

---

418 Case C-315/00, operative part 1.

419 Case C-428/02, [29].

420 'according to settled case-law the exemptions provided for by Article 13 of the Sixth Directive have their own independent meaning in Community law and that they must therefore be given a Community definition.'

421 Opinion in Case C-315/00, [33]: 'in particular in the area of taxation legal certainty is of paramount importance and subjective criteria tend to undermine legal certainty'. However, whilst Opinions expressing different views may clearly be given in different cases, cf. 'The German authorities are in my view justified in considering that a letting is of a long-term nature and qualifies for exemption only if there is evidence of an intention from the beginning that accommodation is to be provided for a period of at least six months.'

422 Opinion in Case C-315/00, [40].

houseboat, it is, for those parties, immaterial, from an economic point of view, whether it is a building incorporated into the ground in a fixed manner, for example by piles, or a simple houseboat such as that at issue in the main proceedings.'[423] Were the houseboat regarded as a moving boat-restaurant, and therefore as goods, it would have been put at a fiscal disadvantage in respect of traditional restaurants in the vicinity.

E.   Interim summary

The current state of the rules on the distinction of land and goods drawn by the CJEU for the purposes of the VAT Directive may be summarised as follows. First, the distinction has been held to require an EU autonomous meaning and the exemption from VAT for land must be interpreted strictly. Tents, caravans and mobile homes are goods whereas prefabricated buildings and the kitchen appliances of a restaurant are land. Non-moving houseboat restaurants are land whereas boats attached to mooring berths are land yet taxable as goods because they fall within the parking exception. No purposive interpretation of the VAT exemption has been explicitly held other than to distinguish between land and goods. Land is not formally defined in the directive, but must be consistently applied throughout the directive, so that the inclusion of 'any structure fixed to or in the ground' in Article 12(2) thereof also applies to the exemption in Article 135 (1)(l). A 'natural meaning' of the distinction has been adopted, can the object be moved easily? Physical mobility is supplemented by the idea of 'permanency of location', followed by the notions of 'integral parts', 'completing' a building and potentially the beginnings of a theory of accessories. The letter criteria may be seen as evidence of objective intention – what a bystander would regard as intended to be part of land – whilst subjective intention has been considered to be irrelevant. In terms of policy considerations, the CJEU has referred to the strictness of interpretation of land, which means in cases of doubt favouring characterising something as goods in order to exclude as few transactions from VAT as possible. Other policy considerations include the legal certainty from clear-cut criteria and fair competition between businesses.

---

423 Case C-532/11, [26].

F.   Purpose

1.   Difference in purpose between national law and EU VAT law

The difference in purpose is palpable between national law and EU VAT law where certain potential rules of national property law have been discarded in the elaboration of the distinction for tax purposes. To return to the facts of Case C-315/00, to take but one illustrative example, that case involved the lessee and occupant of the land renting prefabricated buildings from the taxpayer whereas the other involved the lessee of the land erecting the prefabricated buildings which he owed and then renting those 'buildings' to another. The CJEU held that that that difference in legal relationship was irrelevant. It also held, as a finding of fact, that the prefabricated buildings were not 'inseverably fixed to or in the ground'.[424]

In English law, from the perspective of property law, the buildings would undoubtedly, as fixtures, be part of the land yet subject to the tenant's right vis-à-vis the landlord to remove them.[425] Subletting the part of the land constituted by the buildings the tenant would be renting land. Where the lessor of the pre-fabricated buildings, without any legal interest in the land, merely rented such 'buildings' to the lessee, they would arguably be regarded as goods.[426] In the event of the lessee's insolvency and unpaid rent on the buildings, however, the lessor would undoubtedly have a right to reclaim the buildings but the lessor of the land could lay no preferential claim to them (as they would not form part of the land which he leased).

In French law, since the buildings were not inseparably incorporated into the land they could not be *immeuble par nature* and could only potentially be *immeuble par destination*. However, in both scenarios, the absence of unity of ownership of land and prefabricated buildings would mean that they could only be regarded as movable property, as goods.

In German law, from the courts of which the questions were referred to the CJEU for a preliminary ruling, it is clear from § 95 BGB that the prefabricated buildings, constructed for a temporary purpose, would not have acceded to the land and would remain legally distinct goods. However, had the buildings been erected permanently and had the owners of those pieces of land an option to take over the building, they would have been regarded as integral parts of land for the purposes of property law and any third party right of their lessor would have been

---

424 Case C-315/00, [33], DE: 'untrennbar', FR: 'indissociablement incorporé'.
425 Cf. in Chapter 5. Nursery plants, German Christmas trees and transplantation, the lessee nurseryman's right to remove nursery plants.
426 *Elitestone Ltd.* v. *Morris and Another* HL [1997] 1 W.L.R. 687.

extinguished. The lessor of the buildings would have only a contractual right to the value of the buildings and could in no way have been considered to be a 'lessor of the land' as he had no right in the land. He would have no more right to the buildings as the purchaser of standing timber contractually licensed to fell. Turning now to the current state of positive law, for the purposes of property law at national law, prefabricated buildings in circumstances where the owner of the prefabricated structure rented their use to a lessee of the land, erecting the structure at the beginning of the rental agreement and dismantling it on expiration, the structure – even when sunk into the ground – is still goods. However, for the purposes of VAT law at EU level, the prefabricated structure is part of the land to which it is fixed. As a result, a person without any right whatsoever in the land in at least three of its Member States,[427] has leased immovable property for the purposes of EU VAT law!

These brief expositions of national property law in relation to prefabricated buildings in similar legal relationships clearly demonstrate the difference in purpose – and often applicable rule – of the imposition of a tax on goods and an exemption for the leasing residential or commercial property.

2.   The purpose behind the distinction of land and goods in EU VAT law

As stated in Article 2 of the First Directive on VAT in 1967, 'The principle of the common system of value added tax involves the application to goods and services of a general tax on consumption exactly proportional to the price of the goods and services, whatever the number of transactions which take place in the production and distribution process before the stage at which tax is charged'. The fifth recital to that directive specified that VAT is intended to '[cover] all stages of production and distribution and the provision of services'. However, as stated by Advocate General Jacobs in his Opinion in Case C-346/95, 'Unlike ordinary goods, land is not the result of a production process; moreover, buildings, once constructed, may change hands many times during their life, often without being subject to further economic activity'. The key idea underlying the exemptions from VAT of 'second hand' sales of, and leasing, land in Article 135(1)(j), (k) and (l) is that it is 'a relatively passive activity, not generating any significant added value'.[428] Transactions in land are not, as such, exempt under the scheme of the VAT Directive, merely those which do not entail an economic activity adding to their value. Thus, the first sale of newly-developed land is subject to VAT whereas its subsequent sale is not. In this sense, it is irrelevant for VAT purposes whether

---

427 Considering the United Kingdom as a Member State at the time of the facts of the decision.
428 Case C-326/99, [52].

the other party to such a transaction in land becomes its owner or acquires mere rights of occupation (notably in the form of a lease). As a factor of production or capital good for the purposes of commerce and otherwise as simple housing, transactions in land fall outside of the purposive scope of the VAT Directive, to tax economic activity leading to an increase in value. The distinction in the VAT Directive between taxable transactions in goods and tax-exempt transactions in land thus lies in the distinction of economically active and passive activities, respectively. This is also clear from the exceptions to the exemptions from VAT whereby a passive activity can 'return to the economic circuit' and consequently taxability. The VAT Directive thus excludes the provision of accommodation in the hotel sector (Article 135(2)(a)), letting of land for parking and of machinery and safes permanently attached to land (Article 135(2)(a), (b) and (c)).

It is not the legal concept which determines whether VAT applies but its economic concept. Goods and services, on the one hand, and land on the other are, for the purposes of the VAT Directive, shorthand for economically active and economically passive activities. The CJEU has stated as much in relation to the concept of a lease, which in the civil law tradition is a contractual right and not a right in rem. However, for the purposes of the VAT Directive, it ignored the legal clothing for the economic reality. 'The particularities in question, arising from the fact that these legal institutions belong to distinct legal categories, are secondary in relation to the fact that, economically, a right such as the usufructuary right in question in the present case and leasing and letting present the essential common characteristic'[429] of 'conferring on the person concerned, for an agreed period and for payment, the right to occupy property as if that person were the owner and to exclude any other person from enjoyment of such a right'.[430] The grant of a usufruct in land is therefore also exempt from VAT.

G.   Recalibration

It is difficult not to see a casuistic approach in the CJEU's case-law. In several respects, there are a number of inconsistencies in the decisions. A degree of tension is present between the physical attachment approach and the intellectual connection approach, the latter of which is constituted by considerations of permanency of intention and function. It is submitted that the principal reason for this lies in the fact that concepts of, for instance, private law when used in tax law carry over their definitions in private law, either wholesale or with adaptations specific to the purpose of the tax concerned. In adopting an autonomous

---

429 Case C-326/99, [58].
430 Case C-326/99, [55].

approach to the distinction of land and goods, cut off from notions of national law, and without any EU law on the original basis for which the distinction is drawn in property law, since property law still remains a field of law within the prerogative of the Member States, the CJEU has effectively built up the elements of a property law definition of the distinction, perhaps even a general, over-arching definition capable of application across several fields, which has no application in EU law but is to be applied for the specific purposes of the VAT Directive.

The attempt to provide a uniform legislative definition in the form of an implementing regulation follows the same approach. It will ultimately lead to the same inconsistencies, as appears to have already been the case in the two judgments of the CJEU to have arisen since its entry into force. Whilst providing non-exhaustive enumerative lists of what shall constitute immovable property, it introduces general concepts such as 'integral parts', a 'complete building', 'title' and 'possession', not only without indicating why they are regarded as immovable for the purpose of the VAT Directive but critically concepts which bear different meanings in the Member States' national laws as they currently stand. The risk has arisen of a vicious circle of the introduction of a national law concept, not rooted in a clear purpose of its meaning in the legislative context in which it is used, interpreted autonomously, supplemented by further national law concepts, interpreted autonomously, which in being severed from purpose require further clarification and so the wheel turns again.

It is submitted that two approaches exist for improving the law as it stands. On the one hand, the autonomous interpretative approach could be replaced by a common tradition approach, given that the distinction of land and goods is common to the laws of all Member States. Rules common to the Member States' laws could then be used to determine what is land, and that distinction used for the purposes of the VAT Directive. Although feasible in judicial decision-making because the CJEU is always faced with the specific factual circumstances of a given case, and so its interpretation of the law is already circumscribed by those circumstances, it would perhaps be more optimal for such an approach to be taken at a legislative level.

On the other hand, the present autonomous distinction could be moulded for the specific purposes of the VAT Directive. Once those purposes are recognised and taken into account, there will be a solid basis for determining which distinguishing criteria and policy considerations are most adapted to the pursuit of those purposes.

As has been set out above, the main purpose of the exoneration of land from VAT is the distinction of active and passive economic activities. This is already settled case-law in the definition of the taxable legal institutions of 'leasing and letting' but has not yet been brought to bear on the object of that institution, land.

Land as a social good is a factor of production or place of dwelling. In that sense, it is equally passive to the productive process of consumable goods, which is here the object of taxation. The whole formed by an individual area of the earth's surface, or any three-dimensional construct, a building, houseboat, restaurant, etc., must therefore relate to either passive activities of an economic factor of production or the non-economic function of housing. It is submitted that for both activities, it is permanency of location at the time of taxation which best reflects the purpose for which the distinction of land and goods is drawn in the VAT Directive. This is consistent with the nature of VAT as a tax on consumption. It is not a tax on wealth[431] or on income,[432] which remain the prerogative of the Member States. For the European Union to tax land used as a dwelling or factor of production would therefore simply fall outside of the scope of the VAT Directive.

For a uniform approach consistent with the purpose and scheme of the VAT Directive, the distinguishing criteria and policy considerations for the distinction of land and goods ought to be interpreted in the light of permanency of location at the time of taxation as a dwelling or factor of production. The current rules developed in the case-law may already, to a large extent, be seen in that light.

In the first place, as far as policy considerations are concerned, it has already been demonstrated that the alleged simplicity of relying solely on strength of physical attachment, and thereby jettisoning intention completely, is largely illusionary. Not only can the assessment of the economic cost of removability require complex analysis but the exertion of considerable effort is a relative concept, which is therefore ultimately subjective, and one that can be determined only in the light of permanency of intention.[433] The policy consideration of fair competition, however, has a strong connection with permanency of location because it provides the proximate market for comparison of the use of land.

In the second place, permanency of location at the time of taxation as a dwelling or factor of production is largely borne out by account of the applicable rules given above. First, subjective intention is irrelevant to the distinction of land and goods for the purpose of VAT. It is irrelevant, however, precisely because it is not determinative of permanency, that can be ascertained only objectively. This is in contradistinction to, for instance, the subjective intention expressed in a juridical act such as a contract for the severance of parts of land for the purpose of determining the respective rights and obligations of the parties to that act.

---

431 Such as land acquisition tax (see Chapter 2).
432 E.g. the inclusion of rent from land for the purposes of income tax on private individuals.
433 See above, in relation to prefabricated buildings. How ought it be determined whether the effort of eight persons over ten days for dismantling is an indicator of difficulty of removal rather than ease of removal?

Second, a further illustration is provided by the criterion of strength of physical attachment. That rule is indicative of permanency of location, but the threshold of strength need not be as high as it might otherwise be when the distinction is drawn for other purposes. Inseverability or severability at such a high cost as to be impractical is certainly not necessary. The prospective removal or severance of a part of land as a distinct possibility at an as yet undetermined future date is far less relevant to the collection of VAT than it would be to determining, for instance, whether that part of land may be the subject of third party rights.

Third, the intellectual connection of land and goods will support the transformation of the former into a part of land at a relatively low threshold for the purposes of VAT if that connection relates to the use of the land as a dwelling or factor of production. It is submitted that this is a better yardstick for the assessment of the 'completeness' of a building or structure, despite the enumerative list in Article 13b(c), which merely refers to structurally necessary items, such as windows. Intellectual completeness applies to easily removable kitchen appliances 'incorporated' into the kitchen of land adapted for the permanent operation of a restaurant. On the ground of permanency of location at the time of taxation, it is entirely justifiable for such equipment to be exonerated from VAT when leased with the land despite the fact that, in terms of property law, such appliances would most likely be capable of forming the subject-matter of third party rights in goods separately from the third-party rights pertaining over the land. It has already been seen, for instance, that prefabricated buildings are regarded as parts of land for the purposes of VAT despite the fact that if they were characterised as parts of land for the purposes of private law that would, in certain legal relationships, deprive the lessor of the buildings of any proprietary right over the object which he has leased.

Fourth, the criterion of ease of movability or dismantling does not, for the purposes of VAT, relate as much to movable/immovable property in a literal non-legal sense (e. g., can it be moved?) but to the criterion of permanency of location. This may appear prima facie to be splitting hairs, however, when applied to specific factual circumstances the latter formulation is clearly more appropriate to VAT. It explains more coherently why a houseboat restaurant merely attached to its mooring berth by anchor, rope and connections to public utilities falls within the exoneration from VAT of land. That boat, whilst eminently 'movable', has an intellectual permanency of location for use as a factor of production in the operation of a restaurant business.

This chapter is an illustration of how the conceptual framework developed in Chapter 4 can be used to analyse a particular body of case-law. It has thus concentrated on elucidating first and foremost what the purpose behind the use of the distinction in EU VAT law is. It has extrapolated guiding policy considerations in keeping with that purpose. In that light, it is submitted that permanency of location at a given point in time in respect of the passive activity of an economic factor of production or the non-economic function of housing provide the key test for determining whether a tangible item is in such a close relationship with land so as to fall within the definition of land and thereby escape liability to VAT. This, it is submitted, would provide greater legal certainty and a more accurate yardstick than merely considerations such as whether something can be moved, completes a building or objectively demonstrates a permanent attachment to land.

Conclusion

This chapter on conclusions and perspectives takes the form of a summary of the analysis conducted in the previous chapters (A), a discussion of the main conclusions which can be drawn from that analysis, in particular the perceived need for recalibration in the exposition of the rules for determining when something is a part of land or goods (B) and then a restatement of such a recalibrated framework, as developed and proposed in the previous chapters (C). In terms of perspectives, that proposal is put into the context of the multi-layered vertical reality of modern legal systems, whether federal in nature (United States), different legal systems within a single constitutional framework (United Kingdom) or a blended juxtaposition of supra-national law and national law (European Union), as well as legal families with a common origin in certain fields (Commonwealth) and the consequences of a newly-found legislative sovereignty in areas hitherto attributed elsewhere (Brexit). The conclusions are, however, also readily applicable to discussions undertaken exclusively at national level across different fields of law.

A.   Executive summary: taking stock

In the first chapter, a brief comparative overview was given of the distinction of land and goods in English, French and German law.

Whilst universally drawn, that distinction is, first of all, embedded in the same or different legal schemes (or 'hierarchies of norm').[434] Thus, at the highest degree of abstraction, on the one hand, the distinction in German law of *bewegliche/unbewegliche Sachen* is a subcategory of property which is first and foremost corporeal in nature. On the other hand, as for the distinction of *biens immeubles/*

---

434 At least as far as the general rules/theories of the classifications of property are concerned, i.e. §§ 90–103 BGB, Articles 516–543 Code civil and the functionally equivalent expositions of the case-law on the distinction in English-law treaties on property law.

meubles and real/personal property, in French and English law respectively, 'property' falls into one of those binary categories first, before then being subdivided into corporeals or incorporeals. Thus, there is corporeal realty or *immeubles* (i. e. land) and incorporeal land (i. e. rights in land), on the one hand, and corporeal personalty (i. e. goods) and incorporeal personalty (i. e. all other rights, e. g. debts, shares etc.), on the other.

More specifically in respect of the distinction between *bewegliche/unbeweglich Sachen*, corporeal *biens immeubles/meubles* and corporeal realty (i. e. corporeal hereditaments) and corporeal personalty (i. e. choses in possession), that is to say in respect of the distinction of land and goods, the national theories underlying the rules for determining whether something is (a part of) land or goods all centre around a combination of physical attachment and intention, be it subjective or objective. Those theories differ greatly, however, in emphasis and scope. Whilst reference is made to the various applications of the distinction, that is to say those legal rules the outcome of which turns on whether property is characterised as land or goods, little attention is given to the question whether the characterisation of property as land or goods various according to the specific application of the distinction.

At an even greater level of specificity, various things growing out of the ground, such as standing timber or crops, are regarded as integral parts of land or as goods in one or the other of the legal systems in question.

The vast majority of national law expositions of the rules for determining when something is a part of land, and therefore partakes in its legal nature, or leads a separate existence in the other category of corporeal property, goods, leaves a distinct impression of a naturalistic approach to the categorisation of property. What must be determined is whether or not something is firmly attached to land, attached in its natural state to land, affixed to land with the intention of remaining attached, or even, in French law, intended for the use of the land to such an extent that it may be regarded as part and parcel of the land. All such rules suggest a continuum according to which at some point in the combination of such indicators the balance is tipped and something may be regarded either as part of land or goods. What such accounts of the rules do not suggest that there may be different continuums according to the purpose for which the distinction of land and goods is drawn. That is, however, precisely what is suggested by the legal characterisation of certain vegetation in certain circumstances, at least in English and French law.

The possibility that there may be different continuums according to the purpose for which the distinction of land and goods is drawn is apparent when comparisons of national law are restricted to a particular question of law and/or certain factual permutations or legal constructs. There are often both different factual permutations and policy considerations which tip the balance in favour of classification in one category or the other. A number of illustrative examples have been explored in Chapters 2, 3 and 5.

The second and third chapters provide examples of specific questions of law. In Chapter 2, which takes the case of land acquisition tax applied to contracts for the severance of parts of land, the distinction of land and goods is relevant to all three legal systems. The analysis was therefore able to home in on the inter-relation between, on the one hand, maintaining the uniformity of a distinction borrowed from one field of law in another and, on the other, admitting exceptions for the specific purposes for which the distinction is drawn in that field of law. Ultimately, although discrepancies do arise in specific situations from the characterisation of parts of land contractually agreed to be severed between their treatment in property law and tax law, the underlying reasoning in the tax law decisions is manifestly couched in property law terms. Divergencies from the distinction of land and goods borrowed from the law of property only appear at the margin, such exceptional faultlines are, however, highly instructive.

In Chapter 3, requirements of form for sales contracts in land were considered in respect of contracts for the severance of parts of land, in particular in respect of standing timber. Here, the distinction of land and goods was found to bear different degrees of relevance, ranging from irrelevant to partially relevant and to conclusive. That was the case of German law, French law and English law, re-spectively.

In the light of the fundamental differences arising in the Chapter 3, a con-ceptual framework proved necessary to present the findings clearly, which was developed in Chapter 4. The need for an analytical framework is due to the interrelation between two factors, (i) whether or not the distinction provides the basis for a given requirement, such as of form, and (ii) whether or not the distinction is relevant to the characterisation of contracts for the severance of parts of land and, if so, which contracts. Such considerations of legal systemics and purpose were therefore incorporated into the framework for a complete statement of the law in the legal systems under consideration. The abstract legal distinction in question (land/goods) was broken down into the distinction itself and the corresponding legal requirement (writing/publication/description etc.), then the function of the former in terms of the legal construct concerned (contract of sale/gift) and the effect of (non-)compliance in the system of na-tional law (invalidity/third party unenforceability), which allows for the con-textualisation of the underlying policy considerations (solemnity/expediency etc.) and any related factual distinctions (*fructus industriales/naturales* etc.) to be taken into account independently.

Having analysed specific questions of law in respect of the distinction of land and goods as applicable to contracts for the severance of parts of land, Chapter 5 compared the national distinctions from the perspective of specific factual circumstances, those of nursery trees, Christmas trees and transplantation. By holding the variable of certain factual permutations constant, greater attention could be paid to the different legal constructs to which the characterisation of plants rooted in the soil as goods has been applied. By breaking down the relevant factors in respect of the distinction of land and goods a critical regard was able to be adopted for the purposes of ironing out inconsistencies in national discourse, in particular, in respect of the characterisation of Christmas trees in German law. The exposition of French law in respect of nursery plants revealed greatly diverging points of view from the literature, relating to the distinction of land and goods and, in particular, in the transformation of property from one category to the other (and back again). The divergencies expressed in many of the classical treatises of French law appear not to have been resolved, but merely relegated and hidden from modern discussions.

Chapter 6 provided a brief case-study outlining how the proposed framework could be brought to bear on the emerging case-law of the Court of Justice of the European Union on the distinction of land and goods. It provided an illustration of the practical application of the conclusions of the present analysis further afield than the specific example of standing timber. Rather than calling into question the decisions or outcomes of the decisions of the CJEU, that analysis concentrated on elucidating what the purpose behind the use of the distinction in EU VAT law and extrapolating guiding policy considerations in keeping with that purpose. It was concluded that permanency of location at a given point in time in respect of the passive activity of an economic factor of production or the non-economic function of housing provide the key test for determining whether a tangible item is in such a close relationship with land so as to fall within the definition of land and thereby escape liability to VAT.

B.   Main conclusions: a need for recalibration

Aside from the individual conclusions on the state of the law in each of the legal systems considered, it is submitted that the most important and overarching conclusion of this study is that national law accounts of the rules governing the distinction of land and goods need recalibrating. The idea that the accession or severance of things to and from land, respectively, is a 'natural scientific enquiry' based exclusively on blends of physical attachment to or socially-expressed intention in respect of land is misleading, or, at least, not decisive. Such accounts fail to take account of purpose.

Purpose, or the legal reason why land is being distinguished from goods in a particular situation, is crucial. It is as crucial within a single legal system as it is when compared with others as well as when supra-national is at issue. The question of whether something may form the subject-matter of a distinct third party right is not necessarily coterminous with the question of what shall pass in a given conveyance of land; the former is a pure question of property law, whilst the latter is supplemented by the contractual intention of the parties. By its nature, the fundamental distinction of land and goods is applied directly in several different legal contexts, and tangentially in many others. It thus serves many legal purposes, the underlying policy considerations for which may pull in different directions, leading to certain factors being more important in certain contexts than in others. Consequently, merely asking whether something, even something as mundane as standing timber or crops, is fixed to the soil or intended to remain there will not answer the question of whether it is an integral part of the land for all of the purposes for which the distinction of land and goods is drawn.

No matter how 'natural' a classification may appear – and that of land and goods or immovables and movables is the most natural (or physical) of the general private law classifications ('can it be moved?') – its use in law always has an underlying purpose, a *ratio legis*. As a general classification of private law, that classification will encompass several *rationes*. The preceding chapters have pointed to a number of illustrative purposes outside of property law to which the distinction of movable and immovable property, or land and goods, has been put. These lead to different characterisations and different justifications according to each particular purpose. It is apparent that the justifications (physical attachment, objective/subjective intention, etc.) for any particular characterisation (of standing trees, Christmas trees, etc.) must be calibrated to the *ratio legis* in question (i. e. the reason why the distinction has been applied to the particular point in law (land acquisition tax, default rules of contractual interpretation, the requisite level of formalities for the conclusion of a juridical act, value-added tax, etc.)

C.   Propositions: a new framework

It is submitted that in order to have a principled approach to the distinction of land and goods account must be taken of purpose. Without its legal purpose, the distinction of land and goods is a very blunt tool ('can x be moved?'), even when allowance is made for the criterion of permanency of intention. It could otherwise be seen as a sub-optimal administration of justice in the sense that like would not treated alike, and also conducive to legal uncertainty in that no hard-fast method has been proposed for determining, along the spectrum of physical attachment to permanency of intention, when the balance is tipped from characterising something as land to goods or visa-versa.

The present study has attempted to propose a framework, first of all, for integrating the various facets of legal purpose into the characterisation of property as land or goods and, second, relating legal purpose to policy considerations which have been expressed in that regard and the factual circumstances of the case at hand. These facets of legal purpose have been grouped according to a number of sub-questions: (i) what legal consequence is effected by characterisation as land or goods? That subquestion may sometimes itself be broken down into (a) the particular legal requirement and (b) the consequences of (non-) compliance with that requirement. Then there is (ii) the legal construct and its place in the legal systemics of the relevant legal system. When taken together these three constituent elements of the legal purpose for which the distinction of land and goods is drawn will determine which policy considerations and legal criteria/factual circumstances will be conclusive in any given case. Differences in outcome according to the factual circumstances were taken into account under the heading of factual permutations.

D.   Perspectives: international and interdisciplinary

It is submitted that the framework proposed here may be applied extensively whenever the distinction of land and goods is decisive to the solution of a particular point of law, particularly in the light of multi-layered regulatory contexts which exist across globally-connected legal systems.

1.   Geographical scope

Modern legal systems are characterised by a multi-layered patchwork of sub-national, national and supranational law. In incorporating legal purpose into the framework for the general legal concept of the distinction of land and goods, there is no need for the rules at one level to interfere with the rules at another level. It is entirely conceivable for the content of the distinction to differ from one regulatory level to another.

This is particularly applicable to the legal systems of the European Union. General legal concepts – which provide the building-blocks of legal discourse in several legal systems – will ultimately be used both in national law and EU law. However, by distinguishing between the purposes of the two it should be possible to avoid indirect interference. This is of course subject to cases in which divergence in legal concept unjustifiably hinders attainment of the EU internal market, in which the case for harmonisation, replacing diverging national concepts with a single EU concept, is strongest.

The phenomenon is of course not limited to the European Union. In the United Kingdom, for instance, the distinction of land and goods is already fragmented. In the distinct legal systems of England (& Wales (and, depending on the circumstances, Northern Ireland)), one the one hand, and Scotland, on the other, the general foundations of private law are different, and thus the distinction of land and goods is, in principle, different, but a single uniform Sale of Goods Act applies to both in that it lays down a uniform definition of goods. Further afield, many legal systems of the Commonwealth countries maintain a residual core of private law ultimately derived from English law, one of the concepts of which is its distinction of realty and personalty (land and goods). Although, for instance, such countries may have similarly worded Sales of Goods Acts or Law of Property Acts those pieces of legislation are particular to each country, from which the common core common law distinction of land and goods may diverge according to the legal purpose in question.

The United States, with its strictly federal system, also has a multi-layered system into which the distinction of land and goods is required to fit. Despite a Restatements of the common law with a view to harmonisation, of which the distinction of land and goods forms a part, as well as a Uniform Commercial Code, each state has its own system of private law. Those different systems of private law, whether codified or not, provide for different rules governing the distinction of land and goods.[435]

2.   Regulatory scope

The purpose of this paragraph is merely to state that the conclusions from the present comparative analysis are also readily applicable to discussions undertaken exclusively at national level across different fields of law. This is precisely in light of the argument that legal purpose has – or has the potential to have – a direct impact on the outcomes which are dependent on the distinction of land and goods. Recognition of that proposition should lead to more consistent decision-making. To take but one illustration, in determining whether something is a part of land or goods, there should – contrary to some views which have been expressed – be no binary choice in French law between the equally settled case-law statements, on the one hand, that the movable or immovable character of property 'is determined primarily by the perspective of the parties to the contract' or, on the other hand, that that character is 'laid down in law and cannot be influenced by the agreement of contracting parties'. The question is rather which

---

435 See, for instance, the discussion of common law jurisdictions in Chapter 3. Requirements of form for sales contracts in land.

of those two statements is more appropriate to the specific purpose for which the distinction is being drawn in its application to the case at hand, such as, for instance, determining the respective rights and obligations of contracting parties or the enforceability of third party rights. Within a given national law it is highly conceivable for the distinction of land and goods to be drawn for different purposes and, consequentially, be given a different meaning for several or each of those different purposes.

E.   A final word

The distinction of land and goods is a legal institution. It does not operate in a vacuum but is governed by the purpose for which it is drawn. This is no different from the question of when does a standing tree become timber. The answer depends on perspective. It is submitted that greater account of purpose informs outcome and allows for clarity of analysis.

Bibliography

Table of Cases

In order to provide a uniform method of citation which provides the reader with the exact means of finding the decision itself a particular single method of citation has been adopted:

> *Party name* v. *Party name* Abbreviated National Court and Chamber or town (date in numeric form; reference of the case): [year of law report] volume ... Name of Law Report ... Initial page of report, particular page cited [particular paragraph cited]

> E. g., *Caquelard* v. *Lemoine* Cass. (26. 12. 1833): [1834] 1 S 205, 206

If the law report has been annotated or commented in the law report itself, the citation is followed by the word 'note' and the name of the author, as given or as can be deduced from the law report. Whilst the day and month are not necessary in locating the decisions of Common Law jurisdictions, they are given here in the interests of consistency when they appear in the law report. For some of the oldest English cases, merely the year is given.

Final brackets are used to add miscellaneous information, such as whether the opinion of the advocate general is also published in the report or, where for example the decision comes from an American court, the name of the state in which it is located.

The decisions are presented, firstly, according to jurisdiction and, secondly, in chronological order. Whether the case is cited at an earlier instance, that citation is given with the highest appellate court, unless the case is appealed on another point of law. In the latter case, the earlier decision on the actual point of law cited is given in its chronological order, followed directly by the appellate court.

aff.: affirmed

Common Law decisions[436]

England and Wales
SC: Supreme Court (from …)
HL: [Judicial Committee of the] House of Lords (prior to)
CA: Court of Appeal
HC: High Court
KB: King's Bench (QB: Queen's Bench)

Scotland
CSIH: Inner House of the Court of Session
CSOH: Outer House of the Court of Session
Sherriff's Court

Common Law Jurisdictions
HC of Aus.: High Court of Australia (…)

Herlakenden's case KB (1589) 4 Co. Rep. 62a; 76 ER 1025

Anon KB, (1604) Owen 49, 74 ER 891
Liford's Case (1615) 11 Co. Rep. 46b; 77 ER 1206
Stukeley v. Butler (1615) Hobart 169; ER 316

Duppa v. *Mayo* KB (1669) 1 Wms. Saund. 275; 85 ER 366 (case-note Williams)

Waddington v. *Bristow* Common Pleas (09.06.1801): 2 Bos. & Pul. 452; 126 ER 1379
Penton v. *Robart* King's Bench (23.11.1801): 2 East 88; 102 ER 302
Elwes v. *Maw* KB (13.11.1802): (1802) 3 East 37; 102 ER 510
Watherell v. *Howells* (26.02.1808): 1 Camp. 228; 170 ER 939
Bostwick v. *Leach* (1809) 3 Day (Conn.) 476 (Connecticut)
Stanley v. *White* (1811.06.29) 14 East 332; 104 ER 630
Wyndham v. *Way* (27.04.1812): 4 Taunton 316; 128 ER 351; 13 Rev Rep 607

Teall v. *Auty* (14.06.1820): (1822) 4 Moore 542, *Teal* v. *Auty*, (13.06.1820) 2 Broderip & Bingham 99; 129 ER 895
Evans v. *Roberts* (1826) 5 Barnwell and Cresswell 829; 108 ER 309
Bullen v. *Denning* KB (1826) 5 B&C 842; 108 ER 313
Smith v. *Surman* (1829) 9 B&C; 7 LJ KB 296; 33 RR 259
Erskine v. *Plummer* (1831) 7 Greenl. 447; 7 Me. 447 (Maine)

Rodwell v. *Phillips* (1842): 9 M&W 501
Claflin v. *Carpenter* (1842) 4 Metcalf 580; 45 Mass. 580 (Massachusetts)

---

436 and Scottish cases.

Cain v. *McGuire* (09.12.1852) 13 B.Mon. 340; 52 Ky. 340 (Kentucky)
In re Baldwin, ex parte Foss (1858) 2 De G&J 230

Oakley v. *Monck* (1865–1866) LR 1 Exch 159; 14 LT Rep NS 20
D'Eyncourt v. *Gregory* (07.12.1866): L.R. 3 Eq. 382
Bain v. *Brand* 16.03.1876 Privy Council: (1876) 1 AC 762
Lavery v. *Pursell* (23.02.1888): 39 Ch. D. 508
Hostetter v. *Auman* (09.03.1889) 119 Ind. 7; 20 N.E. 506 (Indiana)
Coody v. *Gress Lumber Co.* (08.07.1899) 82 Ga. 793, 10 S.E. 218 (Georgia)
Marshall v. *Green* (06.11.1875): (1875) 1 CPD 35
Hirth v. *Graham* (24.01.1893) 50 Ohio St. 57; 33 N.E. 90 (Ohio)
Hobson v. *Gorringe* CA (19.12.1896): [1897] 1 Ch. 182

Fluharty v. *Mills* (30.03.1901) 49 W.Va. 446; 38 S.E. 521, 522 (West Virginia, United States)
Alianza Co Ltd v. *Bell (Surveyor of Taxes)* HC (01.07.1904): [1904] 2 KB 666
James Jones & Sons, Ltd v. *Tankerville* (09.07.1909): [1909] 2 Ch 440
Whittington v. *Hall* (15.11.1911) 116 Md. 467; 82 A. 163 (Maryland)
Morison v. *Lockhart* [1912] SC 1017 (Scotland)
Kauri Timber Co Ltd v. *Taxes Commissioner*, Privy Council (New Zealand) (10.07.1913): [1913] AC 771
Griffith v. *Ayer-Lord Tie Co.* (07.07.1913) 159 SW 218, 109 Ark. 223 (Arkansas)

Kursell v. *Timber Operators and Contractors ltd* CA (10.03.1926): [1927] 1 KB 298
Spyer v. *Phillipson* CA (01.27.1931): 2 Ch 183

Munro v. *Liquidator of Balnagown Estates Co* (16.11.1948): [1949] SC 49
Smith v. *Daly and Booth Lumber Ltd* Ontario Supreme Court (29.06.1949): [1949] 4 D.L.R. 45 (Canada)
Saunders v. *Pilcher* CA (24.11.1949): [1949] All ER 1097
Smith v. *Daly* Ontario High Court of Justice [1949] 4 DLR 45 (Canada)
Gunn v. *Inland Revenue* CSIH (11.03.1955): (1955) SLT 266
Hood Barrs v. *Inland Revenue Commissioners* (13.03.1957): [1957] 1 WLR 529

Hopwood v. *CN Spencer Ltd* HC (19.11.1964): 42 Tax Cases 169

Ashgrove Pty Ltd v. *DFCT* [1994] 28 ATR 512 (Australia)
Melluish (Inspector of Taxes) v. *BMI (No. 3) Ltd* [1996] A.C. 454
Elitestone Ltd. v. *Morris and Another* HL (01.05.1997): [1997] 1 W.L.R. 687
McDonnell Estate v. *Scott World Wide Inc* Nova Scotia Court of Appeal (1997) 149 DLR (4th) 645 (Canada)
Fischer v. *Zepa Consulting A.G.*, (09.07.1999) 263 A.D.2d 946, 695 N.Y.S.2d 456, 41 U.C.C. Rep. Serv. 2d 772 (4th Dep't 1999) (New York)

Epstein v. *Coastal Timber Co.* (11.07.2011) 393 S.C. 276, 711 S.E.2d 912, 75 U.C.C. Rep. Serv. 2d 85 (South Carolina)

German decisions

The courts of places, such as Nuremburg, Munich and Brunswick, where an English spelling exists, are cited with the name of the place in German to facilitate its retrieval in the law reports.

Vermögensverwaltungsstelle für Offiziere und Beamte v. Z Reichsgericht, II. Zivilsenat (24.03.1905, II 368/04): 60 RGZ 317

Gasmotorenfabrik D. v. *Sch.* Reichsgericht, V. Zivilsenat (19.04.1906, V 528/05): 63 RGZ 171

Allg. Elektrizitätsgesellsch. v. H. & Co. Reichsgericht, V. Zivilsenat (23.06.1906, V 584/04): 63 RGZ 416

S J. v. G Reichsgericht, IV. Zivilsenat (04.12.1911, IV 179/11): 78 RGZ 35

Ehefrau E v. *P* RG, 5th Chamber (23.03.1905, V 433/04): 60 RGZ 31-

K v. preußischer Fiskus RG 7. (08.12.1905, VII 119/05) 62 RGZ 135

T und Gen. v. *R und Gen.* Reichsgericht (27.04.1907): 66 RGZ 88

Schnellpressenfabrik v. *W. Ehel* RG (02.11.1907, V 53/07) 67 RGZ 30

A v. *R* RG (17.12.1909, VII 132.09): (1909) 72 RGZ 309

Wesche v. *Zuckerfabrik M* RG, 2nd Chamber (03.02.1914, II 625/13): 84 RGZ 125

RG (23.01.1918): [1918] *Zeitschrift für Rechtspflege in Bayern* 221

Akt.-Gesellschaft Wollwäscherei und Kämmerei v. *R* Reichsgericht, V. Zivilsenat (04.10.1922, V 611/21): 105 RGZ 213

D & R v. *S* RG (16.05.1924): 108 RGZ 269

Beslau (present-day: Wrocław)(23.10.1925, VI 243/25): [1926] RG LZ 109

LG Neuruppin [1927] JW 2538

L v. *Kommunalbank in M* RG 5. Zivilsenat (21.03.1927, V 381/26) 116 RGZ 363

OLG Naumburg, 5. Zivilsenat (14.11.1929, 5 U 211/29): [1930] JW 845

P.-M. AG v. *R als Verwalter im Konkurse über das Vermögen der Mitwe G* RG (11.11.1932, VII 143/32): 138 RGZ 237; [1933] 62 JW 694, case-note Bernhöfe

Gesamthaus Braunschweig-Lüneburg v. *Land Braunschweig* RG (14.11.1938): 158 RGZ 362

OLG München (31.03.1955, 6 U 1556/54): [1955] MDR 414

BGH (03.12.1957, VIII ZR 401/56): [1958] MDR (Ls.) 334

BFH (25.03.1958, II 193/56): [1958] 3 BStBl 239

Fa. S v. *W* BGH (30.05.1958, V ZR 295/56) 27 BGHZ 360

BFH (02.09.1959, II 239/57 U) 69 BFH 521; [1959] 3 BStBl 454

BFH (01.06.1960, II 181/57): [1960] 3 BStBl 294

BFH (28.08.1963, II 150/61): [1964] Höchstrichterliche Finanzrechtsprechung (HFR) 245

BFH (11.05.1966, II 171/63): [1966] BeckRS 21005621

BFH (22.06.1966, II 130/62): [1966] 3 BStBl 552; 86 BFHE 424

BGH (11.11.1970, VIII ZR 242/68) 55 BGHZ 20

Fa. R. & S. oHG v. *L. Bundesgerichtshof,* VIII. Zivilsenat (27.06.1973, VIII ZR 201/72): 61 BGHZ 80

BFH (22.06.1977, II R 22/71): [1977] 2 BStBl 703; 122 BFHE 565

Bundesfinanzhof (BFH) (27.10.1978, VI R 8/76): 126 BFHE 217; [1979] NJW 392

K v. *B GmbH* BGH (13.03.1979, V ZR 71/67): 53 BGHZ 324

BayObLG (26.10.1979, BReg. 2 Z 51/79): [1979] BayObLGZ 361

BGH (20.10.1999, VIII ZR 335/98): [2002] NJW 504

OLG Hamm (28.02.1992): NJW-RR 1438

BGH (24.03.1994, X ZR 108/91): 125 BGHZ 338

BGH (19.07.2005, X ZR 92/03): [2005] NJW-RR 1718

French decisions

D: (1) where preceeded by a volume number, *Dalloz périodique* (DP); (2) where
no indication of volume, *Dalloz hebdomadaire* (DH)
  The first abbreviation refers to the court, the second to its chamber or location.
  Cass. Cour de cassation
- Cass. Ass. pl.: Assemblée plénière de la Cour de cassation
- Cass. civ.: Chambre civile de la Cour de cassation

CA: Cour d'appel
- CA Lyon: Cour d'appel de Lyon

Rumpler v. *Diemert* CA Colmar (09.11.1802; 18 Brum, an 11) [1802] S 93

Michel Schott v. *Wolff* (02.10.1805; 10 vendémiaire an 14): S 166 & (10.11.1805; 19 ven-
    démiaire an 14) 1 S 65

Baumier v. *Thomas* Cass civ (26.01.1808): [1809] 1 S 65; Rep de droit (1847), [45]

Ministre des finances (10.06.1810): JE 3881, cited in Championnière & Rigaud, *Droits
    d'enregistrement*, vol. 4, [3166]

La Régie de l'enregistrement v. *Rocquigny* Cass. req. (08.09.1813): [1816] 1 S 15

Mourier v. *Carrichon* Grenoble (19.12.1815) cited in Dalloz, *Rep. de législation, de doctrine
    et de jurisprudence* (1847), biens, [129]

Les héritiers Delavergne v. *Ligneau-Grandcour* CA Orléans (10.08.1815): [1816] 2 S 382

Berruyer et Dubosc. v. *Ligneau-Grandcour* Cass. Civ. (21.07.1818) 1 S 375

Humphreys v. *Harrison* (06.05.1820) 1 J. & W 580

Lambert v. *Saint* Cass. Req. (21.06.1820): [1820] S 257

Enregistrement v. *Japy* Cass. Civ. (19.11.1823): Dalloz, *Rep. de législation, de doctrine et de
    jurisprudence* (1847), biens, [129]

Poupart v. *Dupont* Cass. req. (09.08.1825) *Rep de droit* (1845), vol 6, Biens, p. 206

Enregistrement v. *Laget-Valdeson* Cass. civ. (04.04.1827): [1827] S 563

Luce-Alexis v. *Follope* Cass (03.08.1831): [1831] 1 S 386

Caquelard v. *Lemoine* Cass. (26.12.1833): [1834] 1 S 205; [1834] 1 D 118

Le préfet des Vosges v. *La commune de Bresse* Cass. (13.02.1834): 1 S 720; 1 D 71

Logette v. *Lemaigen* Cass. (09.05.1836): [1836] 1 S 958

Legendre v. *Debras* CA Rouen (01.03.1839): 2 S 421

Garnier v. *Lemarrois* Cass. (06. 04. 1841): [1841] 1 S 414, case-note Devilleneuve

Porte & Bruni v. *Desarbres* Cass. Req. (10. 06. 1841): [1841] 1 S 484, case-note Devilleneuve

Johnston v. *Firbac* Bourges, (31. 01. 1843), cited in *Dalloz, Rep. de législation, de doctrine et de jurisprudence* (1847), biens, [132]

Legigan v. *Legigan* Tribunal de la Seine (12. 06. 1844), aff. in Cass req (01. 05. 1848): [1848] 1 S 501; 1 D 220

Pont v. *Roux et Devienne* CA Lyon (29. 05. 1849): [1850] 2 S 25

Péchin-Gourdin et Aubert v. *Meurisse* CA Paris (12. 04. 1851): [1853] 2 Journal du Palais 184

N. v. *Gallard* Limoges (08. 12. 1852): [1852] 2 S 687

Req. (14. 11. 1853): [1854] 1 S 105

Rodet v. *de Lachapelle* CA Lyon (18. 05. 1854): [1854] 2 S 426

Delhomel v. *commune de Senlecques* Trib. Civ. Boulogne-sur-Mer (23. 05. 1856): 2 S 513

Gontard & Gravier v. *ville de Neufchâtel* Cass Req (15. 12. 1857): [1859] 1 D 366

Epoux Duclerfays v. *Ville de Douai* Civ. (18. 05. 1858): 1 S 661; 1 D 218

Gassowski v. *synd. Mallard* CA Besançon (14. 12. 1864): [1865] 2 S 127

Michoully v. *syndic Chamerin & Fontaine* CA Besançon (16. 01. 1865): [1865] 2 S 127

Synd. Chamecin & Fontaine v. *Mougin* CA Besançon (27. 02. 1865): [1865] 2 S 127

Commune d'Orchamps-Vennes v. *héritiers Millot et consort* Req. (05. 11. 1866): [1867] 1 D 32

Didier-Sequier v. *Benoît* Req (30. 03. 1868): 1 S 201; 1 D 417, case-note Moreau

Collignon v. *Lemaître-Allard* CA Nancy (08. 02. 1870 & 10. 08. 1871) on appeal Cass. civ. (27. 05. 1873): [1873] 1 DP 465

Carl v. *l'État* Civ. (16. 12. 1873): [1874] 1 DP 249; [1874] 1 S. 457

De Boudard v. *Trimoly* Cass. civ. (29. 05. 1872): [1874] 1 DP 143

Millot et Dufournel v. *Langlois* CA Dijon (28. 03. 1876): [1877] 2 S 193

Epoux de la Rougefosse v. *Commune de Boynes* Req. (21. 11. 1877): [1878] 1 D 301

Usine de "la Dillon" v. *Crassous* Cass. civ. (07. 01. 1880): [1880] 1 DP 129

Syndic Sénéclauze v. *Sénéclauze* Cass. (05. 07. 1880): [1880] 1 D 321; [1881] 1 S 105; [1881] 1 P 238

Guingand v. *De Béhague* CA Orléans (11. 08. 1880): [1881] 2 D 38

Vassel v. *Commune de Bazincourt* Civ. (08. 11. 1880): [1881] 1 D 28

D'Albon v. *Duval et Rœderer* Cass. Req. (09. 08. 1881): [1882] 1 S 369, case-note Labbé

Simon et Bondaux v. *Enregistrement* Cass. (27. 06. 1882): [1883] 1 S 382; 1 P 965

Compain v. *Gillet* Cass. civ. (25. 01. 1886): [1886] 1 S 269; 5 D 39

Caisse commercial du Quesnoy v. *Syndicat Valin* CA Douai (16. 12. 1886): [1888] 2 S 115

De la Haye Jousselin v. *Amaury Simon* Cass. civ. (29. 07. 1890): [1893] 1 S 521

CA Poitiers (23. 12. 1890), appeal rejected in *Leparc* v. *Barré* Req. (21. 07. 1892): [1892] 1 D 455

CA Aix (21. 03. 1891): [1892] 31 Rec. Aix 1; Gaz. Pal, Rep. Jur. (1892–1897), v° Vente, [205]

Gauchy & Cie v. *Letombe* TC Péronne (05. 06. 1891): [1891] 2 D 92

Gauchy & Cie v. *Letombe* CA Amiens (13. 08. 1891): [1891] 2 D 92

SA des ardoisières de Bacara v. *Lejeune-Brichet* CA Nancy (30. 01. 1897): [1897] 2 D 457

Brisabois v. *Ravel* Cass. civ. (02. 03. 1902): [1902] 1 Pand. 303

Millien v. *Gay* Req (18. 03. 1902): [1902] 1 DP 190

Syndic B v. *B* CA Agen (12.12.1904): [1906] 2 DP 33

Hesnard et veuve Legrand v. *Anicens établissements Duperrou* Cass. Civ. (01.05.1906): [1909] 1 D 345

Armand v. *Lautier* CA Nîmes (31.10.1908): [1911] 2 D 103

Laurentide Paper Co. v. *Baptist* (1908) 41 SCR 105 (Quebec)

Avril v. *Vidal-Engaurran* Cass Req (24.05.1909): [1910] 1 DP 489, case-note Loynes; [1911] 1 S 9, case-note Naquet

Julien v. *Popon* Cass. civ. (16.12.1912): [1914] 1 DP 115

CA Rennes (31.05.1917): [1917] 1 *Receuil de Nantes* 278; [1912–1920] *Gazette du Palais* (tables), Vente, [339bis]

Mulin v. *Ferras* Cass. req. (14.12.1921): [1922] 1 D 179

Mallet et Uro v. *Dame veuve Le Visage* Cass. Civ. (03.04.1922): [1924] 1 D. 12

Favier v. *veuve Rochette de Lempdes* Cass. Req. (12.07.1922): [1923] 1 D 61

Société des miniums d'aluminium v. *Société des produits chimiques* CA Montpellier (23.10.1922): [1923] 2 S 1

Heusch v. *Lecomte, Belozersky et La Dendronne* CA Amiens (24.10.1922): [1924] 2 D 141; [1923] 2 S 6; Solus, case-note [1924] RTD civ 180

Lacombe v. *Jay* Cass. civ. (17.12.1923): [1924] 1 D 14

S^{té} de la blanchisserie de Thaon v. *Le Gonidec* Cass. Req. (13.06.1925): [1925] 1 S 251

Morgand v. *de Chézelles* CA Amiens (22.10.1925): [1925] D 637

Lombardino et Galli v. *Filippis* CA Lyon (08.03.1923): [1929] 2 D 91, case-note Fréjaville Cass. civ. (13.04.1929): [1929] DH 265

Émorine v. *Long et autres* Req. (18.01.1933): [1933] 1 D 193, case-note Fréjaville

Anduze v. *Lengereau* Cass Civ (02.06.1934): [1935] 1 DP 65, case-note Fréjaville; [1934] 1 S 270, case-note Désiry

Cour d'Alexandrie (14.05.1935): [1936] RTD civ 1021, case-note Demogue; 48 *Bulletin de législation et de jurisprudence égyptiennes* 307

Corbier v. *de Chabannes* CA Bourges (13.07.1943): [1944] 2 JCP 2543, case-note Gény

S^{té} parisienne du matériel Coder v. *SA Ossude* CA Paris (24.05.1944): [1944] 2 S 4

Bouillette v. *Armandon* Cass. Soc. (01.12.1944) [1946] D 56

Mencière v. *Saizelet* Tribunal de Vouziers (10.07.1946): [1946] 2 JCP 3303, case-note Gény

Saizelet v. *Mencière* CA Nancy (11.03.1947): [1949] 2 JCP 3869, case-noter Gény

S^{té} des Combustibles de Vence v. *du Rouret* Com. (09.03.1949): [1949] 2 JCP 5075, case-note Becqué; [1949] RTD civ 536, case-note Carbonnier

Société d' "Approvisionnements Vinicoles" v. *Guiaud* Cass. com. (02.04.1952): [1952] 3 Bull. civ. 122, [n° 160]

Dutant v. *Dutant* Cass. civ. (18.02.1957): [1957] 1 Bull. civ. 67 (n° 80); [1957] 1 D 249

Gratien v. *Audoin* Cass. com. (18.02.1957): [1957] 3 Bull. civ. 47 (n° 57)

CA Paris (27.03.1963): 1964 D 27

S^{té} Kauffmann v. *S^{té} Edel* Cass. com. (13.04.1964, n° 59-12.542): [1964] 3 Bull civ n° 180

S^{té} Rivals v. *Gerboux* Com. (15.06.1965): [1965] D 823

Cass. com. (08.07.1965): 3 Bull. civ. n° 435

Civ^3 (03.07.1968): [1969] D 161

Bresson v. *Tricornot* Cass. civ³ (04.07.1968): [1968] 2 Gaz. Pal. 298

Le Sann v. *Sᵗᵉ Elevage* CA Rennes (25.06.1969): [1969] 2 Gaz Pal 201

Guillot v. *Abel-Coindoz et Durand* Cass. Com. (21.12.1971, n° 70-12033): [1971] Bull civ 290

de Flamain v. *de Azevedo* CA Reims (08.10.1979): [1981] 2 D 40

Bergeot v. *Le Gentil* Cass civ¹ (08.10.1980): [1981] 1 Gaz Pal (Panorama, 25-27.02) 40, case-note Piedelièvre; [1981] D. (IR) 445, case-note Audit; [1981] RTD civ. 647, case-note Cornu

Janisson v. *Ducloux* CA Reims (10.05.1982): [1984] 2 JCP 20225, case-note Dagot; [1984] RTD civ. 334, case-note Giverdon

Sarl Partin CA Montpellier (09.06.1982): Juris-Data no. 600753

Nouvel v. *Yves Jacobelli* CA Aix-en-Provence (15.02.1985): [1985] 2 Gaz Pal 442, case-note Dureuil

Ville de Genève et Fondation Abegg v. *Consorts Margail* CA Montpellier (18.04.1984): [1985] D 208, case-note Maury

Ville de Genève et Fondation Abegg v. *Consorts Margail* Cass. Assemblée plénière (15.04.1988, n° 85-10262, 85-11198): [1988] Bull. AP 5 (n° 4); [1988] D. 325 (opinion Cabannes), case-note Maury; (1989) 78 *Rev. crit. dr. int. pr.* 100, Droz; [1988] 1 JCP 21066, case-note Barbieri.

Richon v. *Castagnet & Belasse* CA Agen (09.12.1992; n° 1088): [1993] 4 JCP G 1772; [1992] JurisData 048301

Drouhault v. *Olry* CA Pau (24.06.1993): [1993] JurisData 046715

Cass. Civ.¹ (7.01.1992): [1994] I Bull. civ., No 4; [1992] 2 JCP 21971, case-note Ramarolanto-Ratiary

Cass. civ¹ (14.12.1999, n° 97-19620): [1991] 1 Bull. civ. 221, [340]

Civ. 3ᵉ (23.01.2002): [2002] D 2365, case-note Depadt-Sebag; 2504, case-note Reboui-Maupin; [2002] 1 JCP 176, case-note Périnet-Marquet

HVB Ostertag GmbH v. *Office national des forêts* CA Nancy (13.05.2008): [2008] JurisData 372089

CA Nancy (13.10.2009)

Commune de Mandres sur Vair v. *Société Anonyme Poli* CA Nancy (13.10.2009, n° 2708/09): [2009] JurisData 023332

Decisions of the CJEU

Judgment of 27 janvier 1994, *Herbrink*, C-98/91, EU:C:1994:24

Judgment of 3 July 1997, *Commission* v. *France*, C-60/96, ECLI:EU:C:1997:340

Judgment of 16 January 2003, *Maierhofer*, C-315/00, C-315/00, ECLI:EU:C:2003:23

Judgment of 3 March 2005, *Fonden Marselisborg Lystbådehavn*, C-428/02, ECLI:EU: C:2005:126

Judgment of 29 April 2010, *M and Others*, C-340/08, EU:C:2010:232

Judgment of 15 November 2012, *Leichenich*, C-532/11, ECLI:EU:C:2012:720

Judgment of 19 December 2018, *Mailat*, C-17/18, ECLI:EU:C:2018:1038

Judgment of 2 July 2020, *Veronsaajien oikeudenvalvontayksikkö*, C-215/19, ECLI:EU: C:2020:518

Literature

Achilles, A., *Protokolle der Kommission für die Zweite Lesung des Entwurfs des Bürgerlichen Gesetzbuchs* (Berlin: Guttentag, 1897)

Anon, 'Growing Crops – the passing of property before severance' (1949) 93 *The Law Journal* 259

Anon, Note to Bullen v. Denning, (1827) 5 Prop. Law. 89

Anson, W. R., *Principles of the English Law of Contract* (Brierly, J.L. (ed.)) (Oxford: Clarendon Press, 20th ed., 1952)

Atiyah, P. S., et al., *The Sale of Goods* (Harlow: Longman, 10th ed., 2001)

Aubry, C., & Rau, C. F., *Cours de droit civil français d'après la méthode de Zachariae* (Paris, Marchal et Billard, 1897–1922, 5th ed.)

Aubry, C., & Rau, C. F., *Cours de droit civil français*, (Paris: LGJ Marchal, Billard et Cie, 4th ed., 1869–1883)

Barbieri, J.- J., case-note on *Ville de Genève et Fondation Abegg* v. *Consorts Margail* Cass. Assemblée plénière (15.04.1988, n° 85-10262, 85-11198): [1988] 1 JCP 21066

Beitzke, G., (ed.) *Staudingers Kommentar zum Bürgerlichen Gesetzbuch* (Berlin, Sellier-de Gruyter, 11th ed., 1954–1967)

Bell, Andrew P. *Modern law of personal property in England and Ireland* (London, Butterworths, 1989)

Benjamin on Sale (1974), see Guest (ed.)

BGB (Nomos), see Ring

BGB-RGRK: *Das Bürgerliche Gesetzbuch mit besonderer Berücksichtigung der Rechtsprechung des Reichsgerichts und des Bundesgerichtshofes* (Berlin: de Gruyter, 12th ed., 1974–2000), see also Hoffmann and Busch

Blackburn, C., *Treatise on the effects of the sale of personal property* (1845)

Bunsen, 'Zur Lehre von den nicht getrennten Erzeugnissen' (1906) 26 *Archiv für bürgerliches Recht* 11

Burge, *Commentaries colonial and foreign laws* (London: Saunders and Benning 1838)

Busch, L., et al., *Das bürgerliche Gesetzbuch: mit besonderer Berücksichtigung der Rechtsprechung des Reichsgerichts* (Berlin: de Gruyter, 4th ed., 1922)

Charlton, S., 'How far factory machinery follows the land in England, France and Germany' in Apers et al., *Property Law Perspectives III* (Leuven: Intersentia, 2015), 217–237

Chaveau, 'Des meubles par anticipation' [1893] *Rev crit* 573

Cheshire & North, *Private international law* (London: Butterworths, 1999, 13th ed.)

Cohn, *Manual of German law*, vol. 1, General Introduction Civil Law (London: Oceana Publications, 1968, 2nd ed.)

Coin-Delisle, J. B. C., *Commentaire analytique du Code civil. Livre III, titre II. Donations et Testamens* (Paris: Le Normat, 1844, 2nd ed.; 1st ed. 1841)

"Coke on Littleton" (Co. Litt.) – Coke, *The First Part of the Institutes of the Laws of England or Commentarie upon Littleton* (London: Societe of Stationers, 1628)

Collin, *Dictionary of Environment and Ecology* (London: Bloomsbury, 2011)

Commission, *The law of property in the European Community* in Studies: Competition – Approximation of Legislation Series 27, (Brussels: 1976)

Comyn, J., *A Digest of the Laws of England* (London: Butterworth, 5th ed., 1824)

Dalloz, D., & Dalloz, A., *Répertoire méthodologique et alphabétique de législation, de doctrine et de jurisprudence en matière de droit civil, commercial, crimminel, administratif, de droit des gens et de droit public* (Paris: Bureau de la Jurisprudence générale, 1845–1870)

Davis, 'Sale or contract for sale of standing timber as within provisions of statute of frauds respecting sale or contract of sale of real property' (1949) 7 *American Law Reports (2nd ed.)* 517

Delvincourt, C. E., *Cours de Code Napoléon* (Paris: P. Gueffier, 1813)

Demogue, R., 'Des droits éventuels, hypothèses où ils prennent naissance, nature et effets' [1905] & [1906] RTDciv

Demolombe, C., *Cours de Code Civil* (Paris: A. Durand, 1845–1882)

Diamond, A. L., et al., *Sutton and Shannon on Contracts* (London, Butterworths, 1970, 7th ed.)

Dicey & Morris, *The Conflict of Laws* (London: Sweet & Maxwell, 2000, 13th ed.)

Dörner, H., & Staudinger, A., 'Einführung zum Gesetz zur Modernisierung des Schuldrechts', Gesetz zur Modernisierung des Schuldrechts (26.11.2001), 1 BGBl 3138

Duranton, *Cours de droit français*, (Paris, Thorel & Guilbert, 1844, 4th ed.)

Dureuil, case-note on *Nouvel v. Yves Jacobelli* CA Aix-en-Provence (15.02.1985): [1985] 2 Gaz Pal 442

Ferard, C. A., & Howland Roberts, W., (ed.), *Amos & Ferard on the Law of Fixtures* (London: Sweet & Sons, 1883, 3rd ed.)

Flandin, L., *De la transcription en matière hypothécaire, ou Explication de la loi du 23 mars 1855 et des dispositions du Code Napoléon relatives à la transcription des donations et des substitutions* (Paris: Cosse et Marchal, 1861)

Fréjaville case-note on *Lombardino et Galli v. Filippis* CA Lyon (08.03.1923): [1929] 2 D 91

Fréjaville, case-note on *Anduze v. Lengereau* Cass. civ. (02.06.1934): [1935] 1 DP 65

Fréjaville, case-note on *Émorine v. Long et autres* Req. (18.01.1933): [1933] 1 D 193

Fréjaville, M., *Des Meubles par Anticipation – Questions juridiques et fiscales relatives aux cessions de droits d'extraction, aux ventes de matériaux de démolition, d'immeubles par destination, de coupes de bois, récoltes sur pied, etc.* (Paris: De Boccard, 1927) (Thesis)

Gazette du palais, *Répertoire universel de la jurisprudence française* (Paris: Gazette du palais, 1892–1897)

Goode, R., *Commercial Law* (London, Penguin, 1982)

Gow, J. J., 'When are trees timber? (or the Mystery of the Woof from the Trees)' (1962) SLT 13

Grady, S. G., *Law of fixtures* (London: O. Richards, 1845)

Gray, K., & Gray, S., *Elements of Land Law* (Oxford: OUP, 4th ed., 2005)

Guest, A. G., *Anson's Law of Contract* (Oxford: Clarendon Press, 1969, 23rd ed.)

Guest, A. G., et al (ed.), *Benjamin's Sale of Goods* (London: Sweet & Maxwell, 1974)

Guyot, C., *Droit forestier* (Berger-Levrault, Nancy, 1921)

Harpum, C., et al., *Megarry & Wade: The Law of Real Property* (London, Sweet & Maxwell, 2012, 8th ed.)

Hart, G., 'The impact of property law and contractual principles in taxation law' (2004) 14 *Revenue LJ* 92 (Australia)

Hoffmann, G., et al., *Das bürgerliche Gesetzbuch: mit besonderer Berücksichtigung der Rechtsprechung des Reichsgerichts* (Nürnberg: Sebald, 1910)

Hudson, A. H., 'Goods or Land?' (1958) 22 *Conv* 137

Josserand, L., *Les mobiles dans les actes juridiques du droit privé* (Paris, 1st ed.: 1928, reprint Paris: Dalloz, 2005)

Jurisprudence générale (1847), see Dalloz

Ker (ed.), *Benjamin on Sale* (London: Sweet & Maxwell; Toronto: Carswell, 1920)

Kommission für die II. Lesung BGB, see Achilles

Kramer, E., 'Kann der Grundstückseigentümer stehende Früchte rechtswirksam übereignen?' (1902) 6 Das Recht – Rundschau für den deutschen Juristenstand 609

Landsberg, 'Kauf von Holz auf dem Stamme' [1899] *Juristische Monatsschrift für Posen und Westpreußen* 177

Laurent, F., *Principes de droit civil* (Bruxelles : Bruylant-Christophe; Paris : A. Durand et Pedone-Lauriel, 1869–1878), vol. 5

Marcadé, V., *Eléments du droit civil français* (Paris: Cotillon, 2nd ed., , 1844)

Marcadé, V., *Explication théorique et pratique du code civil* (Paris: Cotillon then Delammotte, 1873, 7th ed., first published in 1841)

Mark, M., *Chalmer's Sale of Goods Act* 1893 (London: Butterworths, 15th ed., 1967)

Maury, J., case-note on *Ville de Genève et Fondation Abegg v. Consorts Margail* CA Montpellier (18.04.1984): [1985] D 208

Maury, J., case-note on *Ville de Genève et Fondation Abegg v. Consorts Margail* Cass. Assemblée plénière (15.04.1988, n° 85-10262, 85–11198): [1988] D. 325 (opinion Cabannes)

Megarry, R., & Wade, W., *The Law of Real Property* (1984, 5th ed.)

Megarry, R., *A Manual of the Law of Real Property* (London, Stevens & Sons, 1962, 3rd ed.)

Mestrot, M., 'Le rôle de la volonté dans la distinction des biens meubles et immeubles' in (1995) *Revue de la recherche juridique*, vol. 3, 809

Münchener Kommentar:

Ontario Law Reform Commission, *Report on sale of goods* (1979)

Picard, M., in Planiol, M., & Ripert, G., *Traité pratique de droit civil français*, vol. 3 *Les Biens* (Paris: LGDJ, 1926)

Pillebout, J.-F., in: *J.-Cl. Civil Code* (2014)

Planiol, M., & Ripert, G., (Hamel (ed.)), *Traité pratique de droit civil français*, vol. 10 (Paris, LGDJ, 1956, 2nd ed.)

Pothier, R. J., *Contrat de vente* (Paris; Orléans, 1768-1761)

Pothier, R. J., *De la communauté* (Paris: Debure, 1770)

Pothier, R. J., *Traités des personnes et des choses, du domaine de propriété, de la possession, de la prescription, de l'hypothèque, des fiefs, des cens, des champarts* (Paris: Cosse et Delamotte, 1846 (re-print), first published 1772)

Pothier, *Traité des fiefs* (1776), ch. 5, section 2, § 1; Bugnet (ed.) *Œuvres de Pothier*, vol. 9 (Plon, Paris, 1861, 2nd ed.)

Pothier, *Traités des personnes et des choses, du domaine de propriété, de la possession, de la prescription, de l'hypothèque, des fiefs, des cens, des champarts* (Paris: Cosse et Delamotte, 1846, first published 1772)

Pufe, W., *Der Kaufvertrag von Holz auf dem Stamm* (Breslau, 1928) (Thesis)

Raeburn, W. N., et al., *Blackburn on Contract of sale* (Stevens & Sons, London, 1910, 3rd ed.)

Ramaekers, E., 'Classification of objects by the European Court of Justice – movable immovables and tangible intangibles' [2014] ELR 447

Rieländer, *Sachenrechtliche Erwerbsrechte* (Sellier, 2014, Osnabrück) (Thesis)

Rigaud, E., & Championnière, P., *Traité des droits d'enregistrement* (Paris, Cosson, 1839), vol. 4

Säcker, F. J., & Rixecker, R., (eds.), *Münchener Kommentar zum BGB* (München: Beck, 6th ed. 2012–2014)

Säcker, Franz, J., & Rixecker, R. (ed.)) *Münchener Kommentar zum BGB* (München: Beck, 6th ed., 2012–2015)

Salier, G., *Verkauf von Bäumen auf dem Stamm* (Berlin: von Struppe & Winckler, 1903)

Sauvalle, A., *De la distinction entre les immeubles par nature et les immeubles par destination et spécialement de l'outillage immobilier* (Paris: Giard & Briere, 1902, thèse)

Sealy, L. S., '"Risk" In the Law of Sale' [1972] CLJ 225

Staudingers Kommentar zum Bürgerlichen Gesetzbuch mit Einführungsgesetz und Nebengesetzen (2011–2015)

Story, *Commentaries on the Conflict of Laws, foreign and domestic, in regard to marriages, divorces, wills successions, and judgments* (Boston, Hilliard, Gray & Co., 1834)

Sutton & Shannon, Contracts (London, Butterworth & Co, 5th ed., 1956)

Sutton and Shannon on Contracts, see Diamond

Terré, F., & Simler, P., *Droit civil, Les Biens* (6th ed., Dalloz, Paris, 2002)

Terrenoir, R., *Les droits du créancier hypothécaire sur les immeubles par destination* (1944)

Thomas, M., *Stamp Duty Land Tax* (CUP: Cambridge, 2006)

Tilsley, H., *A Treatise on the Stamp Laws* (London, Steven & Sons, 1871, 3rd ed.), vol. 1

Tomlims, *Lyttleton, his treatise of tenure* (London: Sweet, 1841)

Treasury, [2014] *Stamp Taxes Bulletin* (Issue 2), p. 3

van Erp, *European and National Property Law: Osmosis or Growing Antagonism?* (2007)

van Erp, Akkermans et al., *Cases, materials and text on national, supranational and international property law* (Oxford: Hart Publishing, 2012)

Vanuxem, S., *Saisie de récoltes sur pied* (2013) *in* RDC

Vazeille, F.-A., *Les Successions, donations et testamens* (Clermont-Ferrand: Thibaud-Landriot, 1837)

von Bar, 'Real Things' Loss of Capacity to be owned when subsumed within a Parcel of Land' (2013), 448

von Bar, 'Why do we need Grundstücke (land units), and what are they?' (2014) 22 *Juridica International* 1

von Bar, 'Wozu braucht man und was sind Grundstücke?' in *Festschrift für Ulrich Magnus* (München, 2014)

von Bar, *Gemeineuropäisches Sachenrecht* (2015)

Weil, Terré & Simler, Droit civil, Les biens (Paris: Dalloz, 3rd ed., 1985)

Williams's case-note on *Duppa v. Mayo* KB (1669) 1 Wms. Saund. 275; 85 ER 366

Wirtgen, K., *Der Kaufvertrag über Bäume auf dem Stamme* (Neuwied: Raiffeisen, 1931) (Dissertation)

Wolff, E., case-note in OLG Naumburg, 5. Zivilsenat (14.11.1929, 5 U 211/29): [1930] JW 845

Legislation and International Conventions

ALR *Allgemeines Landrecht für die Preußischen Staaten* (Prussian Civil Code)

BGB: Bürgerliches Gesetzbuch

CC: Code civil
Code général des impôts

Council Directive 2006/112/EC of 28 November 2006 on the common system of value added tax (OJ 2006 L 347, p. 1)

Council Implementing Regulation (EU) No 282/2011 of 15 March 2011 laying down implementing measures for Directive 2006/112/EC on the common system of value added tax (OJ 2011 L 77, p. 1).

Council Implementing Regulation (EU) No 1042/2013 of 7 October 2013 amending Implementing Regulation (EU) No 282/2011 as regards the place of supply of services (OJ 2013 L 284, p. 1)

Einführungsgesetz zum Bürgerlichen Gesetzbuch

Finance Act 2003
Fraudulent Conveyances Act 1571 (13 Eliz 1, c. 5)

Gesetz zur Modernisierung des Schuldrechts (26.11.2001, BGBl. I. 3138)
Gesetz zur Anpassung des nationalen Steuerrechts an den Beitritt Kroatiens zur EU und zur Änderung weiterer steuerlicher Vorschriften (25.07.2014; BGBl. I, 1266)
Grunderwerbsteuergesetz (17.12.1982) BGBl I, 1777 as modified on 26.02.1997 (BGBl. I, 418 & 1804)

Law of Property Act 1925
Law of Property (Miscellaneous Provisions) Act 1994
Loi du 22 frim. An 7

Loi Bonald (08.05.1816)

Loi n° 2011-331 du 28 mars 2011 de modernisation des professions judiciaires ou juridiques et certaines professions réglementées

Statute of Frauds, 1677
Statute of Frauds, RSO 1990, c. 19 (Ontario)

Sale of Goods Act 1893
Sale of Goods Act, SO 1920, c. 40 (Ontario)
Sale of Goods Act (New South Wales) 1923
Sale of Goods Act 1979
Sale of Goods Act, RSO 1990 (Ontario)

Conveyancing Act 1919 (New South Wales)
Law of Property Act, 1925
The Conveyancing and Law of Property Act, RSO 1970, c. 85 (Ontario)
Law Reform (Enforcement of Contracts) Act 1954
The Registry Act, RSO 1970, c. 409 (Ontario)

Stamp Duties Act 1783 (23 Geo. 3), c. 58
Stamp Act 1815 (55 Geo. 3), c. 184
Stamp Act 1891 (54 & 55 Vict.), c. 39

Uniform Commercial Code
Uniform Sales Act 1906 (United States)
Uniform Commercial Code (United States)

ZGB: Schweizerisches Zivilgesetzbuch/Code civil suisse (1907)